I KISSED THE BULLY – WOULD YOU?

RYLEE RYDER

authorHOUSE®

AuthorHouse™
1663 Liberty Drive
Bloomington, IN 47403
www.authorhouse.com
Phone: 833-262-8899

Published by AuthorHouse 08/10/2021

ISBN: 978-1-6655-1473-6 (sc)
ISBN: 978-1-6655-1472-9 (hc)
ISBN: 978-1-6655-1471-2 (e)

Library of Congress Control Number: 2021901405

DEDICATED TO

ALL OF THE AMAZING WOMEN WHO FIND
THEMSELVES SOUNDLESSLY STRUGGLING
UNDER THE THUMB OF A MAN WHO IS

SUPPOSED TO CARE
FOR THEIR WELL-BEING.

ABUSE IS ABUSE; BE IT PHYSICAL PAIN, SOCIAL
CONTROL, SEXUAL MISTREATMENT, VERBAL
MANIPULATION OR MENTAL TORTURE.

REMEMBER WHO YOU ARE; ONE OF GOD'S MIRACLES!!!

QUOTES FROM THE CRITICS

"As someone once said, suffering is never for nothing and this book stands as living proof, as a beacon of hope, for those who have likewise suffered".

Peggy Ross

"The reader comes to feel that anyone has the ability to overcome adversity. A good read for everyone who has struggled in difficult relationships with determination to overcome and understand the journey".

Ing J.

RN, BA, BSN, MBAS

"A tale of how so many women focus on the good in a man and refuse to recognize the bad, who chose the relationship over common sense and safety. Rylee Ryder holds nothing back, spares the reader none of the horror, but entices you to preserve, just as she did".

Dr. Bonnie M.

Recovered Alcoholic

This is a genuinely true story. The names and places have been changed to protect the guilty.

INTRODUCTION

I Kissed the Bully – Would You?

The wrinkled old fortune teller with penetrating, dark liquid eyes neglected to mention paying attention to warning signs of addiction or abuse. There was never a word about why I should not deny or minimize the abuse I would encounter. Nor did she advise leaving the abuser after the first incident, making certain that it would be the last. There was never a verbal warning about making too much of a commitment, trusting beyond betrayal or cautioning that I couldn't change my man, no matter how hard I tried.

PART ONE

HERE WE ARE

CHAPTER ONE

Throughout our marriage, I assumed Darth's drinking would dwindle and life would possibly be normal. Usually, I tried to perform Darth's demands, but deep inside I felt restricted for serving his personal agenda. Yet, I constantly strove to make the best of what we had in our marriage. Simply put, I honestly did not understand what a genuinely healthy relationship was, nor did I know how to co-exist in one, as I never had. All I really wanted was for us to be a happy family. I honestly thought that we could, but I was so wrong.

Feelings I could not deal with gathered on my horizon. The turbulent winds blew and thrashed at our doorstep, still I wanted to weather the storm. The relentless downpour was going to sluice the life right out of me, but I was not aware my life would implode; I was not prepared and did not know how scared I should be. Nor did I understand that only misery could come from hoping for the wrong thing, even if my reasons were right. I didn't know that living with an addict was equal to living in the epicenter of dysfunctional madness.

Late one afternoon five years into our marriage I stepped through the back door into the family room where Darth was unexpectedly appearing bleak, as he reclined in the easy chair. His face was pale and there were noticeable red rims on his lower lids. I thought he was going to tell me that someone had died.

In earnest, I asked him what was wrong. His voice resonated with malice, "I'm leaving you." My feet froze, and I stood rigid in the doorway, unable to enter the house. He must have recognized my inability to digest his words, so he stated them again as I let the door swing shut behind me. Then he added that he was taking Joey with him. My panicked thoughts were racing forward and going nowhere. I could barely speak and ask him what he meant?

"I'm sick and tired of living with someone who doesn't appreciate me and give me the sex I want whenever I feel like it," which he interpreted to mean that I obviously didn't love him. He continued to confess, "I've found somebody who does what I want," and he said that he wasn't going to leave his son behind, so he was taking Joey with him. Sitting on the floor next to Darth's chair was a brown paper grocery bag stuffed full of Joey's clothes. When Darth stood up, I realized he had his leather jacket on and had been sitting there waiting for me to come home from work.

He hollered down the hall at Joey that it was time to go. I had absolutely no idea that any of this had been planned. Four-year-old Joey tiptoed into the room in tears and obediently went to stand beside his father. Darth had apparently already told him they were going to be leaving. I didn't know what to say to Joey. Should I tell him not to worry that he would be home soon? Should I tell him that everything would be alright? Could I tell him normal parents always had their problems and Daddy would change his mind? I felt horrible for him. How could he understand when I knew I didn't? He was only a toddler. Darth picked up the grocery bag of clothes, took Joey's hand, and started towards the door. Joey just stared at me over his shoulder as he dutifully followed his father. I'm certain that I was staring back. I didn't dare to utter a word because in my heart I believed that if I had been a better person, Darth would not be leaving me.

I believed that I could cover up all his father's incredibly, impossible behavior. If I could just keep all manner of life in its proper order. I wrongly contemplated that Joey would grow up unaffected by Darth's blatant drinking. Now I was losing control and having second thoughts. How could a child grow up around dysfunctional behavior and learn to pattern his own life in normalcy? Unfortunately, Joey would probably learn to base his ideals on his perception of what he needed to do in his own life.

Long after I heard Darth slam the truck doors, start the engine, and drive away from the house, I just stood where I was. I felt like an undetected prankster had glued my soles to the linoleum floor. I couldn't move, and I couldn't comprehend my circumstances. I thought that Joey would be safe with his father, but I didn't know where they were going. Darth had just ripped our child away from his mother and his home, Darth had just left me. I lived unhappily with him, and I did it to keep a family together and I thought that I was succeeding. How mistaken I had been.

I was immobilized in a veil of uncertainty and shock as it began to turn a pale shade of gray outside. Habit was my only recourse, so I turned and back tracked out the door. I followed the sidewalk we had built together along the winding path to the barn. The horses still needed to be fed. After my barn chores were finished, I didn't bother to build a fire in the wood stove or turn on the house lights. I plopped down on the sofa in barn shoes and coat and stared off into space wondering.

My solitude was startled when the phone rang. It was my best friend, Nellie. She sounded frantic which caused me to wonder what had happened to her. She said that Darth had stopped at her house, and he had Joey in truck, and she could see him crying through the window. The poor kid, he wasn't even old enough to think that if he just ignored his pain, it would eventually go away. I'd learned to cope with emotional pain in that fashion; it was how I survived in my relationship with his father.

By the time Nellie arrived, the bitter dealings of the afternoon had warped into a deep, dark gloom and I was still sitting alone with the lights out. I was in a state of confused distress trying to understand the reality of Darth's actions. Even though I did not care for many of the things that Darth would partake of, I did love him.

After years of friendship Nellie and I shared a history between us. It was a wholesome relationship that we weren't going to give up even if Darth was so insecure that he was threatened by our time together. I felt that he had no logical reason to disapprove of our alliance. I went out of my way to make certain that Darth came first, and Nellie never undermined my loyalties to my husband. When Darth accused us of being lesbians, we both found that comment hysterically funny and then disregarded it. He attempted to ruin our friendship in every way that he could, which probably fueled his frustration at our ongoing commitment to one another.

As a twenty-four-year-old married adult I knew that Darth frequently stopped at Nellie's rental house when he was in town. I was pleased that he could at least be friends with Nellie when she and I weren't together. I trusted my best friend. Tonight, in the shadows of my empty house Nellie was coming to my aid. She explained with resolute objectivity that Darth had recently confided in her that he had been cheating on me. He had also promised her that he had stopped. Nellie felt at that juncture that telling me the truth would only be hurtful to me and serve no positive purpose. Keeping her mouth shut, she trusted Darth when he promised her that he would never cheat again.

Nellie paced back and forth across the family room carpet. As I absentmindedly twisted strands of hair through my fingers, she explained to me that on many occasions when Darth had told me that he was working late he was really getting laid. This made sense to me since he was never at the friends' houses where he claimed to be. This affair also explained why he wasn't pressuring me for sex every time I rolled over.

This is what my life had come to. I'd always worked diligently at being a good wife and mom. I endeavored to build a career so that I wasn't working for a pittance. I made and kept a beautiful home, and no one ever had to ask me to cook dinner or mend their socks. I was married to a man who had a temper. He was the same man who could be exceedingly immature. He possessed a multitude of traits that were identical to his father even though he had vowed he would never be violent or mean in similar ways. It didn't matter anymore how hard I tried to be compliant. Darth was gone. He had taken our son and abandoned me for another woman.

He took Joey and left me to return to his original high-school girlfriend Elise, because she was such a marvelous mother and took great care of her three little kids. I automatically rationalized Darth's behavior as my fault, even though I did not feel that I deserved that type of treatment. As his alcohol consumption increased, I did not realize that the irrational rationalizations I made had become a normal thought process and way of life for me. I had learned to focus on various problems but disassociated that our troubles were a direct result of our dysfunctional behavior.

I had never felt anything so vastly devastating.

CHAPTER TWO

I drifted in my own ebbing tide of delusion, and dubiously believed all, Darth's accusations of what an aberration I was. I tried but, couldn't find a way to sink into nothingness. Several days had passed and I still didn't know where he had gone, who he was with or what had happened with Joey.

On the fifth day the phone rang. It was Joey calling me. I was so relieved to hear from him. Joey sounded tired and uncertain just like a frightened little boy. While I tried to talk to him his father interrupted us on a connecting line.

Darth stated that Joey wanted to see me, so he would bring him out to the house the following morning and he hung up. I had no idea who had been taking care of Joey or if his father had even been going to work. Uncertain of what to expect when they showed up in the morning, I was still adamant that I didn't want my son to come from an emotionally bankrupt and physically broken home. That left me with one choice. If possible, I would do whatever it took to reconcile with Darth. I didn't begin to know how I could accomplish such a feat. For years I'd attempted to stand my ground while playing doctor to his drinking illness. Now all I could contemplate was how our lives had turned to rubble and ruin.

Making amends with Darth left me limited options, but I knew what those options would be. I would no longer be positioned to oppose his drinking and I would have to gratefully perform the exploited sex he demanded. The only other answer would be to prolong the separation.

Darth would have nothing to lose. He still had Joey, a sexpot woman on the side, his good old girlfriend Elise from high school, and apparently a place to stay. He was a con-artist, a liar, an adulterer, and he had the upper hand. Viewing myself as a victim, I thought that Darth had more influence and authority than he did. Abusers who have inflated impressions of themselves generally convince their victims that they are more powerful and significant than they really are or should be.

As worried as I had been, I was also delighted to see both my husband and son. They seemed somber, reserved, and quiet. I wondered exactly what Darth had been telling Joey. I got the distinct impression that I was not to approach either, so I just stood in my invisible space while Darth directed Joey to go play in his room. Joey acted like he wasn't supposed to speak a word or touch me. I just smiled at him and told him that I had really missed him while he was gone, and I was glad he had wanted to come and see me. He blinked blankly at me as he obeyed his father and proceeded down the hall to his bedroom, creating static cling as he dragged his small feet across the carpet.

Distracted I took one step closer to Darth and he took a step backward. He informed me that if I thought I could seduce him; I was totally mistaken. I knew that I was fully dressed, and I hadn't touched him in his privates. His remark was another that I didn't quite understand or know how to respond to. I stood looking up at him feeling completely off balance and uncomfortable in my own house.

My clearest memories of this morning are mostly of my feelings and not of my words. I knew that Darth wasn't giving away any information other than he was happier with another woman who would accept him just like he was, and that he should be entitled to be the man he deemed himself to be. He stated that I was way out of line to expect anything different of him.

As he continued his lecture, I realized that he was laying down the ground rules that I would have to accept if he were ever going to come back home. He showed absolutely no remorse about any of his lies or infidelities. He devoutly claimed his lying was necessary and that I had brought all my suffering upon myself. I recognized that I could not defend myself or he would simply walk back out the door. My self-defense would have caused his immediate exit and he would have taken Joey with him.

I knew that the only way I could keep my husband and son at home was to admit to Darth my inadequacies which included driving him into other women's arms. I told him that I understood that I was wrong not to accept him as the fine human being that he was. I promised to repent of my ways and always see him in a new light. I told him I would never interfere in his life again and that I now understood my true place. I apologized for the terrible pain that I had caused him by not understanding that he needed to be himself.

I gave up on the concept of mutual dependency, where mutual trust is built by partners in a healthy relationship while caring for each other in ways that are not destructive, where life can function rationally without constant manipulation of one another.

However, there was no mutual dependency in our marriage as I was now a classic enabling, bonifide fraud trying to agree to whatever Darth wanted to hear, in a struggle to save my family. Surely, I was the guilty party in this family breakdown. How could I have ever caused the two people that I loved so much unhappiness? I obviously deserved what I was getting, according to Darth. He claimed he didn't think I could change into a better person and that he still thought he should take Joey and leave me for ever.

I didn't know what else I could do, so I swallowed my last bit of pride, dropped to my knees blocking Darth's path from the back door and beseeched him not to go. I frantically told him I really loved him. In the rhetoric of my mind, I decided that it was not an issue that I no longer genuinely liked Darth. I didn't want him to leave me again. I knew that I could change if he would just give me the chance, however, I didn't know exactly what I should change. I believe those were the words that my father had expressed to my mother over twenty years before. I meant them, and I knew my biological father never had. Maybe they were stuck in my subconscious somewhere. Yet, I convinced myself of my promises and committed myself to my obligatory sacrifices.

Darth looked down at me, pitifully crying on my knees and said, "I want proof and I'll have to think about it." As he turned away from me to leave, he granted his permission for me to speak with Joey for a few minutes. I summoned him from his room and tried to appear, and act as if our lives were still functioning in the normal daily routine. In the adjacent garage I could hear his dad digging through the metal tool trays next to the door on the work bench and I tried to ignore the sounds. Seizing my window of opportunity, I asked Joey where he had been and what had he been doing.

He told me that he was staying at his Grandparent's house. That would be my in-laws who had said nothing to me or attempted any type of contact. I was getting the impression from my child that he had been left at his grandparents', without his father being there. I did not want to pressure Joey about where his father had been. I mentally questioned if he already felt uncomfortable telling me the few details he was disclosing and then of his own accord he proceeded to inform me that I wasn't going to be his mother anymore. This statement petrified me and enraged me simultaneously. I asked Joey what he meant because of course I was his mother and always would be. He told me that his father and Elise had told him that she would be his new mom and that I wasn't his mother anymore.

Anxiously, I tried to explain to Joey not to worry, that I was his mom, and everything was going to be fine, then Darth walked in. When I glanced out the family room window, I could see the hood on his truck was up. Faking contentment and trying to control my indignation I asked what was wrong with his pickup. Darth said that he had taken the distributor cap off before coming into the house. I knew that engines had distributor caps, but I didn't know how one functioned. Obviously, a vehicle wouldn't run without one.

When I questioned Darth about the distributor cap, he said that he parked in front of the garage door to block my car and then took the distributor cap from under the hood so that I couldn't steal Joey in his truck and run away with my own son. I was amazed that Darth had ever thought I would do such a thing. Stealing our child from our home had never even occurred to me, only to Darth. He fixed his truck, slammed the hood down and they drove away. I did not know when I would hear from them again.

The following day Darth phoned and said that he wanted to see me. I took his request as a good sign. He said that he would be home in awhile and it sounded like he intended to show up by himself. I thought that talking was preferable to his complete absence. When Darth arrived, the house was as silent as a vacated chapel, and it was completely dark outside. I had the coffee brewing. Darth appreciated my coffee making efforts but let me know that like everything else in life, I hadn't done it quite right. While pouring the remaining brew down the drain he informed me that he had been thinking about how I could prove my good intentions to him.

He stipulated that we go directly to bed, and he would bring the first set of new rules. I was expected to obey these rules as he wished. If I did not obey the rules to his personal satisfaction then all bets were off, and he was permanently leaving me, at which time he intended to reserve all rights to his son which meant his full custody. I absently nodded as I listened to Darth lay down the law.

We would strip and get into bed where we would proceed to have great sex. I would know when he was ready to come as he would physically withdraw from me, and I was instructed to take his erect penis directly into my mouth. Delicious sex was to continue with his penis planted in my mouth until he was finished ejaculating, at which time I was expected to enjoy swallowing every single squirming sperm. After swallowing, I was required to smile at him as if I had wanted this demanded sexual act that he was pleased to force upon me. It was my job to make him feel like the man he was born to be.

Deftly closing my mind to Darth's erection and struggling to inhale air as he ejaculated into my mouth, I convinced myself that I was indeed preserving my family. Swallowing without gagging, I looked at Darth sitting triumphant with a scathing grin, straddling my bare chest with his wet erection pointed directly between my eyes. I looked up into his face which bore a façade I'd learned to distrust, and now despise. I patronizingly smiled the very broadest, beaming grin I could muster.

I hated his medieval domination and mocking betrayals. I think I even hated Darth. I tried to chase the thoughts of his other women and their sexual acts from my consciousness. I felt my self-esteem rapidly leaching away from me. I had to remember that if, for whatever possible reason, Darth was not satisfied with my performance, he would leave me again. I had complied exactly as instructed. I felt like a worthless woman trading my sovereignty for a belief that I could purchase family stability based on sexual acts. Darth liked my smile.

CHAPTER THREE

Sexually deviant Darth and befuddled brooding Joey were home. I was emotionally traumatized but attempted to be cheerful. I practiced being seen but not heard. The worst part is I had agreed to this punishment by giving in to his demands, and by doing so I had diminished my self-worth.

I tended to my household chores with my eyes lowered. I was afraid that Darth would see into my soul and recognize how I had grown to loathe the way he treated me. The only way I could conceal my buried feelings was to avoid eye contact with him. I was still recovering from a severe whiplash injury that occurred the year before, and I tried to hide the neck problems from Darth since he accused me of faking the injury. I didn't dare to cry around him because he was an expert at using my own pain against me.

I thought that I was trapped when I first married him. Now I knew that I was. I decided it didn't matter if Darth didn't love me, as long as he loved Joey. If I could provide our son with both of his parents and a real home, I would dutifully accept my obligations by making myself the martyr of the household. I didn't dare to leave Darth. I was too worried about the impact that would have on Joey, and under Darth's influence I didn't dare to separate him from his son. Given the persistent whiplash problems I could not function full time at my job. I did not believe however that I deserved the degrading treatment I was receiving from Darth. The trend for debasing me was catching on and Joey was beginning to treat me like his father did. I did not know it then, but it was the beginning of the end of a normal relationship with Joey.

Darth would seize any opportunity that he could to remind me of my many shortcomings and the repercussions I would suffer if I did not do his bidding. I felt as if I had fallen into a bottomless pit where I was constantly surrounded by complete lunacy. I was desperately trying to climb from this unending void. I felt totally helpless, a learned behavior that Darth had taught me. I felt powerless in my situation at home, and Darth continued to reinforce the hopeless feelings I struggled to endure.

My attempts to climb from the depth of the darkest reservoir were completely futile. On the teetering brink, there were times I thought that I had a grip on the edge of salvation. The moment that I would grab onto the lip of the pit, Darth would be there waiting. He would look smugly down upon me as I desperately grasped at sanity and struggled for a ledge to lever against. During this advent in my life, I decided that God really didn't exist. Amazingly, I continued with a shred of hope that I might change Darth's conduct, so the abuse would stop, and my idea of a relationship could be rekindled. I'd grown accustomed to a span of time between abusive incidents, a pattern that Darth used to intentionally lull me into a false sense of security after he would abuse me.

The parent teacher conferences of which Darth never attended, was like the last. Joey was doing poorly in school as his grades were barely acceptable and he possessed a multitude of behavioral problems. His teachers wanted to know if something could be bothering him at home. Any child being raised in an addiction atmosphere constantly hears mixed messages that teach mistrust. By not leveling with Joey about his father's real problems, I was allowing him false information, in a pathetic effort to protect him from reality. All the confusing messages and actions probably kept Joey second guessing about what was really happening. I was only trying to keep Joey from experiencing the same pain that I was feeling. His teachers thought he acted belligerent and defiant. I knew he was, and I couldn't blame him.

While I privately wished that I dared to defy Darth, I couldn't tell his teachers that I was no longer supposed to be his mother or that I was constantly frightened about what was happening to all of us. Joey had a lot of legitimate reasons to be disobedient. His elementary school teachers expected me to fix Joey's cantankerous attitudes. I couldn't even begin doctoring Joey's wounds when I wasn't allowed to lick my own.

All was not lost because Darth could still badger me with Elise. When he had previously informed Elise that he would return home to his wife, he explained to me that he had felt guilty for hurting the poor helpless female creature. He had described her three young children and how she was making a great effort handling the expense of raising them. She had to go to work full time and leave her kids with her mother who babysat for free every day. Why at one point she had hocked her wedding ring to purchase milk and bread to feed her kids.

On this note Darth also informed me that he had taken more than ten thousand dollars, all the money from our joint savings account except for the eight thousand three hundred dollars that he claimed as his from my neck injury settlement and had given our savings to Elise. He was controlling our finances and then telling me after the fact, which served to implement additional control. Not only did he make substantial financial decisions without my consent, but he was also giving our money away. It didn't matter that Darth had previously quit his job and had been basically unemployed for several months or that I was trying to recover from what would be a permanent injury.

When I began to protest Darth's monetary decisions, he declared, "If you don't like it, I'm leaving you for Elise." After all, Elise deserved the money because she thought she was going to get him back after years of longing for him in high school and then he left her, once again, for me. I detested Darth and his decisions but all I could do was remind myself of Joey and our pretend home life. The last I heard, Elise left her suicidal husband and bought a new house. This made Darth feel noble because he had purchased the right to do away with his guilt over leaving poor deprived Elise to return to his welcoming wife.

My despair was drowning me in depression. I forced myself to go through the maneuvers of functioning even though I didn't feel that I possessed a purpose. Dozens of times I hid in the formal dining room next to the antique china hutch in a shaded corner staring vacantly at the chairs I had re-upholstered. This was my squatting space where no one would notice me, and I let my loneliness ache inside of me. Hiding there, I could let the tears roll pell-mell. I cried constantly when Darth was not around to witness my agony. He had never apologized and felt no remorse. I wanted to forgive him if only I could convince myself that he really did love me.

Needing someone to rescue me, I frequently turned to my best friend. To some degree Nellie had a handle on what Darth was all about and I knew he would occasionally stop at her house late in the evenings to schmooze her. He thought he was convincing Nellie with his versions of his fantastic husbandry skills. I hoped she knew better, but I could sense that she had difficulty avoiding Darth's manipulations as he always sounded tenacious in his convictions and was easily believable.

One evening Nellie had driven to our house and I had a hunch that what she really wanted was to talk to Darth alone. Finding a household project to busy myself with I escaped down the hall to scrub toilets. Trying to sanitize my life with tidy bowl denial, while living in a dysfunctional life with Darth, I'd felt as if I'd been swirling around in a toilet bowl on the verge of being sucked down the plumbing and drowning like a brown turd in the septic system. Between flushes I could overhear bits and pieces of their conversation which was turning into a heated argument.

After his verbal stream of put-downs, he made sure that I knew that Elise excelled at being someone that I was not. Because she was so extraordinary, he claimed he hadn't slept with her while he was seeing her behind my back. Darth explained that they had been saving themselves for later. The woman that he was having an extra-marital affair with was a successful restaurant owner that he had met in a bar. I didn't know who she was but according to Darth she possessed mega business accomplishments and was a mighty super sex heroine in bed. She relished in all the sex she could get and performed overt sexual acts for Darth whenever he desired, he didn't even have to ask. In the privacy of my own mind, I pictured them as rotund hogs rigorously attempting to boink each other in the confined space of the backseat of my car.

After selflessly confessing these deeply guarded secrets of his private life to me, he wanted to know what secrets I had. I honestly did not know how to respond to this because he was expecting me to tell him all about my unprincipled affairs, and I'd never had one. He continued to pursue the topic knowing that I was surely holding back some tidbit of checkered information about my supposed infidelity. I didn't know what to say other than the truth.

There was one secret that I had kept to myself regarding Nick and the modeling job for the automotive product promotion. Of course, Darth had known about that appointment for an interview. Darth also knew Nick. Darth just didn't know what Nick had said to me and how I had managed to wiggle out of a trapped situation. This was the only story I had to share. I'd grown weak in the head, so I took the bait and shared.

Big, big mistake on my part. I sat in stunned silence as Darth came completely unglued. He ranted and raved as if I had just confessed to being humped by the entire male population. My transgression was far worse than anything he had ever heard, and I was obviously disloyal for never telling him.

My honesty had dug my hole even deeper, and Darth was determined that I was going to pay. He came and went at all hours as he pleased. He allowed Joey to treat me like his maid instead of his mother. Darth drank harder and I sank deeper. My anger over the unfairness practiced by Darth tried to suck me into the pits of living quicksand.

I knew by my frequent abdominal pains that my ulcer was agitated. I could no longer imagine what it was like to have any fortitude left to draw from. I struggled to find my emotional stride. I recognized some innate value within myself and clung to the potential fantasy that Darth might recognize his own faults and eventually treat me with dignity. I felt sick in my soul and didn't know how to heal myself.

In my deepest depression I toyed with an enticing thought. I considered killing myself, so he could no longer batter me. Suicide could be a perfect revenge. It would permanently end my misery and Darth would have to feel guilty the rest of his tarnished life. He would have to clean up the mess and explain to his parents, better yet, he would have to explain to my parents. Darth would be forever tortured by my death and how he had driven me to it. I fully intended to make a gory and revolting mess.

The blinds were tightly drawn, eliminating any natural light and the door into the hallway was securely closed. The sink and dressing table were not visible from the bedroom, and I could not be seen from the bed where Darth slept. I stood somberly leaning over the enamel sink with both sweaty palms resting against the bull nose of the counter. I was facing myself in the gilded mirror that I'd purchased for a bargain because of a slight chip in the bottom left-hand corner. In all my thoughts I felt completely devoid of human dignity, and all I could recognize was grief. All I could see in the mirror was a quagmire of anguish. I could not decipher exactly where it started and felt that it would never end. I just wanted to succumb and let misery have its power. I only saw one way out and I intended to take it.

I was certain that if I died, I could forever escape my internal agony. The razor blades were in the same drawer as the toothpaste. I thought about how grand this would be. It was the worst that Darth deserved; he was the architect of emotional torment. I'd reached the point where taking my life was the final payback.

Inserting the razor blade tightly between forefinger and thumb, I applied it to my left wrist. Joey's bedroom door across the hall was only fifteen feet away from where I stood. He slumbered there in his bed. To my bewildered dismay I realized that he could possibly find my bloody mess before Darth did. That would be horrific to a six-year-old, detrimentally affecting him the rest of his life. What would he think of me and all the values that I'd endeavored to instill in him? It would make him doubt every good thing that I had ever tried to teach him. If I intentionally took my life, every truth that I wanted him to learn and exercise in his own life would be nothing more than a lie from his mother.

As badly as I wanted to hurt Darth, I could not hurt my son in such a way. This was wrong to do to a child, and I knew it. I stood in a perplexing trance, seeing nothing, for the longest time. I had absolutely no idea of what else to do so I turned on the shower and closed the swinging glass door shut behind me. Still wearing my cotton nightgown, I sat down in the bottom of the stall. I stayed there with my knees pressed snuggly to my chest in a fetal position for a long time. The warm water turned cold, and I could not have cared less.

During the predawn hours Darth pulled me out of the cold shower and went to work. I got dressed and went about my daily duties in zombie mode. It had not previously occurred to me that a successful suicide attempt would have never been blamed on Darth. Convincingly he would have used my suicide to further shore-up his complaints against me.

I needed to stop feeding the monster and start slaughtering it. For the last several years I'd asked Darth many times if we could go to counseling and he insisted that he wouldn't allow it. As a last resort I decided that I would do so behind his back. I found a marriage counselor and cautiously kept my weekly appointment with him. Our medical insurance would have covered the cost, but I was afraid that Darth might see the visits on the insurance statements delivered in the mail, so I paid cash. This was difficult to do since I usually didn't have much cash. I wrote my checks at the grocery store for extra cash and shopped more frequently.

Finally, I did convince Darth to attend one session with me. This was intended to be a joint session where we could both talk about our individual views of our problems together with a referee. I was allowed one partial sentence and sat unassumingly while Darth proceeded to tell the counselor about his accomplishments, and my inventory of faults and digressions. At the end of our session Darth announced himself to be cured. Consequently, it would not be necessary for him to return and that I wouldn't be returning either. Since we had a sitter, he took me to dinner to celebrate.

In the think tank of my thoughts, I knew that I had been raised to make a silk purse out of a sow's ear, but what my mother had neglected to teach me was that the purse, no matter how appealing to the eye, was still a sow's ear. I burrowed my behind deeper into my dinner chair and while jabbing at my salad, I made a resolution to try harder to understand Darth.

I had headaches. I had stomach aches. I had chest pains. I was twenty-five years old, and I thought I was going to have a heart attack. I had sleepless sweaty nights and dizzy spells. I felt overwhelmed. My neck still tired easily with painful spasms. I heard things that I knew weren't there and saw movements that didn't exist. I was sick of feeling like a second-class citizen. My monthly periods were changing, and I was hemorrhaging a lot. My list went on and on and I began writing down all my ailments. The yellow note pad I used had almost thirty lines and I'd filled the entire page. I took my list with me and made a doctor's appointment with a woman doctor I'd never visited before.

I could feel the dark puffy circles under my eyes while I sat and impatiently waited. When the nurse took me back to the examination room she asked, "Why are you visiting the doctor today?" "Well, I really don't know, but I'm hoping for a miracle." I handed the nurse my list and she didn't say a word. She glanced at it, looked at me, shook her head and left me waiting.

The doctor was busy, but I could tell she had compassion. I could see it in her body posture while she read my list. Then she looked directly at me and asked, "What is your home life like?" In five hundred words or less I explained what had happened in the last few years. I hoped she would believe me and was afraid she wouldn't. Then she told me I was remarkable! I wanted to know why she would think that, and she told me that any woman that could survive what I had been dealing with and still look like a million bucks was doing something right. I accentuated my girlish grin by baring all my pearly whites and said, "Really?"

The Doc didn't think that I looked like I felt. She responded that if I had the fortitude to get out of bed in the morning then I was on the right track. She suggested that I ride my horse as soon as my neck was able and then she smiled at me sincerely. So, I felt bad but looked good. My heart hosted thoughts of a meager new start.

That weekend when Darth wanted to invite his parents over for dinner, I declined because I had not prepared a menu for that day that would accommodate company. I explained to him that I had only defrosted three pork chops for dinner. Standing in my way in front of the refrigerator door Darth drew a deep breath and showed me his pumped-up chest while informing me that I could drive all the way to town and buy two more.

My feelings crashed in on a wave that threatened to drown me if I turned my back on the emotional storm. So, I turned to face Darth. Armed with dangerous knowledge that I felt awful but looked like a million bucks and knowing that divorce was not a word that existed in my dictionary, I did not hesitate long enough to process further thoughts. Instead, I told Darth that if he wanted to invite his parents to dinner that was fine, he could drive his own butt to the store and purchase two more pork chops. And he did.

Unwittingly, I had just bolstered a microscopic piece of faith in myself. I wanted a new start, but really didn't know what to do about it or how to attain confidence in myself. By addressing a bully, I discovered a thread of lifeline that would empower me with a new beginning.

I'd grown a gonad.

CHAPTER FOUR

As my morale improved, so did Joey's. I thought we did well together, especially when Darth wasn't present. I hoped that my presence added stability to Joey's life. When Darth was home Joey would withdraw from me, leaving me feeling alienated. I worried about whether he would eventually become disrespectful of other females later in his life. Then I conveniently erased this niggling issue from my current concerns as I didn't know what I could do about it, and I couldn't envision my cute little crumb-cruncher growing up to use a female as his chew toy.

It was easier to focus on the daily routine of teaching Joey to care for his pony, but he'd given up on that idea. Joey was shifting gears and talking about a motorcycle. I could understand how a motorcycle would appeal to him. His father had grown up with one and so had I. Joey might be slightly young for this, but Darth was convinced he could handle a minibike with adult supervision.

We decided to look for a used one. Saturday morning Darth announced that he'd found a minibike for sale in the newspaper and he and Joey went to investigate. They came home with a motorcycle strapped into the bed of the truck. It was three times the size of a minibike. This motor-cross bike was not at all what we had discussed, and I knew that it would be way too much bike for a seven-year-old boy, especially a seven-year-old who had never ridden a motorbike and tended to give up easily when something was difficult for him. When he was a toddler, he pushed his plastic big wheels with his feet like Fred Flintstone for six months before he finally decided to pedal. I had clear and distinct visions of Joey airborne with a contorted body like the kids in extreme sports shows.

Joey and his dad unloaded the cycle and Darth buckled the matching white helmet onto Joey's little beanie head. I knew that gravel could peel layers of hide off elbows and knees, so I requested that they move onto the softer orchard grass along the driveway. Darth thought he should be in charge, so I back tracked to the open garage where I watched and waited. The bike was running, and Joey was on it. He couldn't even reach to set two feet down on the ground while sitting astride his humming monster. He pulled on the throttle as Darth stepped back and the mighty bike lurched forward and rolled on its hind wheel. Both Joey and the bike fell backward and sideways in a twisted, tangled heap with the cycle's engine still throttling and the back tire spinning in circles like a big beetle trying to turn upright.

I couldn't hear what Darth said to Joey, but I knew what I wanted to say. Joey should have never been put on a machine that was too much for him. It didn't bother me when the cycle got parked permanently in the garage for several years, collecting dust. Joey never did attempt to ride the motorcycle again and decided that he really liked his bicycle instead.

Feeling consumed with resentment, I contemplated skinning Darth alive for being such an ignoramus. As he frequently reminded me, he was the grandest father who ever lived, and he loved his son more than anything else on earth. Darth and I were moving our motorcycle discussion from the garage into the family room when I pushed the issue about finding Joey a smaller motorbike. Sitting down in the center of the family room, appearing to ready himself for an important meeting, Darth began polishing his set of metal gulf clubs. I had never been to a golf course or seen him play, but he seemed to think that he had grand golf potential. I was standing behind the loveseat when I realized Darth had let fly with one of the heavy ended golf clubs. I felt the air rotate as the weighted club whizzed right past my right temple and smacked directly into the table lamp, hinging itself in the thin metal miniblinds as it went thud against the window making the adjoining patio doors shudder.

I looked at Darth in sheer disbelief. He could have killed me. He yelled something obscene at me and I tried to diffuse the violent situation by kneeling to pick up the broken chunks of the porcelain lamp from the carpet. Darth glared at me as he stomped out of the room making a beeline for his truck and drove to who knew where until he decided to return the following day.

Many times, he had disappeared as my punishment, only to return with no apology or explanation. Most abusers return and promise to change. Darth never promised to change, even though I kept thinking he would. I didn't know about how a marriage with physical abuse could do severe damage to me, even though Darth's violent actions frequently frightened me, swamping me with a bitter sense of injustice.

Abusers are likely to evolve from an abusive childhood themselves and tend to foster substance abuse that exacerbates their other problems. Usually, Darth would stop his abusive behavior for limited periods of time. I thought it was because he was trying to be kind because he felt badly. However, it was an act of manipulation to get me to trust him again and then he would return to his rancor. He had repeated this typical pattern many times before. Somewhere I had missed the memo that said enablers tend to disconnect their thinking from what they are experiencing as they resist logical reasoning to form an excuse while mentally creating a chain of illogical reasons.

The future aggressive actions Darth would display had no way of warning me in the present. There were warning signs I didn't recognize, such as Darth's possession of unusual weapons that he designed and manufactured for himself. He stashed a pair of pointedly sharp, deadly brass knuckles in his bed stand. Frequently, he would sit on the edge of the bed admiring his handywork. It was puzzling to me that anyone could be so enamored with such an ugly weapon. Because I did not understand his actions, I chose to overlook Darth's lack of emotional self-control. His tendencies to "blow up" over minor incidents and his ability to express strong negative emotions in an unacceptable manner could be dangerous. Darth had displayed a history of violence, and I knew that he grew up in a home where his father physically disciplined him with beatings when he was young. Children who are victims of brutality often grow up to be perpetrators of violence themselves.

When Darth returned home after his last tantrum, he was talking about how he wanted to quit his job as a heavy construction journeyman. Now he wanted to build and market his invention, stainless steel sawhorses that would fold into a compacted unit for easy storage and carriage. Darth and his recently acquired drinking buddy were excited about their clever idea. Ned Parker was a retired paint salesman and old enough to be Darth's grandpa. He insisted that selling paint had gone to hell in a hand basket for several reasons, none of which were his fault.

Ned drove me nuts. He was always at our house after dinner in the evenings and he constantly jabbered nonstop. He was a true know-it-all on any subject matter. Darth thought Ned was great because they both thrived on one another's goombah ideas while sharing several cold brews. Claiming it was necessary to relax while they worked on their mind taxing and inventive marketing plans.

I could do the math. They would have to sell hundreds of stainless-steel sawhorses to pay for the equipment that was required to manufacture them. We still had the eight thousand three hundred dollars from my neck injury claim and since Darth had long since announced that the money rightfully belonged to him, he decided to spend it on metal fabricating equipment. If he were a miser, he could find used equipment that would jump start his worthy endeavor.

My car was ousted from the garage and the proto-type metal sawhorse was constructed. I had to admit the idea was nifty, but it seemed too expensive for carpenters to afford. Any carpenter could buy plastic sawhorses for much less money or handily make his own quadrilateral braced semi-horizontal stabilizing carpentry device from scraps of two by four lumber. What did I know? I was just a dumb girl.

Now it was Ned's job. He was going to sell a gazillion of these even though he couldn't sell paint. I knew Ned's wife had a good job with benefits and I knew I didn't. Our house payment was on an adjustable scale interest rate, and it had almost doubled since we built the house. At this juncture Darth quit his job to manufacture collapsible stainless-steel sawhorses and Ned Parker never sold one.

Still resenting this venture, I didn't dare to remind Darth that he had given away all our life savings to Elise. Instead, I tried to focus on his positive attributes. I knew he wasn't lazy. Darth acquired used sheet metal equipment and a welder, and then he used our two-car garage as his workshop. He took out a loan against the house and moved the wood fence across the front yard and built a shop in what used to be the pasture.

The front corner was walled off for a functioning office and two bay doors were installed, one with a slanted concrete loading ramp. We chose a name, paid the appropriate fees, and incorporated. Darth negotiated with large manufacturing companies and spent hours calculating estimates for project bids. We offered quality work for a reasonable price with the service to back it up. We were now in business to build commercial grade restaurant equipment that was eventually sold and installed in restaurants across the nation, Hawaii and Alaska.

There was paperwork, payroll, invoicing, bill collecting, union dues and materials to be ordered and picked up. I ran all the errands, accomplished the banking, and paid the taxes. I worked for free. I sent Joey to school in the mornings and went to work in the shop office after breakfast. My neck injury still wouldn't tolerate long periods of sitting which I remedied with a short nap during mid-afternoon. Darth hired a couple of the journeymen he had worked with in the past and purchased additional used fabricating equipment. The business grew. Next, we added a professional cabinet maker and became certified to install our own fire systems into exhaust hoods. We bought an enormous flatbed truck with rusty wheels and a crane for heavy overhead installations.

We added a two-story addition to the shop with its own bathroom, so the employees could steer clear of the bathroom in the house. The top story was a larger office with room for another secretary and private office space for Darth, the boss man. Darth bought a couple of company trucks with racks and a black T-top sports car which he eventually traded for a Mercedes with a spacious trunk and sat phone. I hired a secretary and kept working supplementary hours.

Our modest shop ran two shifts and Darth always worked on weekends. He hired a few more men and then his father and brother. Our driveway was a parking lot, and our yard was never again a peaceful country retreat. I liked the gal that I hired to handle part of my workload. She did her job and managed to put up with Darth. Occasionally I found her in tears and understood how she felt when Darth was blowing a minute detail out of proportion.

To keep track of the paperwork and influx of money, I hired a certified public accountant to be certain that taxes were completed professionally. Darth's dad and brother were putting in a lot of overtime, but not as much as Darth. His father was complaining about working so many extra hours, his brother was still single and didn't seem to mind. Darth was not willing to pay overtime to any of the family members, including himself and his father was not willing to continue with such a heavy work schedule.

The practical solution to the problem at hand was company stock shares and splitting them three ways. Darth was the nucleus, took all the financial risks and worked more hours than his sibling. The stock that belonged to Darth also technically belonged to me and I had been working long hours for months for absolutely no wages. We also personally shouldered the burden of all the financial liabilities and the debt on the shop building. Darth argued that since his dad and brother had also invested eight thousand three hundred dollars each toward additional equipment, that the share holder's splits in stock should stay as the three of them had agreed. Never mind me. I decided that I was lucky that Darth didn't want to hire his mother.

I'd never been under the impression that Darth considered his brother an equal partner, but my opinion didn't count, and they split eighty six percent of the stock equally. Darth's dad agreed to acquire the balance of fourteen percent and never work overtime or weekends. Darth was so busy that I felt my life had improved slightly. Time permitting, I taught Nellie to ride my old swayback sorrel gelding. We giggled between ourselves because Darth accused us of riding properly seated in our western saddles to give ourselves orgasms.

We let him think what he wanted.

CHAPTER FIVE

The end of that summer Mom gave me a pink dancing needlepoint pig, framed in a small oval plastic frame. Embroidered in bold letters under the dancing pig's feet it said, "BE HAPPY". I was trying, but what Mom left out of the equation is when you wrestle with a pig, you both get rolled in foul pig poop, and only the pig likes it. I was figuring out that being nice wasn't going to cure Darth, and neither was logic. Attempting to have a normal, logical conversation with an addict was akin to pulling my bottom lip over my head.

But I wasn't yet ready to accept that enablers allow debris to accumulate with no exit drain, while rubbish swirls and clutters in the catch basin of their homes, until the water level becomes so intolerable that you can no longer find a way to squirm onto a safe ledge, because there isn't one.

So, it was worth it to me to give up my lofty ideals for a somewhat respectable marriage if Joey had a father who loved him, and I could pretend to live in some semblance of normalcy. I reconciled in my mind that Darth no longer loved me, and I questioned if he ever really had. I knew that I loved him but no longer liked or respected him. I did not consider him my friend or confidante. However, I devoted myself to making the best of our relationship. After all, life was a series of punts, rolls, and occasional field goals.

Understanding that I was not without my own foibles, I chose to overlook as many of Darth's faults as possible. Instead, I tried to focus on

Darth's good qualities. He was smart, talented, and compulsive about his work. I also realized that I could not expect Darth to give me credit for my talents unless it served a purpose to him.

Knowing that I existed in two different dimensions where one was real, and the other was based on my contrived perceptions of reality, I decided to strive for happiness, have faith, and never give up. The word "tenacity" took on an entirely new meaning in my life.

I cajoled Darth into church attendance on a regular basis, privately thinking that it would reduce his alcohol intake. If he wasn't drinking, he might begin to resemble the guy that I thought he was when we were dating. Once again, I was undertaking a feat to control my drinking spouse. Still denying the reality of our relationship, I was diligently attempting to change my man. What I didn't consider was that Darth could use church attendance as a cover for insisting that I comply with ideas he wanted to institute into our relationship. We had each agreed to attend church for completely different selfish reasons, even if my reason was for a good purpose.

I was hoping that we might be able to build our marriage on Christian ethics and only God knows what Darth really thought. I believed we were off to a great start when Darth promised that he would stop drinking. To rise through the ranks of the Priesthood that was offered to male church members, each male had to adhere to prerequisites and no alcohol was one of them. If I wanted to arise to my full status as a woman member, I would have to do so by being married eternally to a husband that would abide by all of church principles. The church goal was to eventually dwell in the highest kingdom of heaven. The result would be jointly creating our own worlds without end in the afterlife. This was not something that I had desired but if worlds without end were affixed to a husband who did not drink, I was willing to try it.

We attended church every week for a couple of years. We obeyed all the regulations, except that Darth was still drinking behind my back. However, at the time I chose to believe that he was being honest with me about his sobriety. I sang in the choir and did special church assignments and paid our ten percent pre-tax tithe.

Darth frequently reminded me that since I was lacking in the motherhood department what I really needed was another child to enhance my maternal skills. I was in total disagreement. My instincts told me not to trust Darth completely with this idea. The truths that I knew I could count on from him would be immaturity, self-serving manipulation, and control. I didn't think that another child needed to be a new ingredient in the same old household recipe.

Darth's insistence grew as we were the only husband and wife at church with just one child. Darth had a vasectomy years ago, so he thought that we should adopt. This was his genuinely half-baked idea. He insisted that if I would do this one modest request for him that he would treat me like a queen for the rest of my life. Surely, I must understand that adopting a child would make us a completed family and it would be selfish of me not to participate.

After being relentlessly badgered for months with his obsessive idea, I felt that I had to prove I was a worthy woman, so I consented. We filled out reams of paperwork from the State and were eventually approved to be adoptive parents. I was astonished, but I decided that what the State didn't know wouldn't hurt them, nor would I ever dare to tell an adoptive counselor about the alcohol and abuse issues, Darth had seen to that.

Painting pretty pictures in my head, I went on a mission to the mall. I shopped for the perfect pattern of pink wallpaper that any little girl would adore. Not stopping short I searched for matching bedspread and creamy colored paint to turn the bedroom furniture into a little girl's paradise. Since I had agreed to this commitment, I might as well make the best of it and "be happy." With any luck this new little girl would have a special fondness for horses, and I could teach her to ride.

Weeks later the big manila envelope arrived. It was full of information and photographs of a dozen children that fell into the age bracket we had requested. I'm sure that any one of them would want nothing more than a real Dad and Mom with a family to love them. Darth thumbed through the black and white photos, picking the child he wanted, and it wasn't a little girl. Instead, he chose a boy. I decided that was manageable because I hadn't hung the pink wallpaper yet.

Darth was on the phone to the appointed counselor to announce his choice. When he found out he wasn't allowed to pick the kid he wanted, that the State was going to do that for him, Darth was irate. "Nobody tells me what to do and that includes some dumb desk jockey employed by the government". Darth knew which child he preferred from previewing the photos and if he couldn't have the kid, he picked then he wasn't taking anyone of them.

I stood unwavering in the center of the room listening to his conversation and to my aplomb; I wasn't the least bit surprised that Darth wouldn't accept just any orphan. Privately I let a wave of relieve wash over me. I knew that it was a mistake to bring another child into our household, even though our house could accommodate one. I think it was the only time that I was ever thankful for Darth's immaturity and volatile temper,

Like many values in life, I felt that there was the good, the bad and the somewhere in-between. I found that moderation in most things was the wisest choice. I was also an adult who still wanted to please her mother, by attending church with Darth I was doing so. The more that I examined church doctrines the more certain I became that I was not a believer in the "one and only true church". I didn't think that it was the only true church; some of the teachings were certainly notable but not every principle was based in what I believed to be spiritual truth. Darth didn't think so either, we eventually left the church membership.

Free from church and the no drinking zone, Darth was reigning supreme and busy running his business, surrounded by his friends and relatives. When an opportunity presented itself, I'd approached Darth's father about his drinking. I had a feeling that Dick knew more about Darth's alcoholic intake than he was willing to discuss. In earnest I was hopeful that Dick would have some positive influence on his son. Dick told me to grant Darth his liberty, as he claimed, "You can catch more flies with honey than vinegar." I interpreted this to mean that I should be nice and quit bugging Darth, feeling berated by my father-in-law when I was seeking his help, I picked up my marbles and went home.

CHAPTER SIX

The following spring, business was booming, and we were running out of room to handle the needs of our present, and future customers. We required more space and equipment. Through town and a few miles past the main intersection was a parcel of raw acreage that bordered the city limits and was adjacent to commercially zone land.

The original shop building in our yard was still mortgaged against our home, but Darth had a plan. We borrowed against the business revenue and started construction. Darth's scheme was to build a residential house which would really serve as an office to coerce the City Council into giving him a zoning variance changing the shop acreage zoning from rural to commercial.

Darth decided that I didn't belong in the secretarial pool, so I had an oak roll top desk located in the far corner of the living room isolating me from the secretarial pool.

My job description was unusual. I handled the problems that no one else was willing to manager, any tax issues with the government reports, past due collections, catering to the boss, emergencies, job interviews, budget projections, etc. Once the house was built and converted into office space, the City Council approved permits for our new commercial shop accommodations. It was gigantic. Darth obviously had full blown goals and intentions. Several of our corporations could operate under one roof. All the engineering layout, welding, pressing, cutting, polishing and assembly would be performed in the new shop. The roof was designed as a helicopter pad.

Darth decided that we could save some overhead if the company owned an additional out of town house for the installers to occupy, instead of spending funds on hotel rooms. I did not argue with this idea because I knew what we were spending on travel expenses and if those funds could be diverted toward a solid investment, purchasing a house-hotel made some sense to me. Darth felt the house was a great buy.

Since Darth frequently made the one-way four-hour drive, he would now have a place that he could stop and rest or stay over for the night. He told me that he met the previous owners and inquired of them if they knew someone who could clean up after the installation crews vacated to return home on the weekends. The previous owners knew the perfect cleaning woman, their own daughter. This woman cleaned the hotel house on a regular basis as I paid the monthly invoices that she submitted.

One weekend afternoon Darth answered the home phone line and had an underhanded conversation on it. Was this strange or just theatric on his part, since only our friends and family members were privy to the private household number and used it strictly to make personal calls. Darth was clearly agitated by this call and acted as if he didn't want me to overhear the conversation. He also made it clear to the party on the other end of the line to never call his home about business again.

I was thinking that our home was supposed to be my oasis, as Darth told me he was talking to the stupid cleaning lady who took care of the hotel house. I asked why she would be calling him at home on the weekend and he said her apartment had been robbed and she was very distraught. I couldn't imagine why the cleaning woman would call Darth about her problem and he told me she didn't have anyone else she could call. I privately wondered why she wouldn't have phoned her elderly parents who had recommended her in the first place. I did not realize then that she had moved to an apartment near our home and no longer lived in another state next door to her parents.

I began to connect the dots the following week when Darth hired the cleaning lady as an additional secretary. When she arrived at the office, I met her for the first time and a tsunami wave of reality hit me. She was not an old crone with a hair net, thick soled shoes, and dirty dish rag. She was younger than I was and attractive, she possessed absolutely no office skills to speak of. I was informed that she had just relocated to work with my husband even though she couldn't type. I wasn't blind to how she and Darth whispered and lingered around one another when they thought that no one else was paying attention. Then one day without warning, she was gone.

The fact that we were only twenty-seven years old and running a successful enterprise that we had built from the ground up had little effect on me, I still felt that I was the same person that I had always been. I lived in the same house, wore the same clothes, and rode the same horse. I was still the same mom and wife. I was just a girl wanting a boy to love me, albeit for all the wrong reasons.

However, I suspected that a lot of Darth's success was going to his head and his drinking was a contributing factor. Darth thought he could do anything he wanted. He'd started a new routine with eight-year-old Joey. Frequently, they would leave the house together. There was never a mention from either of them about their plans. I would simply find them gone. Generally, they left when I was at the opposite end of the house. I could be in the shower or making the bed on a Saturday morning and they would simply vanish.

Eventually later in the day they would reappear, and Joey would talk about how they had shopped for baseball cards, gone roller skating or spent the afternoon at the bowling alley. These circumstances seemed bizarre to me but when I would attempt to question Darth, he would simply close the door on the conversation. In time I quit worrying about it, knowing they would both come home before the day was over. It bothered me that I was not included in their plans or their fun, but they seemed to prefer to be with each other. I chose to banish worry and be pleased about Darth spending quality time with his son.

In addition to being intentionally left behind, I was the only disciplinarian. It was always me, the mean mom who had to insist on brushing teeth, going to bed at a decent hour and not eating dessert first. It became my fulltime duty to monitor Joey's schoolwork, the cleaning of his room and picking up after himself. I was the enforcer who oversaw feeding the dogs and carrying in firewood. I resented being the task master and not being allowed in on their covert fun activities.

I thought that the father and son bonding sessions were great for a child, but the infra-arrangement was lopsided and teetering. I didn't know what to do so I kept forging ahead with my daily tasks and office duties in a feeble attempt to reaffirm the value of my own life. Denial was my natural human response to situations that I was unready to cope with. I lied to myself to minimize our problems and go on pretending that our lives were functioning normally. Regardless of why I continued to live in denial it was like gravity, eventually it was going to pull me under.

CHAPTER SEVEN

Near the elementary school that Joey attended, was a babysitter who had been referred to me by the mother of one of Joey's classmates. I developed an immediate affection for this bemused teenage girl. She was quiet but would eventually open-up if I prodded her with several questions about high school. She was fifteen and looking forward to getting her learners permit to drive. She seemed sensitive and pensively sad, and I wasn't certain why, but Joey liked her.

We rarely required a sitter as we no longer had mutual friends who invited us over, and it had been years since we'd borrowed Darth's folks' camper for a weekend getaway. If anybody went somewhere to do something recreational it was usually Joey. He enjoyed trips to the beach on the weekends with Grandma Dodie, visiting her beach house that wasn't really on the beach.

It had been ages since Darth, and I had been to the movies. Darth would insist that we view purely sexual movies in degrading downtown theatres. Initially the movies he chose were produced with an undeveloped plot and a lot of raucous sex performed by women with perfect bodies, voluptuous lips and inflated breasts. Movies that were sexually satisfying to him eventually plummeted to the sleazy theatres that showed kinky sex between men. These movies were not arousing or interesting to me; they were chalked full of obscene and lewd actions causing me to sit seething, preoccupied while silently studying the smutty crannies of Darth's cranium. One night in a filthy flea bag theatre in the dilapidated section of town Darth took me to a show of two men having anal sex with Vaseline lotion as a lubricant.

Disgusted with him, I sat perched on the edge of my seat in the clammy, musty theater, and wondered who had sat in the seat before me. Thrumming thoughts of dread throbbed through my head. I wasn't going to sit through more of the big screen show. On a morbid impulse I walked out. Only to find myself on the sidewalk in the scary end of town, in the middle of the night, all alone with no car keys, as I stood staring down a creepy alley. Darth appeared and took me home. From then on, he rented the sexually arousing VCR movies that he wanted to watch.

For a week in August Joey was going to be gone to California with both my mom and dad for his first visit to Disneyland. I'd been excited for him to have this opportunity and I knew he was eager for the trip. I planned and asked Sally if she would like to help me paint for pay, so I could complete Joey's bedroom project before he returned. Halfway through the week I recognized resentment in Sally's attitude toward her father whenever the matter of her home life came up. My thought gave me pause. Her father had been sexually molesting her. I felt outraged with him while I felt absolute compassion for her. I finally came right out and asked her if her father was touching her in ways that he shouldn't. She hung her head as the tears rolled down her sorrowful, pallid cheeks. The problem with trying to help her was that she really wasn't willing to discuss the issues, and I did not know how to crack her protective veneer.

To get Sally away from her father, she would have to be the one who disclosed the sordid details. The following day I picked her up as usual and we continued with our painting project. When I felt the timing was right, I asked her some specific questions that she was willing to partially answer. When I inquired about what her mother knew Sally somberly told me that she had gone to her mother for help the previous year and her mom had been infuriated that Sally would tell such shameful lies about her own father. I suspected that her mother knew the truth and preferred to deny it for her own reasons, at Sally's expense. Sally cried, "My mom told me if I ever told lies about my father, she'd throw me out of the house." This was finalized when her mother insisted, "You should be grateful your father puts a roof over your head and food on our table."

Currently, I was unaware of information claiming that parental sexual abuse to children frequently begins when the sexual relationship between the parents is deteriorating. Later I would read material that indicated there is frequently a connection to alcohol and drug abuse associated with sexual abuse of anyone, including children. Although children may be abused by strangers, they are in more danger with familiar neighbors and family members. Sexual abuse and incest damage children's lives to the core of their being, right into adulthood. Typically, these children are embarrassed, frightened, and feeling shame. The assault upon their young bodies and minds is especially confusing to them because the predators reward them with gifts, promises or special privileges.

As careful as possible, I explained to Sally that I could get her help, but she would have to be willing to tell on her own father. There were homes where she could stay, she could even stay with me, but first she had to disclose the details regarding her father's cruel advances. She agreed that she could inform the proper authorities. I had already talked to them, and they wanted to help her. They would come to my house and her mother would never have to be involved. All Sally had to do was explain the repulsive truth. She agreed that she would.

The next day I picked her up and we waited at my house until the authorities arrived. They were kind and gentle with Sally and explained that she could either tell them everything, write it down on a piece of paper, or speak in private to the Dictaphone they had brought with them, but she had to be the person that divulged the details of her father's molestations.

Instead, she shrank into our sofa pillows and cried. She wouldn't talk or write so the Family Services representatives left her with a card covered in telephone numbers that she could call anytime day or night. Sally had told me that she had a lock on the inside of her bedroom door. She was careful to keep it engaged and she could always use the telephone in her bedroom. Generally, the problem for her was getting to and from the bathroom and back down the hall to her room. I wished she would tell but I don't think that she ever did. Finally, she refused to come back to baby-sit for me. I told her that if she ever needed me, all she had to do was call and I would immediately come straight to her house, no questions asked. Sally never did phone me.

From then on when I occasionally needed a sitter, I would call my neighbors teenage son. He was sixteen, the eldest of my friend's three children. They lived across the street from us and even though we were each busy with our own lives, we managed to occasionally go on horse-back trail rides together. We had lived across our country street for several years and frequently one or more of her children would ride with us. When I mentioned that I needed to find a reliable new sitter, Lydia suggested her eldest son, Jordan.

One day when I was picking Joey up from his best friend's house, I had a few minutes to visit with Jimmie's mom. I asked her if Sally had babysat for her in the last few months. Apparently, Jimmie's mom had heard a few rumors but hadn't seen Sally. Jimmie's mom did say that she had overheard her kids talking the other day and possibly I should be aware of their conversation.

Lydia's oldest boy, Jordan had recently baby-sat for Jimmie and his brothers, and had approached one of them sexually. They didn't want him to come back to sit ever again. Jimmie's mom didn't know any exact details because her kids weren't telling, but she did know that she would intentionally avoid Lydia's son as a sitter. This was really bad news and the only way I felt I could get to the truth was to have a discussion with Joey. He would talk with me about most things if his dad hadn't yet been involved in the conversation. If a worst nightmare were unfolding, I didn't know how I could keep Darth out of the picture. I was hoping that Joey could tell me what his best friend Jimmie was talking about and that an enemy had not touched my son.

When I asked Joey about Jimmie's experiences with the Jordan, I knew immediately that the truth was lurking somewhere below the surface. I could tell that something happened that involved Joey. I wasn't going to stop probing just because it got incredibly uncomfortable. I wanted to know exactly what had been going on when the sitter was alone with my child. Then I was determined to address whatever profane ugliness existed.

Gleaning answers as I could and putting them into chronological order took time and effort, but I think Joey felt better after he was able to open-up and reveal his feelings. The sitter used a good old stand by with him, "You can stay up past your bedtime if you'll do whatever I want, and I'll let you watch late night television and not tell your parents."

Joey would lay face down on his bed with his pajama pants around his ankles while the sitter straddled him naked from the waste down, deliberately rubbing his erect little teenage penis back and forth against Joey's buttocks until he reached ejaculation. This made me furious. Every cell in my body was saturated with repulsion. I wanted to snap that stupid kid's scrawny freckled neck with my bare hands and nip off his nuts with rusty scissors.

I wanted Joey to be in counseling where he could really talk and work his way through being molested. I didn't think he was going to do that in detail with either of his parents. Then I thought again about Darth, and I knew he would be irate. I was afraid the situation would be even more complicated if Darth were spiraling out of control in a heated tirade. I had command of my own situation when I siphoned grocery money to pay for my marriage counseling but there was no way that would work with Joey. His dad would find out. It was best for me to just level with Darth.

That evening I explained everything that I'd been able to uncover to Darth while he ranted and raved about how he was going to "kill the molesting teenage bastard with an uncontrollable cock." I was afraid that he meant it literally, and I didn't think that it would help Joey if his dad marched across the street and blew the kid's head off with a shotgun.

When Darth simmered down and finished his fist clenching, he said he was going to talk to Joey alone. Already I was being shut out of the situation. Darth was going to take control and do it his way, so I sat down in the family room and waited as I absently studied the texture of the vaulted ceiling.

When Darth emerged from the hallway, I felt my heart line go flat and my chest sink, as he told me that Joey had talked all about it and everything was now fine. In other words, this was my complimentary warning that I wasn't supposed to bring the subject up ever again. I told Darth I didn't care how embarrassing it was for any of us, I wanted to report it to the authorities. In my unvarnished view the sitter's parents had to know what was going on and take appropriate actions. I really didn't care what would happen to the demented molesting Jordan. I wanted him to be punished and I didn't want him near Joey again.

I was uncertain if Joey had told me the entire truth. I knew there would have to be emotional consequences, but what about any physical injury? I wanted to have him examined by a doctor. Darth came unglued at this idea and said, "absolutely not", forbidding me to do any such thing. He vowed, "Joey told me everything and there wasn't any physical penetration from the sitter." I was thinking to myself that I hadn't seen any signs of blood on Joey's underwear, and he told me that when the sitter was finished, he would clean Joey's back off with a washcloth. I supposed that it would serve to further humiliate Joey by taking him for an examination.

The following morning when Darth went to work, I phoned Jordon's mom, and talked to her at length. She wasn't difficult to convince, and she whimpered along as I explained what I knew about the situation. I told her I couldn't bring it up with Darth but that I wanted proof from her that she would report her son. She stuck to her word and called Family Services. Lydia's entire family had to go to counseling and the eldest son was required to do some special community service along with his own private therapy.

Darth forbid me to discuss the ordeal again with Joey, but we did talk about it a few times when I felt Joey was open to the subject. It was wrong to sweep it under the rug like dust balls and pretend that the situation would heal itself. I made further attempts to convince Darth that we should take Joey for therapy but he steadfastly forbid it.

I followed up on a regular basis with Lydia and to her own shock and humiliation; she found out that her eldest son had learned his sexual perverted-ness from his older cousin who had practiced on him.

CHAPTER EIGHT

Pushing my pencil, I had designed a horse barn complete with a covered arena. The barn would house fifteen matted stalls, overhead hay storage, feed, and tack room, viewing area, bathroom, miniature grandstands, heated wash rack and enclosed shavings bin. The concrete aisles led to sliding doors for plenty of light and ventilation.

I'd been backward and forward through my figures and calculated all my overhead costs. If I kept my barn full of boarders, I could make the monthly payments on the building. I could afford a payment on a new truck that would always be at my disposal if I traded in my car. It was the same automobile that Darth had screwed-around-in with the restaurant owner. I thought about her every time I sat behind the steering wheel. I would be relieved to get rid of the car. Now, all I had to do was present this information to Darth in a manner that would appeal to his ego, construct the barn, and fill it with paying boarders.

After being in dozens of other barns, I had left no possibility unturned in my design. I hadn't wasted a single inch of space. Darth agreed with the design drawings and said that he could engineer the plans. I wanted to get three different contractors to give us bids, but Darth disagreed. He wanted to be his own contractor and use our company's employees to do the construction and only subcontract the electrical. I wasn't certain that this was the best route to take but if it meant getting my horse facility, I wasn't going to argue about who built it.

Reviewing all my calculations for costs and overhead, Darth agreed that I could net the funds that I had projected if I kept the barn full of boarders' horses. I was one step ahead of him when I presented my marketing plan and contingencies for a full stall barn. I listened carefully to Darth as I knew him to be the man who frequently agreed to one scenario and then dispelled all plans in mid-stream without a warning. My instincts were telling me that he had agreed to my barn business because it could carry its own weight and he'd sound good telling his friends, parents and employees how he was building a horse barn just for his wife.

In the mud of early spring, we started production of the barn structure and Darth's ego all at the same time. I had assumed that we would apply for a loan at the bank we used for our business. Darth wouldn't explain why but he wanted to construct the building first using business funds and then finance the barn after it was completed. I did not want to involve the business in this personal undertaking, but Darth had the final say and he had previously decided that he would make use of his employees for labor, so I was out of the decision-making loop.

As with most construction project completion seemed to take forever despite my efforts. I was busy with the small details that added to the big picture and the additional horse that we had purchased. After agreeing to my projection for the barn business, Darth insisted that I needed to go all the way with my abilities and the manufacturing of his ego by purchasing a stud horse.

They had major hormones. You couldn't ever relax around a stud because you could never trust them completely, not to mention that I had never handled a stud horse before. Horses, as much as I loved everything about them, are inherently dangerous. They are powerful, flighty animals that can hurt you in less than a second in a thousand different ways. I had no desire to deal with a stud horse.

I knew of a woman who owned a stud she had raised from a foal. She had ridden and trained this horse for years. She bred mares with him every spring and hauled him to the fall circuit shows. For a stud horse, he was quite docile. One evening she entered the stall to put on his winter blanket for the night. His owner had probably done this over a thousand times. However, on this night her beloved stud horse bit her on the neck while she was fastening the chest straps on his blanket. A stud horse can force a mare to the ground this way. This unfortunate woman's stud bit right through her jugular vein and she bled to death in his stall and there wasn't a damn thing she could do about it. I really didn't want to deal with a stallion, yet Darth insisted that I raise, train, ride, show and breed one to promote the barn and provide additional income.

Not only does it take major capitol to purchase quality horse flesh, but it also takes even more money to promote one. The idea works if the horse is a supreme athlete, he's properly promoted, and he can pass on all his outstanding traits to his offspring. The idea could work, providing the stud horse doesn't go lame or impotent and you don't become a fatality when you're in his stall.

I stood overlooking the construction site where one of Darth's employees spent eight hours on a bulldozer excavating three thousand dollars' worth of footing into the wrong spot. I regretted that this employee was Elise's older brother and one of Darth's favorite employees who was required by court order to appear at the pharmacist once a week to swallow an Antabuse pill that made him sick if he ingested any type of alcohol.

Running the facility was an enormous amount of work. I'm sure I could have worked that hard at something else and made more money but that wasn't the point. I was happy when I was in the barn. It was like walking into an entirely different world from the world where I lived. My barn and equines gave me a sense of balance and serenity. Some evenings in the winter when it was pouring and blustery, there would be a misty layer of fog that would settle into the arena. I loved to ride through it. My arena was my escape to heaven on earth.

Perhaps only a horse enthusiast could understand what it felt like to ride. So much of my life was out of whack, and no matter how hard I tried to compensate or compromise for it, I couldn't fix it. Yet, on the back of my horse, I was at one with the universe.

However, there was a price to pay. You were always expected to pay a price to Darth. He had allowed me our barn with his strings attached and now I owed him. Since I owed him, he was once again, doing whatever he wanted. He was coming home at all hours of the night, with no explanations. I thought there was more than a just another woman involved.

Should I push the issue of where he was or what he was doing, he would remind me that if my barn did not start producing additional funds, he was going to tear out the stalls, pour a concrete floor in the arena and turn it into another shop because he wanted space that was more expansive. It served no positive purpose for me to remind him that all the boarding stalls were full. The barn was consuming less bedding shavings than I had originally planned, and the barn budget was right on track, the same budget that he had initially approved.

When submitting all the application paperwork that Darth had authorized to the bank, I had also submitted our financial statements. The appraiser had been out and completed the bank required evaluation on our property and home. Our banker had approved the additional mortgage against the barn structure, and underwriting was working on the red tape. The following week we received a check from the bank for over seventy thousand dollars. This amount was slightly more than what we owed our company for labor and materials. The check was made payable to both of us, so after I endorsed the back of the check, I gave it to Darth to sign. Standing in front of his desk I told him that I had to run to town on errands and I could do the business bank deposit that day. Darth told me, "Nope" that he had an appointment, so he would do the banking and he took the barn check with him. I trusted Darth with the banking; my brain must have left the building.

CHAPTER NINE

One of the activities that Joey enjoyed was baking. He wasn't into cooking unless it was a TV dinner, but he did like to bake cakes and cookies. Together we would feast on the raw cookie dough. The mixing bowl sat deeply in the stainless-steel kitchen sink where Joey could handle the electric beaters for combining ingredients. We were busy stirring batter one evening when Joey asked me if I thought he'd beaten the batter long enough. I peered over his shoulder at the brown flour lumps and told him he needed a few more minutes of mixing. While we were having this conversation, Darth came walking into the kitchen. He had overheard our discussion and as he sauntered between us up to the sink, scrutinizing the bowl he said to Joey, "Don't listen to your mother, she doesn't love you like I do."

I couldn't believe my ears or the lie. Even if what Darth said was true, which it wasn't, why would you say such a thing to an eight-year-old boy. Wondering if Darth wanted a fight, I chose not to say a word. I wanted to stand my ground and poke my finger into his hairy chest and tell him to shut-up because he was a lying bastard. I couldn't because I didn't know how to fight Darth's lies with concrete evidence, so I stayed in my sheltered denial and proceeded to unload the dishwasher.

Unaware that as the addiction penetrates deeper into the family infra-structure, destructive alliances are formed between family members, usually the alliance is formed between one parent and one child against the other parent. As Darth developed his posturing with Joey, I reacted in a manner where I was trying to make life easier and protect Joey. I was desperately attempting to stabilize our family as Darth's addictive behavior grew more unpredictable.

Careful not to position Joey in the middle and give Darth the fight he wanted, my thoughts bounced up and down in my head. I was beginning to understand all too clearly that this must not be the first time that Darth had told Joey I didn't love him. In a pivotal moment I realized that Darth had been poisoning my son against me. If he genuinely loved his only child as he professed, then he would never indoctrinate such hurtful and hideous lies into our son's tender mind. I was beginning to realize that Darth had been undermining me for years.

When lunch was over, and the mess cleaned up I had just enough time to scrub the kitchen floor, if I hurried. Since it was hot outside, I decided now was a good time with the windows wide open to strip the old wax build-up off the linoleum. I was on my hands and knees with a hard-bristled brush scrubbing up the gunk. After I'd sufficiently removed the old wax, I switched to my push mop to clean up the messy grunge I'd scoured. I'd also been mentally preparing for the best way to present the horse for sale, and I was running out of mopping time.

Along came Darth, barefoot and in his shorts, he strode across my mopping project. He wanted a drink of water and wouldn't get one out of any of the three available bathrooms. While pausing at the sink for his drink, he began to quibble with me about how I couldn't sell a thermo blanket to an Eskimo and I'd never be able to sell the horse. I told him that since I was totally useless, he could go out to the barn, bathe, and clip the horse and have the mare saddled and ready for the potential buyer.

Darth opened the refrigerator door and snagged himself a Coors, as he took the first cool pull from the beer, he made a snide remark to me. Turning his back, he arrogantly strutted off. That did it. I refused to mentally stomp out my burning fuse; I kicked the hornets' nest instead. I didn't pause to consider the consequences of my temper; I just unleashed it. For seconds, my temper felt forceful and strong and ever so willing to oblige me. I struck. The mop I'd pushed about the floor slid hard past the refrigerator door and right into the back of Darth's bare heel. I was astonished how high he could jump for a big bulky bully.

I drew blood and I liked it. With one final swoop I struck again, and blood appeared on the back of the opposite heel. Peering at me over his shoulder with his beer in-hand, he shot me a look of disbelief and exhibited amazing speed in exiting the kitchen. I didn't understand why he didn't retaliate. I privately wondered if he thought he deserved it, or he was afraid he'd have to ride his mare for the potential purchasers. He didn't ride nearly as well as he drank. I felt a small victory and smug satisfaction, but I didn't deceive myself into thinking that chasing Darth with a mop was something that I would get away with very often.

I gave up on selling Darth's horse; he announced that he wanted to keep her as a brood mare. She was well pedigreed, but she filled a stall I could have boarded out for income. I quit training her and started riding the gelding I'd purchased. He had scars and bowed tendons from his previous owner because of being run over a cliff and through a barb wire fence. There were additional fresh scars on both of his shoulders from his last rider's spurs. I hated his previous owner and loved the horse I knew he would become. I thought he needed me as much as I needed him, strange how I had thought the same things about Darth.

After months of difficult training, I took my palomino gelding to a four day "A: circuit show". By the end of the circuit we had won the all-a-round amateur championship. I was more than a little excited, I was ecstatically glowing. Darth wanted to reward me by selling my horse.

But I'd hidden his registration papers and wasn't buying into Darth's self-indulged idea.

What I was going to do instead was schedule myself for necessary surgery. My periods weren't normal, I would constantly hemorrhage for weeks at a time, and the worst part was the excruciating pain. I explained to my doctor that when I'd sit down on a padded chair it felt as if I was jamming a broom stick deep into my crotch. My doctor was certain that I had endometriosis and he explained there was a cure for it.

Getting pregnant usually cleared it up and kept it from coming back for a while. As far as I was concerned surgery was my only option, another baby in my marriage was not. Aside from going through a complete hysterectomy my biggest concern was who could manage the barn chores while I was recovering. The only person that I could think of was my mother. She and Dad were retired, and they traveled around the country in their fifth wheel trailer participating in senior citizen activities. To ask her to do all my work for six weeks was an enormous task and favor to request. Mom could stay at the house in the spare bedroom that never did get wallpapered in pink, cook meals, do laundry, and take care of Joey while I was recovering.

Darth informed me he absolutely forbid my mother from staying with us for six weeks. He claimed he would send over an employee every day to take care of the barn. Darth knew that someone had to take care of Joey. The barn chores weren't something anybody could do on a whim, especially those who didn't know how to handle horses. I told Darth I didn't care what he thought or wanted; I was asking my mom for help while I was recuperating.

Mom arrived while Dad stayed at their current campsite location since he'd just taken a job working for the Forest Service on a part-time basis. I felt guilty about my request for help because I knew that my parents would be much happier together than apart. I spent a few days going through the barn work schedule with Mom, so she was familiar with the routine and each horse. She was amazed how much work running the barn was and couldn't believe that I could handle that along with a household, a child and a part-time job at the business. Mom thought that Darth should hire someone to clean house for me each week. I could go along with that.

Joey and Mom took me to the hospital the evening before I was scheduled for surgery. I already had a headache and could tell that Joey was worried. I tried to explain that everything would be fine, and I would be home in a few days, and that he shouldn't worry, Grandma would never make him eat spinach. The following morning during surgery preparations Darth showed up and sat in my room talking business on the phone. He acted like a jerk, and I was relieved when they rolled me down the hall to the operating room.

Still sleeping I vaguely remembered Darth showing up that evening. I was too wasted on the heavy pain medication to be social and relished my escape into sleep. Two days after surgery my doctor released me. Since I ate my hospital food, took myself to the bathroom and walked up and down the hall unassisted pushing my IV bottle, he decided I could recover just as well at home. Mom came to pick me up late that morning Darth's Mercedes, so I wouldn't have to climb into my four-wheel-drive truck. She thought I should stay another day, but I was determined to go home.

Mom was fixing dinner when I stumbled back down the hall directly to the support of the awaiting sofa. To my surprise Darth showed up before six o'clock and had dinner with us. So that was it, one of his reasons for not wanting Mom to stay with us was because he would have to save face and appear to be an attentive husband, being home for dinner and spending the evenings at home where no one was drinking.

My entire uterus, cervix and ovaries had all been removed. According to Doctor's strict orders there was to be no sex, for six weeks. I was hoping that Darth would understand about my condition and be willing to follow the doctor's instruction. I had a nasty incision across my lower abdomen that started at the right hip bone and ended at the left. My surgeon had even cut right through my old hernia incision. I still had all the ugly black staples holding my exterior together along with a lot of pain.

My doctor told me in thirty years of surgeries he had never seen endometriosis in the severity of which I'd had it. It was necessary to remove my intestines and scrape the fibrous disease which is why my bladder bled as it had been surgically scraped as well. At age twenty-eight there would be no more hemorrhaging periods for me.

Getting in and out of our king-sized waterbed with the padded bumper guards was extremely difficult, and terribly painful but a necessity if I wanted a comfortable place to sleep. It was five days after my surgery and so far, so good. Darth had gone to sleep at night but that was about to change. Late that night when he sloshed into bed and sent the mattress waves rolling, he informed me that he wasn't waiting six weeks for sex. I tried to tell him that there was absolutely no way I could have sex for six weeks until I was healed. I still had internal stitches where my cervix had been permanently sliced off.

Darth was becoming more agitated as he spoke, and I was beginning to cry. He genuinely frightened me, and I pleaded with him to understand that there was nothing I could do other than have the necessary time to heal. He wasn't buying it. I felt so vulnerable. I couldn't move fast enough to escape him, and it would take me forever to get out of the waterbed in my condition. I certainly couldn't run and there was nowhere to go, and he knew it. He demanded that if he couldn't have sex, he wanted me to masturbate him. I sobbed harder and told him I couldn't move very well or work my arms because it stressed my sutured abdominal muscles. I had no strength and unlimited pain. He didn't care; he still wanted to be masturbated. I was silently cursing him and the stupid, rolling waterbed. I finally flat out told him as steadily as I could that I simply could not comply.

He erupted and slugged me full-fisted, in a direct hit on the raw stapled incision. Gurgles of memories burst forth in bright blue stars. I wanted to run down the rabbit hole and hide, but I didn't know where it was. I thought I was going to pass out and then he could just rape me and be done with it. All I could do in an incoherent state was try to draw breath. I felt the darkness surround me as I vaguely sensed the lolling mattress while trying to lie perfectly still. Darth flipped over on his side with his back to me and went to sleep. I remembered that Mom was across the hall in the spare bedroom, and I wanted to go ask her to protect me, but I didn't dare. I felt as helpless as a four-year-old and wished that my mother could beat Darth up.

I felt too disgraced and disregarded to even tell my mother. Throughout my teenage years Mom had done a fine job of reminding me that the only way to true happiness was to marry in the temple of the one and only true church. I felt that by running to her now, I would prove to her that she was right, even though I believed in my heart that she wasn't. I believed enough in myself that I could have a happy marriage without belonging to an organized religion that I did not agree with. Defeat wormed its way across my mind, as I tried to marshal my inner strengths, I fell asleep.

CHAPTER TEN

Dad arrived to gather up Mom five weeks after my surgery. I could get around well enough, even though I couldn't stand unswervingly upright. I walked around stooped over like an old woman with a severe case of osteoporosis. I managed to accomplish all the daily barn chores working very slowly and taking rest breaks on a bale of hay.

Alone again, I watched my parent's gooseneck travel trailer roll down the gravel driveway and head out of sight. There I was feeling vulnerable in my undesirable world with no one left to rely on. Darth would return to his own agenda of coming home when he pleased.

Returning to my part time job at the business, I argued with Darth about a new project he wanted to pursue, a tavern. Down the street, kitty corner from our bank was a tavern for sale. Darth wanted to own it. He explained he was the perfect candidate. Our business could afford to purchase the commercial building. Darth said the purchase would be a good investment. It needed a complete remodel, and we owned a business that could renovate at wholesale cost. The tavern was conveniently located just five minutes from our office, making the project easy to supervise.

The last thing in the world that I wanted was to own a tavern. Neither of us had any experience operating a bar with a grill and menu. Darth certainly didn't need his very own liquor license. I couldn't begin to imagine a worst-case scenario. Standing-my-ground, I told Darth, "I am not going to sign the paperwork with the bank to get the loan." I did not realize that Darth would be prepared for my stance.

He snarled back at me, "I can do whatever I damn well please, and I don't need your permission to purchase the tavern." He never broached the subject with me again. Instead, he bought his tavern.

Attending to my office duties, I still had a regular grip on business practices. However, no one ever mentioned the tavern activities to me. I knew that Darth had signed the required documentation and we, I mean he, now owned a tavern. The current remodeling plans were underway. This was the first time in our marriage that I was not asked to supervise the decorating of a project. I had no idea what Darth was spending on this gamble, but I think it had his father and brother concerned. His father's and brother's combined stock totaled more than Darth's, yet to my knowledge they did nothing to hamper the tavern purchase.

Going about my work in the barn and at home, I lived with the assumption that Darth was still supervising the remodel of his latest pet project. I didn't know that the grand opening he had been talking about had already taken place and the tavern had been officially opened for business. I discovered this by accident from my hairdresser.

Tyla told me that she had been to the grand opening. I told her that I knew one was being planned but the remodel was not yet complete. She stopped rolling my hair, stepped back and told me that the opening party had been the previous month and she knew this because she had been there. I was surprised and somewhat embarrassed that I hadn't known this, so I inquired as to how Tyla had known about the party. She said Darth had invited her younger sister, who had invited her. I hadn't seen Tyla's younger sister in years. She would have lagged three years behind me in school and she was the one sibling of all the kids that I had never liked. I'd always found her to be pushy, self- absorbed and bothersome. I contemplated what her connection could be to Darth? Tyla knew. Her mouth was stumbling around with words trying to find a discrete way to inform me that my husband was boning her younger sister.

I had previously felt recent suspicions about Darth's indiscretions, but I had never caught him in the act. When my instincts would speak to me, I learned to answer back with excuses. I reprimanded myself for having dire thoughts about someone I was supposed to love and trust. In my judgments, I always offered the benefit of the doubt to my spouse. Later in life I would learn to listen to my instincts because instincts don't lie.

In addition, that was not all Tyla had to tell me. The night of the grand opening when the freshly modernized building was packed full of celebrating people drinking free beer, Darth had stood on one of the new tabletops and made an announcement to the audience. He wanted everyone to know that his wife wasn't attending the party because she was a disappointing sex object and he deserved better. I wondered what everyone at the party thought of me. I'd grown up and gone to school in the area and probably knew most of the people who had been present for Darth's exaggerated sex speech.

I was recognizing changes in Darth's chemically altered actions and thoughts, but I hadn't a clue of what to do about it. I did not understand the behaviors that were emerging as Darth's addiction took a stronger hold. Perhaps he did not realize what was happening as he adapted to cover-up his increasing addictions that were swiveling beyond his control.

That evening when Darth came home from work, I told him that if he would install a hot tub in our backyard, I would sit in it and drink with him. I really meant what I was suggesting even though I didn't drink. I promised him that I would change to be what he wanted me to be if he would just spend time at home with me drinking in the hot tub, instead of at his tavern. He agreed that a hot tub with a devoted drinking wife sounded good and might satisfy his manhood too. I drew up plans for the installation of a Jacuzzi, but Darth never followed through. He was too busy drinking down at the tavern and courting Tyla's annoying, younger, married sister.

Instead of reaffirming the value of my own life, I made a common mistake of prolonging addiction by my willingness to promote Darth's drinking in a Jacuzzi. I was not extricating myself from the unhealthy addictive patterns. In my desperation, I was willing to join them, if Darth would give me what I wanted and include his family in his life. I was willing to compromise my own well-being, as my efforts to help my addict grew increasing futile.

CHAPTER ELEVEN

A few hours' drive from our house was a sizeable horse show facility that was sponsoring an open show. I thought it would be good practice to haul the stud to this show for exposure to unfamiliar show grounds, constantly reminding myself that the stud possessed rampant hormones, I tried to think of him as just another horse, but then I would remind myself not to trust him. Ironically, this was the same way that I knew I should scrutinize Darth.

I returned home around eight o'clock Sunday evening just as I had promised. Daylight was creeping to dusk when I pulled the horse trailer past the house and down the driveway to the front entrance of the barn. Both horses were fighting with one another, though neither of them could really inflict any real damage with the flat metal stall divider between them. I wasn't comfortable unloading them by myself if help was available.

None of the lights were on in the house but I knew Darth was home because his Mercedes and handy satellite-cell phone was parked on the driveway pad. Deciding to leave the two skirmishing horses in the trailer for a few minutes I jogged up to the house. The doors weren't locked, but the house was silent with a hush of emptiness. Joey must still be with his grandparents?

Flipping on a few light switches as I went, I started down the hallway. Still, no one answered my calls. The unnerving quietness of the house felt thick. In the darkened master bedroom with the tiny bedside reading lamp alight was Darth in his blue jeans and plaid flannel shirt, in bed. This struck me as weird. Darth never went to bed early and since he believed clothes were sexually inhibiting; he certainly never wore work clothes to bed. I asked him what he was doing, and he just stared at me as if I was dense and held up his book. I asked him why the entire house was dark, and he glared at me over the top of the book binder. I then asked, "Would you please come on out to the barn and give me a hand unloading the two feuding horses", he simply nodded recognition.

Thinking that Darth was going to follow right behind me I left the house the same way I'd come in and walked back out to the barn. When I approached the trailer both horses were squealing at one another. Their ears were pinned flat back against their necks, and they were trying to kick one another though the stall divider as the trailer rocked from their shifting weight. The agitated situation was worsening by the minute and Darth wasn't anywhere in sight. I waited a few moments and finally decided that I'd better address the situation by myself. I trusted my gelding more than the stud, so I decided to start by unloading him first. I'd just backed him out of the horse trailer when Darth magically appeared, standing directly behind me in the dark. He insisted that I hand my gelding's lead-rope to him. There was something very strange and steely eyed about the look on Darth's face. It was eerily menacing, and it made me afraid to hand him the lead-rope. I already had the gelding unloaded and under control. The horse that needed immediate attention was the stud kicking up noisy outbursts inside the trailer.

Not wanting or needing to hand my gelding over to Darth I told him that I was putting him into his stall, and I could manage it. Darth didn't say anything, so I assumed that he'd gone to the trailer to unload his stud. I opened the stall door and started to enter with my gelding when I felt a solid tug from Darth on the back of my jacket. I let go of the lead-rope and the horse continued into his stall and his awaiting pile of dinner in the hay trough.

As I brushed past Darth an inner iciness told me that I needed to put distance between myself and my husband even though I was confused about why. I'd stepped about three feet onto the concrete aisle way when Darth grabbed my right wrist and swung me abruptly to face him. I knew I was in trouble, but I didn't understand.

The crest of my head came to the bottom of Darth's chin. I could see the half inch scar etched into his hide from falling off the jungle gym when he was a kid. When he and I were teenagers I thought the rough scar was sexy. I tried to down-play his antagonism by calmly telling him to close the stall door before the horse got loose. He acknowledged me by tightening his grip. I understood that Darth could be violent, but I was never emotionally prepared for the outbursts. Generally, it was his justifications as to why everything that was wrong was always my fault. Tonight, he said absolutely nothing. All I could hear was a pop of tendon and bone somewhere in my shoulder. I winced with the sharp pain that traveled wherever it wanted to go. I still tried to pretend that nothing was wrong, and I asked Darth to let me go. His grip tightened, and I felt my arm forced into an unnatural angle as he spun me around. I tried to continue breathing as grimy pain burrowed under my skin. Darth moved swiftly for the taking and grabbed my left wrist as well, severely twisting it into a deformed position wedged behind my back as he continued to hold my other arm in the same method.

I heard both of my knee's crack when they hit the solid concrete aisle floor. I couldn't move and getting back to my feet was an option Darth was not going to allow. Against my own determination, I cried out that he was hurting me and demanded that he let me go. Simultaneously he twisted both arms further. As I gulped for air, I looked up into the face of my husband and didn't recognize the man I saw.

Fiendishly, he was smiling down at me in a demented smirk. I felt my chest seize because I knew he had no compunction whatsoever about harming me. I felt gooseflesh pimple the sides of my neck as I saw malice in his gaze. I immediately forgot all about the excruciating pain because I was so terrified. Crude brutality emanated from Darth as I knelt at his mercy. I was stunned by the realization that Darth was thoroughly enjoying himself as he purposely twisted harder.

Kneeling on the stone-cold barn aisle I looked at the rancor in Darth's expression and seriously wondered if his eyes would glow in the dark willing his head to spin around exorcist style. I didn't even question what I saw. I knew begging would be the true kiss of death and simply embolden Darth. His smile contorted into one last hostile grin for my benefit. He shoved me over into a crooked heap and walked away without looking back. I was astounded.

When I could work my arms again, I unloaded the stud horse and turned off the barn lights. I was cold and still shaking as I hid in the corner of my gelding's stall and listened to him contentedly munching on hay. I didn't dare to go back to the house. I had no idea what Darth had in store for me there. After a few hours, my terror had begun to subside. Terror is not like dejection or delight it is a discriminating condition that can only last for awhile. I decided Darth would surely be sound asleep and I could get something to eat. Beyond that I didn't know what I should do.

Working up enough courage to walk back to the house I realized that Darth's car was no longer in the driveway. He hadn't gone back to bed, he had disappeared. Still trembling, I practiced selective mental repressions as I went to bed unaccompanied in the empty house where I could make believe nothing out of the twilight zone had just happened. As I chose to do nothing, I was unknowingly joining Darth in a merry–go-round ride of denial, resentment, bewilderment, and guilt.

CHAPTER TWELVE

Darth's mare that never sold was bred to our stud horse and her delivery date was growing close. In anticipation I was checking Darth's pregnant mare constantly. Her udder was swelling and waxing which was an indicator that the foal could be born within the next few days. When the vaginal area under her tail began to droop, I knew the birth date of her first foal was close at hand. I'd never owned a pregnant mare before, so I dutifully set my alarm clock for two-hour intervals each night and regularly trudged to the barn to check the mare. It was frosty winter weather, so I pulled sweats on under my nightgown, my barn jacket over the top of my robe and strode to the barn with the flashlight shining.

She was stalled at the back of the barn in an oversized foaling stall bedded deep with fresh yellow straw. In the bluish light of night, standing with her head down, bottom lip loosely hanging, and one hip cocked off to the side she snoozed lazily, looking excruciatingly pregnant. She had grown accustomed to my frequent nightly visits which was a good thing. I had grown tired.

The alarm was blaring in my head, which meant it was midnight and time to get up, again. I felt as if I was waking in a murky haze, and I would much rather have been left to my slumber. I followed the same ritual I had developed over the last few nights and proceeded quietly out the back door. I knew immediately. I could hear the mare grunting from the back of the barn clear to the porch. I discovered it was hard to run with thick sweatpants under a floor length fleece robe.

Down in her foaling stall on her side with pasty lather on her neck was the distressed mare trying to give birth. There was the soggy baby with his head and neck completely scrunched against the corner of the tongue and groove wood stall. At first, I thought that the foal was dead with its neck broken. Upon further inspection I realized the foal was breathing rapidly with both of his hind legs still stuck firmly in the birth canal.

The mare had decided that she was finished performing her delivery job and she was trying to standup. I wasn't a vet or a foaling expert, but I knew that if she stood upright, she would either break her foal's back legs or disembowel herself or possibly both.

Planting my right foot on top of her hindquarters to hold her down, I tried to talk soothingly to her. Squatting, I wedged my shoulder under the foal's neck and tried to heave him up and away from the corner of the stall and straight back out of the birth canal all at the same time. The mare was getting up. I pulled harder and felt my hysterectomy incision complain and then I had a two-hundred-pound baby horse in my arms as we both tumbled bloody and sticky into the straw bedding.

He wobbled on spindly, long legs as he muzzled me searching for his mother's life-sustaining nutrients. I was so energized about the new baby that there would be no sleep for me the rest of the night. Darth still hadn't come home so he missed the first big foaling event. I had no idea where Darth was, but we had a new baby to show to Joey in the morning.

A few days later under closer inspection of the mare, I realized her udder was smaller and harder than it should have been. Her milk was drying up and the baby wasn't mature enough to get by on solid dry feed. The following morning, I was positive we had a problem. The vet told me there was nothing I could do other than bottle feed the baby myself and watch him closely for any signs of dehydration.

Bottle feeding a foal, how hard could that be? It would give me a lot of one-on-one time to bond with him, except the situation ended up like trying to put pants on an octopus. I could either force the bottle and fluids on him or he could die slowly. I was determined not to lose him.

Every hour I mixed the formula and attempted to persuade the colt to suckle the bottle. He would squeal like an indignant ape and scamper across the stall to hide behind his milk-less mama. I finally managed a system of maneuvers that worked. I would pin my hip against his shoulder positioning him firmly beside the wall and hold one arm over his neck grabbing his halter. With my free left hand, I'd hold the nippled bottle with life giving fluid and elevate his chin so fluid flowing from the bottle ran down my arm and elbow and into my shirt. The foal managed to swallow a few ounces of fluid by force of gravity.

After the first twelve hours of bottle battles, I had bruises under both of my arms, down my sides and cross my chest. Of course, Darth was nowhere to be found and this horse baby business was all his idea. By Saturday morning I'd run out of formula and so had the local general store that stocked what I needed. The feed store, all the way into town had formula so I phoned Dodie to see if she would mind picking up formula and bringing it out to me.

Over the phone, Dodie wanted to know, "Where's Darth"? I told her, "I don't know". She asked again, "When will he be home", I told her I didn't know that either. She inquired twice with the same questions before it occurred to her that I truly didn't know. I was just worn out enough to continue to tell her that this wasn't the first time that her son had disappeared with no explanation.

Dodie showed up an hour later with the powdered formula as promised. I wasted no time attempting the battle of wills to force fluid down the throat of the non-cooperating foal. Dodie and Joey went to the house to play in his room after which they left to spend the afternoon together in town, leaving me with the bottle-feeding regimen.

I went to the house for a breather and skimpy lunch. Where was Darth? He'd once possessed feelings of affection and had always been available to assist me when we'd raised baby claves to add funds to our savings account. Were his positive traits and characteristics deteriorating as he took on new behaviors that were typical of a different person whom I didn't know? Someone I'd never imagined he could be. All he seemed to care about now was achieving the next high or finding the new female flavor of the month. The house was empty except for the regular household furnishings and a paperback book Dodie had obviously left on the kitchen counter for me.

I stared at a used paperback book from a garage sale. The book appeared to be about getting an alcoholic sober. That was a surprise, especially coming from Dodie; she had never once expressed to me any concern about her son having an actual drinking problem. Staring at the book cover, I felt even more confused than I had been.

Darth's drinking certainly caused many problems in our household, but I didn't think that he was an alcoholic. I'd seen drunks on the streets downtown under the Brownport Bridge. I'd always thought of them as homeless bums wearing ragged, soiled clothing. They spent their nights getting drunk and days sleeping it off in cardboard boxes, after begging spare change to buy their cheap booze. That was an alcoholic. Darth was not a tattered, disheveled homeless person, nor had I ever seen him beg spare change. I curiously opened the book to the first page. Since no one else was home I could read in private. I needed a reprieve, and there was no time like the present.

After reading the first chapter of the book, I was positive that the author had been living with my husband for years. She knew exactly what it was like to deal with my spouse even though she had never even met him. I wanted to kiss her for understanding the details of what and whom I was attempting to deal with. Technically, I began to understand the true definition of an alcoholic. For starters, alcoholics and drug addicts are one in the same except they have simply chosen different substance dependencies. If you have alcoholic or drinking parents and/ or grandparents, your risk factor would likely increase. Some people can drink socially and never become addicted and others start their addiction process as indulging youngsters. The time span for becoming addicted varies with everyone based on their gene pool, and rate of consumption. A mathematical formula for determining addiction does not exist. Even if you never touch the hard stuff, alcohol is still a chemical, so it doesn't matter which label you drink.

Most authorities on the subject consider alcoholism to be a cruel disease. It is insidious at best which is why it is so complex to recognize and treat. Unfortunately, the sick person doesn't really know when they've crossed the line between having a potential problem and being addicted. There is no ruler by which to measure their addiction.

You can however evaluate the result and the affected family members. No two alcoholics will look exactly alike, and frequently drinkers are also druggies, but they will always share several similar traits, which left unleashed will eventually destroy the user and the ones who love them. To sum it up, I could lump drug and alcohol abuse into the same category as the devastation, the tears, the addiction, were one in the same.

I had been attempting to live happily with my loved one, yet I generally did not know which end was up, but still I claimed there was not really a massive problem. The first thing I'd have to do is get rid of my denial.

Denial was not my friend and if I allowed it, denial would keep me sick along with the one I loved. I didn't want to spend my life masquerading as an imposter of the person living the life that I really desired to have. Getting rid of my denial didn't mean that I could just admit out loud that there was a problem. Admitting a problem and brushing it aside with continuous excuses is what got me into denial trouble in the first place. Denial is very sophisticated. I could only face denial head on and to do so successfully I'd better be prepared. I'd have to be educated about denial and the journey I was beginning to embark.

CHAPTER THIRTEEN

My used paperback book was pointing a finger at me that I could identify with yet didn't completely understand. An enabler was someone I had never heard of before. It didn't sound nearly as appalling as being an addict. Yet how could I possibly be guilty of contributing to my husband's drinking when I had spent our entire relationship trying to stop him?

Thus far, he could break all the rules because I ran around behind him picking up the pieces. If I was responsible, he didn't have to be. I made apologies for him. I made excuses for him. I tried to be completely indulgent for him. I took whatever he dished out. I covered for him. I was sober when he was drunk. I was the parent at home when he was absent. I said prayers for him when he made fun of me. I pretended nothing was wrong when it certainly wasn't right. I told myself he was a good parent to his child when he was abusive to me. I turned the other cheek a thousand times when I should have stood my ground. I stayed when a normal emotionally healthy person would have left the relationship. I had been a martyr and proud of what I could withstand.

Because I was working overtime at being everything the addict wasn't, I made myself responsible for my actions and his. Since I was responsible for all the everyday tasks, my drinking and drugging enthusiast was liberated to travel the great highway of addiction. I was a major role player in his actions because I was an expert at shouldering the burdens.

Addicts can't survive in a relationship without an enabler even though they don't even recognize the problems they are promoting. I'd been assuming that if what I was trying wasn't working to make me happy, then somehow, I wasn't doing enough. If I hadn't been willing to enable Darth, he probably would have moved on to someone who would.

Being an enabler was a monumental task. I learned how to function on overload all the time. I was so accustomed to chaos that I didn't even recognize my stress load. There is one positive aspect about enabling an addict in their disease and irrational behavior. You can stop. It most certainly isn't easy, but it is simple. For my best interest I had to stop imagining that any trace of positive behavior on Darth's part was an indicator that he was finally changing for the best.

Enablers are not hard to find; the smart ones attend their own AA meetings in rooms adjacent to the addicts' meetings. The yellow pages in the telephone book list a multitude of telephone numbers for Alcoholics Anonymous, which hosts meetings in every municipality on any given day in several locations. Typically, a local school or church building will donate an available room for AA meetings.

Alcoholics Anonymous isn't just for drunks and addicts. It goes together with a program for enablers. All AA requires is a small donation if you can afford one. At AA they don't ask a lot of personal questions and you don't have to participate in the discussions if you choose not to. It is perfectly acceptable to remain totally anonymous as you learn while you listen. A real plus was that other enablers in attendance understood most of my trauma. Many of them were long time veterans in their forties, fifties, and sixties. They had already spent years participating in the addict's dysfunctional world and had finally decided that as enablers they were tired of being codependent.

In AA they don't preach about religion, attendees are personally entitled to believe in any religion they chose. What AA does promote is a higher power and how I could utilize it for my benefit. My higher power could be anything that felt appropriate, be it the Lord, or the man in the moon.

Finally, I would learn to let go of everything that I had been trying to control, because no matter how hard or how long I tried I could never control an addict. I felt enormous relief when I learned to stop trying to control Darth, even if he didn't stop drinking. Sometimes a religious reason helped me; I posted Proverbs 21:3, "Do what is right and just, that is more pleasing to the Lord than sacrifice", to my closet door. I'd been enabling, so I'd been sacrificing a lot.

As an enabler I had been practicing manipulation. Manipulation is nothing more than the clever management of someone else's affairs to attain your own end. I was learning to identify what my intentions were all about. I practiced manipulation with good intentions for a positive outcome for a person who obviously needed management.

However, I was now learning to change my mind about manipulating with nice intentions because manipulation equates to one person controlling the outcome of another person's actions. All manipulation is wrong unless the person who is being manipulated freely assigns his rights to the manipulator. If I tried to manipulate circumstances by words or deeds, in an effort I found necessary for productive reasons, then not only had I assumed a position of responsibility for Darth's actions, but I had done it for my own selfish reasons of control, and I was doing so without his permission.

In truth, manipulation was wrong no matter how I justified it. Instead, I had to face the reality of what Darth was all about. The Darth that I knew liked to keep me guessing about what he wanted. When I was positive, he would blow his stack, he lavished me with praises, but only in front of my friends and family. He had lots of rules that he privately expected me to follow. If I didn't comply, I'd suffer the consequences. When I was diligently following all the rules, the end goals would change, without notice.

Darth's reasons did not have to be logical. No matter how logically I'd argue them, it would not change his mind, and I could never win the argument. I could not make a point with him based on logical and sound reason, and I'd be baffled when he would use irrational logic against me. If that didn't work to his satisfaction, he would move the goal post marker without preempt. He could make plans and agreements with me and enjoy himself as he deviated one hundred and eighty degrees when my back was turned.

I was constantly shocked by his immaturity. He ingested and excreted immaturity on a regular daily basis. Yet, he was always very convincing. He would convince me that I was someone I never wanted to be. Given the chance Darth would convince my friends and family members that I was a musing degenerate selfishly propelling my way through life. He spent years undermining what kind of individual I truly was, until even I believed him. He took his time, as he slowly turned my friends and child against me until all his excuses were justified inside his dubious mind.

His habitual lies became chaotic and all-encompassing. Eventually, I never knew what to believe as Darth smattered the lies with bits of truth. He constantly contradicted himself to the point that it was obvious to me, but never to him. During these episodes he liked to argue, especially if he had been drinking. The arguing frequently escalated to some sort of melodramatic violence. I learned that it was ineffectual to pursue a reasonable discussion with Darth when he had been drinking.

Eventually he became dangerously violent as the verbal onslaught heightened. Darth had a temper and when it was out of control, he always made it my fault. If he hurt me, he said I made him do it. He rarely apologized or showed remorse. When he began going bald, he said I caused that too. He always had an excuse to drink because he said I drove him to it. When he chewed ice from an empty glass, he claimed it was because he was sexually deprived.

His friends were all addicts or potential addicts, and he was frequently compulsive about gambling, excessive credit card charging, and sexual demands or neurotic about his work. He liked to turn mountains of problems into modest mole hills and dare me to disagree. When I dared, I generally suffered more than he ever would.

Darth always claimed that he never had too much to drink and drive. He thought he was a man that could handle his liquor. He insisted only wussies didn't know how to handle their booze and then operate a motor vehicle under the influence. He refused to own his own problems. Rules and laws were written and meant to be enforced upon everyone besides himself as he felt he was entitled to be profoundly irresponsible about many realms in his own life.

One of the scariest recognitions on my part was to accept that I was assisting him down the road to addiction. I spent years enabling him when I thought I was performing good works on his behalf. This was a very intricate and difficult pill to swallow. I'd been a legitimate enabler and I didn't even know it, but it was never too late to change myself, and appreciate that one of the biggest mistakes' women make is thinking that they can save or changing their man. My mother told me I could, but I shouldn't have believed her. She meant well, but I could not change another person. I could only change myself. By trying to change Darth, I was deceitfully robbing him of his own responsibility to fix himself.

CHAPTER FOURTEEN

After being married to the same man for over a decade, I heeded the written advice, and hid my paperback book from Darth as it suggested. Then I sneaked off to my first AA meeting. I felt a guilty twinge for hiding the book that I was reading. It probably wasn't necessary as he was rarely home anyway, but I wasn't taking any chances. I wanted to change. I knew there was nothing wrong with me trying to improve myself which might eventually work to his benefit. I also knew that he would not approve of the book, and he would undoubtedly forbid me from attending any AA meetings.

When needed, I used the excuse of going to Nellie's house and off I went to a new therapeutic experience. I wasn't sure what to expect. I just wanted to find tranquil peace as I pulled into the parking lot. It was a luminous spring evening and the doors to the building stood wide open. There were dozens of cars in the parking lot and a group of preteens playing together under the barricade of a shade tree. People were milling about everywhere, drinking coffee, many of them smoking cigarettes.

It was time for the meeting to start. As I passed a total stranger in the hall, I asked which room the meeting for the spouses was held in and he gave me directions. Several elongated folding tables had been pushed together, end to end and approximately twenty-five chairs had been assembled around the extended seating area.

A sublime looking man who appeared to oversee the meeting sat at the head of the table and brought the assembly to order, he began the meeting by having all of us repeat in unison the AA aphorism. "God grant me the serenity to accept the things I cannot change. Courage to change the things I can and the wisdom to know the difference."

Then the man in charge said, "Hi, my name is Tom and I'm an alcoholic." The same scenario was followed by the fellow on his left and so forth until they came to me. Of course, none of them had ever seen me before and I said, "Hi, my name is Rylee and I'm not an alcoholic." I sat down as everyone glared at me and I attempted to grin at the disbelieving faces. The room was dead silent and the person to my left did not pick up the introduction where I left off.

Finally, Tom said, "These meetings are about openly admitting our problems, there is nothing to be ashamed of and you can admit out loud that you have a problem." I reiterated myself by saying, "but, I'm not an alcoholic, I don't even drink". Everyone stared at me again as if their silence could extricate the truth. I was quickly becoming uncomfortable. Tom was compelled to try again, "Now Rylee, part of your problem is your denial, and you have to learn to accept that you have a problem that is greater than yourself and stop denying it." I replied simply, "I know, but I don't drink."

Everyone continued to stare at me as if I had mad cow disease, until finally; Tom asked me what my last name was. Normally you don't have to give your full name at meetings, but I told him it was Vadies. He asked me if my husband's name was Darth, and amazed at Tom's knowledge, I said, "Yes." Tom glanced around the room and told everyone it was all right, that I was telling the truth. He said he remembered me from high school and that he knew my husband was the drinker. Everyone chuckled into their coffee cups, and somebody told me I was in the wrong meeting room. I was supposed to be across the hall with the other enablers in the Al-Anon group.

Rising from my metal chair to leave, Tom told me I could stay so I would have a better idea of what the addicts talked about in their meetings. Tom was at the head of the table because it was his turn to discuss his journey as an addict. This meeting included a celebration with chocolate cake because Tom had been sober and on the wagon for almost two years. Tom recognized that it would be a difficult lifetime pursuit to stay sober. Tom's wife also attended Al-Anon meetings and his kids attended Al-Ateen. They were all learning about the role that each of them played in the addiction process. For the addict to get healthy and stay that way he needs the people around him to do the same thing. It's exceptionally difficult for the addict to be dysfunctional all by himself.

Even if the addict never gets clean or stays sober, at least the family members lead a better life. In Al-Anon they learn about how not to participate in the disease. I felt this was enormously important for Joey. Given his gene pool, I wanted him to understand how vital it was not to drink. He needed to understand the importance of this. Drinking isn't just a hereditary problem. Addiction is also a learned behavior and thought process.

I went home with additional reading material to protect myself with further knowledge. I felt that I was on the path to new hope and possibly a new beginning. I didn't want to give up. Divorce was still a word that did not exist in my vocabulary. I desperately wanted to find a way for our family to heal. The more I learned about the addiction process, the more complicated it became. Continuing my studies and my weekly AA meeting without Darth's knowledge, I was developing an enhanced understanding of what I had been doing wrong for many years to contribute to Darth's addiction.

Understanding that no matter how good my intentions, my controlling actions were not going to help my family to become healthy. Everything that I was doing right for a normal situation was very wrong for dealing with an addict. I'd come to the definite conclusion that Darth was addicted. I suspected that he had been an alcoholic since he was a teenager. I also thought that his parents realized this, but as typical in a dysfunctional situation they chose not to address the real issues.

Darth's mother was a person that I had always liked. I believed that she meant well even though she tended to exist in her own little ditsy universe where she could disengage from reality. She probably had no idea what a normal reality was supposed to be like. I knew I certainly didn't, but I was willing to accept that normal people didn't run around trying to fix the sick one.

Reading the book that Dodie silently left for me on the kitchen counter, I realized she had placed the burden of responsibility for her drinking son solely on me. Possibly she viewed me as the strong one who could help her son when she was not willing to approach Darth in a family struggle. Instead, she left the battle to me armed only with a second-hand book. Luckily, I thought the knowledge was empowering.

Many times, I didn't feel that I belonged at AA. The whole idea seemed foreign to me. I was a nice person, and I did good things, why should I have to put in time at AA? I had to sneak to meetings because the husband with the problem refused to admit he had one. Still under mental construction, I snuck around going to AA as a work in progress trying to figure out how I was going to deal with our family problems. I was desperate enough to try anything.

At one meeting we discussed how we could deal with a drunk on a verbal rampage. All of us already knew from experience that logic wouldn't work. It didn't matter how calm or pleasant you remained or if you'd been right a thousand times before. It's impossible to reason with an addict especially if he's high or he's been drinking. There is, however, a proper response for anything that the addict could possibly say.

It is amazingly simplistic and easy to pronounce, and anybody can do it. You just say, "O." You can stand in front of a mirror and practice verbalizing your O's. You can practice while driving or while vacuuming. You can get really good at it. There are dozens of ways to say "ooo", Oho, ohhhoo, oHHHHH, OOOho, etc. I was now prepared with the perfect response to any of Darth's verbal badgering.

Now I knew how to defuse verbal battering in the future, "OooohooO", it's an answer or response that means absolutely nothing. Therefore, it gives the illogical, immature addict nothing to argue about. It simply takes away all his leverage and muscle. He soon tires of meeting no resistance and walks away to his next project or drink, which leaves you happily to yourself.

Darth showed up unexpectedly one evening wanting me to do his laundry. I had wondered what he did for clean clothing when he was an absentee husband. Now I knew. He had purchased an entirely new wardrobe and an ample supply of fresh underwear even though he had a closet at home that was stuffed full. I brooded over how he had paid for all his new merchandise. I knew he had taken money out of our joint savings account because he told me he'd made a loan to his shop foreman when the guy's girlfriend had ripped him off. Later I would learn that was another lie.

When the revolving charge card statement arrived in the mail, I learned the truth about how Darth had financed a new wardrobe for himself. He'd charged it to several of our joint credit cards which I rarely used and reserved for emergencies. When I received the statements, I phoned and wrote letters to all the credit card lines and requested them to be cancelled. I cancelled the cards I could that had a zero balance and applied for one in just my name alone. I had a feeling I was going to need it. I hid it in the ash tray of my truck in case of a crisis and I put a wooden club behind the seat. I left the keys in my ignition when my truck was parked in the garage and I began backing it in, so I could pull out in a hurry. I felt ridiculous, but consistently did it anyway.

Mean while, no one was talking to me about any problems at the business, mostly I was treated as if I had a contagious infection. The guys who came to work at the cabinet shop on the home property avoided me at all costs. I didn't hear anything from Darth's parents or brother, but I had a feeling they knew something was wrong with Darth. I also suspected that he was spending less and less time at work and more time at his tavern.

One afternoon I discovered that he had changed the security code on the alarm system at the gated driveway to the business so that I could no longer enter the premises. I phoned the office manager and asked her what was going on. "Darth doesn't want you to have access to the business." Then under her breath, "I know that he is drinking too much." I asked her why she would think this. "I can tell because of the way he's conducting himself and his business affairs." She thought he was not exercising prudent business practices. I couldn't understand why his brother and father, who also owned stock and worked with Darth everyday, weren't trying to prevent a disaster.

A speculative thought came to me. Had Darth wanted a tavern, so he'd have a convenient place to deal drugs? The nose bleeds he was having must be caused by snorting cocaine. I knew coke was extraordinarily expensive. Darth had installed a vaulted safe in the closet of the upstairs master office at the shop. I did not have the code to the safe and I'd thought it unusual when Darth had installed it approximately six months before. When I questioned him about it, he said it was for petty office cash. I made a comment about petty cash, not being worth much. Darth had told me to mind my own business, so I did.

One night at home he was angry with me as he irately complained, "One of my guns has been stolen out of the gun cabinet. It's one of my rifles and I want to know what you've done with it." I said, "Ohh", because I didn't know what else to say. I couldn't tell one of the rifles from another and I surely hadn't stolen one of our own guns. Remembering that Darth kept the gun cabinet locked, I asked him, "How could someone steal a rifle out of our house and out of the locked gun cabinet without any signs of theft?" He accused me of leaving it open, which I had not. "I dust it every week when I clean house and I have never seen it left open." Years later Joey would tell me that his dad staged his own gun theft for the insurance money and pawned the rifle. Joey was nine years old at the time and he knew more about what his dad was doing than I did.

Something else that I had noticed about Darth on the rare occasions that he was present at home was his posture; it had changed significantly. Through years of handling horses, I had developed an eye for how the animals moved and acted. I was always on the lookout for some undetected lameness or soft tissue swelling. Now I was noticing changes in Darth's movements, but I couldn't quite put my finger on it. Then I read about it in my paperback. Supposedly, addicts in final stages of addiction do change their body postures. I'd noticed this in the way that Darth shifted his body position in his car seat when he drove. I'd see him through the windshield and there was something strange about his profile. I thought I was probably involved in more heartache than I could handle.

CHAPTER FIFTEEN

Reading about unlearning enabling behavioral patterns, I greedily grasped an understanding of my predicament. It was imperative that I quit being responsible for the addict. He would either sink or swim on his own. This was a very scary concept for me. I didn't want him to drown dragging the rest of us under. I understood the theory that if I carried the burden of responsibilities, I was eliminating the addict's prospect to be responsible for himself. I comprehended the reasoning but did not want to face the reality of going under. This perception was compounded for me by my deep-rooted feelings that the way Darth conducted himself was also a direct reflection on who I was.

Eventually I would learn that Darth's behavior had nothing at all to do with what kind of person I was. I had to perceive each of us as two separate entities. Once I realized this, it was much easier for me to distance myself from a lot of my old behavior. I was beginning to recognize that I could not be solely responsible for everyone, or their actions. As I began to detach myself from the dysfunctional people around me, my long-lost self-esteem began to bud and blossom.

Saturday afternoon, Joey had invited Jimmie to spend the night at our house. At four o'clock Darth was supposed to take both boys from the house to the firing range to practice shooting their BB guns, after which they would have pizza and return home to watch a rented video.

I'd kept the two boys busy goofing off that afternoon and when four o'clock rolled around Joey wanted to know where his dad was. I phoned Darth at the office, but no one answered. As far as I knew Darth was the only one at the office that day, so I tried the shop. One of the welders answered and said that he'd been working overtime all day and he hadn't seen Darth.

Where was he now? It was after five o'clock and the boys were antsy and hungry. I finally baked them a frozen pizza with extra cheese and continued searching for Darth via his cell phone which was really a satellite phone which he wasn't answering even though he got a signal. When seven o'clock passed us by, I convinced the kids they should go ahead and watch the video without Darth. I was making up excuses to cover for Darth's calloused behavior even though I knew from my Al-Anon attendance that I was not supposed to do that, even if I was trying to bolster Joey's hurt feelings.

When it was almost ten o'clock, the boys were in their pajamas in Joey's room talking about whatever it is little boys stay up to talk about under the cover of a quilt tent with flashlights and sleeping bags. I was silently seething about what a schmuck Darth was, and I could no longer stand to douse my emotions with logical AA thoughts. Darth was not a missing person who could be advertised on the side of a milk carton. I knew exactly where he was, I was betting he was at his tavern. He had probably been there all afternoon. Mentally, I pounded my fists as I refused to tolerate this type of behavior where Joey was concerned.

Patiently I explained to Joey and Jimmie that I thought Darth was in town at the tavern and that I was going to go get him and I would be right back. Jimmie lived just a minute down the street, I told them if they had any kind of emergency, they could call Jimmie's mom. Both boys knew where I was going and why. Not stopping long enough to get dressed I marched out of the house in my worn-out terrycloth bathrobe that zipped up the front. I grabbed my most convenient pair of shoes at the garage door, the blue rubber muckers I wore out to the barn to do chores in each morning and my unsightly old barn coat with dirty cuffs. I was so furious with Darth that I charged out of the house not giving a rat's ass about my appearance.

In five minutes, I pulled down the street that fronted the tavern. It was odd to know that I owned it and had never been in it. Sure enough, I spotted Darth's Mercedes. The car was parked right in front of the tavern entrance. In Darth's mind he probably thought that the parking space should be reserved just for him, the exalted owner. There were vehicles parked on the same side of the street as his car, in front and behind it.

Letting my vehicle idle in the middle of the street for a few seconds I decided that I would parallel park next to Darth's vehicle right in the middle of the street and hope that I didn't get a ticket. I was afraid that if he saw me, he would bolt like a wild animal. I don't know exactly why I contemplated Darth's evasion; probably because I understood he was a quitter at heart. I wasn't taking any unnecessary chances. I wanted him to come home and explain to his son why he was at the tavern breaking his promises.

I blew out a huge breath that hitched in my throat and entered the tavern door. The place was packed with patrons and the stench of cigarette smoke assaulted my sinuses. The ceiling was painted the darkest black with beautiful gold accented ceiling fans rhythmically churning through the dense cloudy haze. One side of the room was full of pool players while other clientele sat at round bistro tables or in front of the bar placing their orders.

Stepping through the entrance I noticed that several pool players had stopped their game and were overtly staring at me. I didn't know if it was because of the way I was dressed or if they knew that I was the wife who had previously been denounced from the tavern table tops as being such a louse in bed. Feeling slightly absurd in my robe and squeaky rubber boots I strode across the wooden floor up to the bar with my head elevated and asked the bartender if he knew where Darth was. He motioned with his thumb that Darth was around the corner, and sure enough there he was. The backside of his left shoulder was facing me, so he didn't notice the fuming housewife in her original farm fashion outfit. Looking beyond his backside I realized there were restrooms, pinball machines and an ill-lit exit door complete with the green neon sign.

Then I saw her, Tayla's younger married sister. She had pulled a bar stool up next to Darth's and had her arm linked through his. She was leaning against him with her plumped up boobies and talking into his closest ear as he slouched toward her. The little slut. She saw me approach before Darth did. She pulled back her shoulders and sucked in air uplifting her big boobs in defiance. It didn't stop me. I walked directly into her space, looked straight into her hostile hazel eyes, and told her to slither back under her own rock. She looked at me like I could go straight to hell, so I poked my nose in front of hers and told her I meant it. She looked to Darth for support and when she didn't get it, she made a grand exodus with her ample hips and retreated to the restroom.

There sat my husband who had been diddling anything female, drunk, and stoned in his bar. In his glass was his favorite social lubricant. I'd witnessed the same stupor and malicious expression the night he'd left me in a twisted heap on the concrete barn aisle. I knew where his bloody noses were coming from and why. No wonder Darth had been so adamant about owning his own tavern. It was the perfect location to deal and partake of drugs.

Was each high for him the time that he said to himself, I need just one more chemical tryst? I thought he must be beyond that thought. Surely, he must have started snorting with the rationalized idea that he could quit whenever he decided. Obviously, there wasn't a high or a downer that didn't turn Darth on, being buzzed and stoned must have never lasted long enough or remained embedded deep enough to last indefinitely.

At some point different theories must have gone through Darth's head. He must have thought he was immune, but he didn't appear immune to anything except loving his family. Perhaps it wasn't just Darth's demands for sex that couldn't keep him satisfied. There probably was never a damsel with a willing crotch that could have given Darth the mental orgasm he got from a good snort of white line. He was probably on the lookout for the nearest climax he could find, anywhere at any price.

Darth protested my unexpected appearance by puckering his pouting mouth into a repulsive expression which represented all the characteristics about the male Vadies lineage that I had grown to detest. I had to resist speed slapping his existence into oblivion along with everything he stood for at that moment. Flexing my jaw muscles while grinding my molars against adversity, I glared into his dilated pupils, and told him that he was going to come home immediately.

He responded with a drug induced slur, "I don't feel like it." I retaliated, "I've blocked your car and you're going to come home with me now." I threatened, "I'm gonna latch onto your arm and if you try to stop me, you'll have to break my arm in front of all your drinking buddies to escape me." To my astonishment he tamely followed me like a puppy on a leash out to my truck and got in on the passenger's side. When I hopped in, I pushed the automatic door locks into lock position and drove away into the forbidden night.

I did my best to sensibly explain to Darth why I wouldn't tolerate his behavior where Joey was concerned. The further I drove; the louder Darth became. The whites of his eyes were branched with tiny red veins and his drug-swollen head looked as if it would explode. I drove a long loop into the next town and back to the tavern. Darth was threatening that he wanted to go back to his own car. I wanted him to come home and wait until morning to get his car, but he wouldn't agree. I didn't take him directly home with me because he was genuinely scaring me.

I pulled back into my temporary parking space in the middle of the street. Darth sidled out of my truck and unlocked his own car. As I pulled out of the way, he romped on his gas pedal and passed me doing fifty miles an hour in twenty-five speed zone. I tried to keep up but soon his taillights disappeared into the unknown darkness. A few minutes later when I approached our driveway, I could see the lights were on in the garage and Darth was loading something into his car trunk.

It was Jimmie's overnight bag. I had not anticipated this development. I couldn't believe it. Darth was going to leave with in the middle of the night with both boys. I tried to enter the house as Darth was crossing the threshold with both little boys being herded out the door in front of him. He shoved me aside, hard enough to knock the wind out of my lungs when my backside hit the wall. I followed behind them trying to reason with Joey. I asked him not to leave with his father who had been drinking. I didn't want either of the kids to get into the car with Darth.

He opened one car door and hurried both the boys into the back seat. I scuttled to the other side of the car and flung that door open telling Joey to get out and stay home with me. Joey told me that his dad said he could drive because he wasn't drunk. The next thing I knew Darth was on my side of the car. He had a death grip on my arm as he was deliberately exerting enough pressure that I worried about being impaled on the radio antenna. In one explosive movement he yanked me hard enough to bounce me off the car allowing him enough time to get into the driver's seat, slam his door shut and race away with two young, trusting little boys. It was after one o'clock in the morning and I had no idea where all three of them were going or if they would arrive safely in one piece.

I went back into the house. I felt like I was a hundred and ten years old when I phoned Jimmie's mom. I was ashamed and panicky as I started to tell her about the situation. She told me she understood and that everything was all right. Jimmie had just walked in the door. I didn't understand how she could understand, when I didn't. Later that summer I would learn that she was divorcing Jimmie's alcoholic father.

Not knowing where Darth was taking Joey, there were no further phone calls I could make. I assumed that they would go to Darth's parents. Realizing that my twisted arm hurt, I took off my barn coat and saw Darth's hand imprint beginning to turn color on my wrist. I thought about how I had not practiced what I had been studying. I tried to reason with an addict who was under the influence. I tried to control his actions by forcing him to come home. I'd also gone to the tavern to look for him. Darth's addictions existed without a doubt, and he was beyond my control. He was losing himself in his own delusional quest. Sooner rather than later Darth's addictions were going to backhand him. Possibly Darth could have never known the person he would become when he took his first drag on a smoke or nursed his first alcoholic brew as a kid. This was where he was really going to end up, social teenage smoker to out of control crack head. He never could have known which person he would become when he lit up his first drag on stolen cigarette when he was only twelve.

CHAPTER SIXTEEN

I was learning to let go of my addicted husband and fend for myself and my child. The addict was no longer my top priority. If, I was not of sound mind and in control of my own destiny, I would not be capable of properly parenting my child. The strong-willed girl I used to be had been missing for too many years. I'd been thinking about her, and I needed her back.

When I was in grade school my mom had a flock of chickens to eat the bugs in her garden. Banties roamed freely around the pasture and garden area, every evening they migrated back into the chicken coop at sunset. They were all hens except for one skinny, brightly feathered, territorial rooster who plucked for bugs and small gravel pebbles while dominating his hens. I made several trips a day to the barn to feed and care for my horse, passing the chicken coop at the gate it was easy to avoid the rooster on ten acres.

One Sunday afternoon, wearing cut-off shorts and scuffed cowboy boots, not something that would concern a tomboy in the sixth grade; I was minding my own business on the way to the barn. I hadn't given a second thought to where the chickens were. Midway between the garage and the barn the rooster stealthily swatted me with his talons on the back of my bare legs. I screamed more at the surprise than the pain and turned to face my tormentor. To my shock he was going to attack again. He was running directly toward me, making an obscene screeching noise. I stood my ground. I could play soccer as well as any of the boys in grade school and I was preparing to kick the red ranting rooster into deep space.

His fluffy chicken chest connected squarely with the hard-pointed toe of my cowboy boot as he lifted off backwards, bound for orbit. I knew I'd won the fight. I turned and continued strolling toward the weathered barn door. I felt it again, this time he drew blood. Spinning to challenge my attacker I drop kicked him a second time for all I was worth. He lay face down in the pasture appearing to be dead. Much to my chagrin, he got back up, charging again with his beak pointed toward me like a speeding arrow. At this point I began screaming for my father who was mostly deaf in one ear. The right toe of my scuffed boot connected and reconnected with the homicidal rooster before my father appeared with a stick and chased him to another corner of the field.

I wasn't going to take this from a cranky male bird. I patiently waited for sunset when the chickens would file one by one into the dilapidated old coop. I took the straw bristle broom from the back porch with me and carefully entered the coop. I latched the door behind me as if I'd come to gather eggs and proceeded to beat the feathers off the cocky old bird. I made my point in a way that a chicken brain could understand and left the coop full of swirling banty feathers. The skinny red rooster never bothered me again. The little girl inside of me who wouldn't tolerate a berserk bird had grown up and willingly lived years with an intolerable spouse.

As a young woman, who had never accepted the concept of divorce, I knew it was becoming a reality. I saw it as my only choice. Yet, I was still investing in the idea that Darth might change. I was going to file for divorce in hopes that he would understand that I was serious about him entering rehab. If bashing him about the chicken coop with my divorce papers didn't make him see the light, then at least I would already be on my way to a new life.

A week after Darth had disappeared into the night with Joey and Jimmie, both Darth and our son re-appeared. I knew they had not been staying at his grandparents' because I'd made a trip to town to talk to Darth's folks. I'd been learning about the intervention process at Al-Anon and I was hopeful that his parents would understand the situation and be supportive. I believed that there was strength in family numbers. I was still trying everything that I could think of to help Darth.

I tried to make the wisest verbal choices that I could muster in suggesting an intervention to Darth's parents. The idea was to approach the addict from a loving perspective. With family members who cared about him unanimously supporting the scheme. I thought intervention would steer Darth into rehabilitation. I'd checked and there was an excellent rehab center in the neighboring town that specialized in chemical dependency. All the addict had to do was admit himself and promise to work the program from start to finish. It was not recommended that family members visit the addict while in rehab. Better yet, all the family members should participate in their own rehab program and begin attending Al-Anon.

I was already attending Al-Anon and investing effort into reading about addiction and its effects on dysfunctional families. Addiction is typically hereditary and frequently skips a generation, but the dysfunctional behavior lives on in each generation as it is a learned behavior transferred by parents who really don't know what normal healthy family function is. I was now beating my head against exactly that problem. Darth's parents were not the least bit interested in assisting me with an intervention to rally round their addicted son. I decided that denial still had a strapping hold on their emotions and viewpoints. Dodie said she could never do such a thing to Darth and stammered about the kitchen pretending she just couldn't deal with an intervention, while continually interjecting that she knew Darth really loved me.

Love has nothing to do with an addict's actions. Personally, I felt that addicts didn't truly love themselves, making it impossible to honestly love anyone else. Nonetheless, Dodie was convinced that Darth loved me in generous heaps; however, she didn't have the stamina to confront him. Dick had a completely different attitude. He blamed me. He told me to grow up, which was exactly what I was doing, whether he helped me, or not.

I countered to my in-laws that if they wouldn't help Darth through intervention then would they please do it for Joey. If everyone could put their fears and feelings aside and attempt to do the right thing for Joey's sake, it wouldn't be such a desperate decision. Perhaps Darth was right, I couldn't sell thermo blankets to Eskimos and I was never going to convince his parents that all of us needed help.

When Darth and Joey re-emerged, after being AWOL for over a week, we finished dinner as if we were your regular run-of-the-mill family. I nabbed the opportunity and explained to Darth, "I've seen an attorney and filed for divorce", secretly hoping that my statement would initiate an attitude adjustment on his part.

As if we were talking about the weather, Darth simply replied, "Don't worry I'll make the house payments, so you and Joey have a roof over your heads." He knew that I didn't make enough money with the horse boarding business to pay for the house and all living expenses. He seemed contrite and quite sincere and then all he said was, "I'm going to bed."

I told him I wanted him to leave, and I did not want him to come back home until he was willing to address his addictions. He denied being an addict and abruptly left the house. He never did come home again, which was not a difficult adjustment for me since he was gone all the time anyway. In many ways it was a peaceful time because I didn't fret about when he would come back home. I just accepted that he was gone, and frequently experienced a quiet respite. I thought about all the reasons that he should go to AA and rehab, and then I wondered how Joey and I would survive as I did not possess the ability to meet our current overhead.

Even though I felt a sense of welcomed relief, there was also a significant sense of loss. The family unit was now officially severed at my command. Although I needed the abuse to stop, I wished that the relationship could continue, and I frequently reminisced about the Darth that I remembered as a teenager. I didn't fully realize that Darth would proceed to lie and manipulate his relatives and my friends to isolate and control me from a distance. We were going to lose our home because he would never honor his promise to make the mortgage payments. He would take drastic measures to gain full custody of Joey and manipulate the legal system to his own advantage, yet I thought he would be willing to eventually seek therapy. I loved and hated Darth. I was constantly torn and confused by his behavior which was always contradictory and unstable while he frequently shifted from kindness to affliction.

I continued to attend my Al-Anon meetings, and I was also traveling to the next town and attending their meetings on a different night. I practiced my own program, and I thought of it as double fortification. I was going to need every ounce of it.

I knew that attorneys cost extraordinary amounts of money and I basically had none. I'd gone to the bank and withdrawn exactly one half of what was left in our joint savings account. My attorney had explained that according to state law, who ever got to the bank account first was entitled to withdraw all the funds. Attempting to be fair, I only took half. There had been a few significant withdrawals over the past several months that Darth had made without my knowledge. I assumed it was money that went directly up his nose, leaving me with a few thousand dollars to spend sparingly. My attorney required the bulk of my remaining funds as his retainer.

Bolstering my bravery, I anxiously tried to convince myself that I could make a hired stranger understand what Darth was all about. I'd never been able to convince his parents or his browbeaten brother. I couldn't create facts with gut instincts and expect the lawyer to believe me.

That is why abused women don't tell. They instinctively know that normal people will not readily believe them. We really don't even believe our situations ourselves. The addict has spent years priming us to disbelieve. What we do understand is that our stories are unbelievable. Whether it is the listener's inability to believe, it didn't matter because as the victim, I willingly believed that I had very limited choices.

It is a monumental mistake for an abused person to hope that their friends or family will initially judge their circumstances for what they really are. People with ordinary, healthy lives could not comprehend or identify with what I was trying to explain to them. I know this because when I tried, not only could I sense the listening person's discomfort; I also knew that they couldn't comprehend my unconventional story.

I should not have expected a sound-minded person, inexperienced about addictions to understand. They can't, because they have never been a qualified veteran of living with an addict. Seeking advice from well-meaning friends, mothers and ministers was a mistake. Well-meaning people couldn't help me. The advice they offered might be sound for someone in a normal situation but was devastating to me in my co-dependent circumstances.

I had grown beyond minimizing the abusive behavior in my marriage, the days of trying to forget incidents and blaming myself for our problems had now diminished with my former wedding vows. I was no longer willing to pretend that the husband who promised to love me would not harm me. If I chose to continue in my denial and self-blame, it would prevent me from effectively changing my situation.

It appeared that my lawyer who dealt with legal powers knew what he was talking about regarding divorce decrees. He only took cases where there was a substantial family business or homestead at stake. He reviewed my financial statements and asked a lot of specific business questions. Then he explained that due to the accumulation of our financial assets, I should reconcile with Darth, if possible.

Exactly what I was afraid of, this guy didn't get it. Darth was not going to play by conventional rules. Darth had no regard for anyone but himself and his own policies, which he continually changed. The more intently I tried to explain what we were up against, the more ridiculous I sounded to my expensive and educated attorney. He insisted that I shouldn't worry because he was going to have all my legal rights under control. I felt that he thought I was a nervous housewife overreacting to my situation and blowing it out of proportion. My attorney thought that it was his job to hold my hand, find a compromise and get paid thousands of dollars. I hoped that he would eventually recognize the difference between what he thought, and what was expected with Darth.

I was learning in Al-Anon that it was possible to deal with impossible situations by controlling my emotions. Initially I had assumed that controlling my emotions was absurd, but I was willing to try. I pretended that my emotions were controlled by a plastic light switch mounted on the wall. With a simple flick of my hand, I could turn the plastic switch on or off, it was my choice.

When my mind flipped the emotional control switch on, I could very easily become a bawling, babbling emotional nincompoop. As an emotional basket case, I only knew what I felt, and I felt a lot: frustration, confusion, disdain, sacrifice, disillusion, pain, loss, betrayal, determination, and fear. Or I could choose to turn the emotional switch to the off position. The off position meant that I distanced myself from my disturbing feelings and focused on the immediate problem at hand. When focusing directly on a singular solution or just one problem at a time, I could think rationally without being overwhelmed. I honed my emotional switch until I became a logically lethal, determined thinking woman with a cause.

Several weeks had passed and Darth had not entered a treatment program for his addictions. Occasionally he stopped at the house without warning and collected Joey. Joey generally came home mad at me and unwilling to talk. He would disappear with his father for a few hours or a few days, but he eventually would come back home. Darth was teaching Joey to keep his secrets. Joey was learning to hide the truths about his parents. For Darth this was another tactical maneuver to create isolation for his victims. With his victims as captives, he was building a stronghold around himself. Mixed messages and repressing feelings and fears were just a few of the misconceptions that Joey was adjusting to at his father's command.

I knew I needed to get Joey into the program for children. I'd mentioned the subject to him several times and he would insist that nothing was wrong with his dad and that he would never need to go to Al-Anon with me. I made an executive decision. The kid was going to go. I explained to him that he didn't have to talk. He didn't have to like it. He didn't even have to like me, but he did have to attend Al-Ateen once a week.

The evening of his first meeting, he belligerently got in the car with me. His arms were defiantly crossed across his chest. His furious brown eyes stared straight ahead through the windshield as if his intent gaze could melt the glass. I finally gave up trying to communicate with a hurt and angry nine-year-old. When we arrived in the parking lot he refused to get out of the car. I opened the passenger door and told him he did have to do this. He responded by yelling obscenities at me and refusing to budge. I pulled harder and he came off the seat swinging and kicking at me.

Partially dragging and pulling him into the designated classroom I felt like the worst mother in the world, but I didn't know what else I could do for him. It was crucial that he understand what his father was doing and how he could cope with it. I didn't know where else to drag him, to reinforce him with the tools he needed. I told him I would be in the room around the corner, and I went to my own meeting.

Most of the other wives in the Al-Anon group were annoyed with me. I had done the unthinkable and filed for divorce. Several of the other women felt that I was wrong. Now was not the time to leave my addict. He needed my support, and I should not pursue damaging my family.

I was in total agreement with them but pondered if they were somehow threatened by my steadfast attitude of refusing to remain a doormat. Perhaps they saw themselves as flabby housewives with wrinkles who didn't possess the nerve to be homeless, and man-less. Al-Anon did not support abusive relationships. It did instruct us to find and act upon what we felt was right for ourselves and that was what I was determined to do. I also respected their right to remain married to their husbands even though I was beginning to understand why having no man was better than living with a bad one.

I questioned their co-dependence, a relationship where one partner tries to fill their own needs by controlling the other partner's life. The addictive partner would typically refuse to accept responsibility for his own actions, by passing those responsibilities to the co-dependent who readily accepts. Co-dependency is one partner's inability to separate their identity from the addict's because in a sense they are addicted to the addict. Like all addictions, the process begins at a subterranean level with denial.

However, I explained to the women that they weren't factoring in all the details. Yes, I had always honored my wedding vows. Yes, I was very dedicated to my commitments. Of course, I wanted to keep my family intact. I had tried this for over ten years, but when I married Darth as a young hopeful girl I never once agreed to be abused. I never gave him permission to repeatedly hit me or sexually abuse me. Our vows didn't say that I should love, honor and obey while my husband lied, cheated and ran around. I never agreed to be mistreated and I wasn't going to take it anymore. I reiterated to the incensed females that AA teaches us that actions speak louder than words, and I was learning to listen to the addict's actions.

I thought that the first time Darth hurt me and betrayed my trust, that I was a victim, and now I understood that after the first offense I had simply become his volunteer. Looking up the definition of the word "victim", it was defined as "a human being sacrificed to a deity." I certainly did not consider Darth to be a deity, even though I had honored him like one. A victim is also defined as a dupe, one who is easily deceived.

Phoning my lawyer, I instructed him to have divorce papers served on Darth. Then I wondered how much that would cost. I was analyzing how I could have ended up in such a drama. I felt as if I were living in abnormal psyche class 101. In hindsight I was beginning to realize a lot. I brooded over memories with trepidations in my internal search to understand where I had gone wrong. While absent-mindedly chewing on a tootsie roll, I attempted to comprehend my problems by drudging up old memories from high school.

PART TWO

IN THE BEGINNING

CHAPTER SEVENTEEN

I had never viewed a website that quoted statistical information reporting that thirty percent of the world's female population would be subjected to abuse and/or coerced into sexual acts that they did not willingly want to commit. My properly stoic mother never broached the topic of pregnancy, hormones or erect penises and statistics of battered women were never sketched across the classroom blackboard. What did I know? I was just a ninth grader.

There was one other girl in geometry class, she was extraordinarily brainy, and she didn't say much so I spent most of my time attracting attention from the male sector. Darth was more than happy to participate. He was fun, tall, dark headed and attractive. He seemed to be friends with everybody, the druggies, the jocks, and the geeks. Darth was comfortable in class, the cafeteria or assembly hall. Everyone appeared to be his friend. He even understood geometry.

I was still too hung up on my old boyfriend Stew, to give Darth very many of my considerations. I'm sure Darth had figured out that thoughts of Stew filled most of my spare moments. Darth was not deterred; perhaps he liked a challenge. I was aware of him and appreciated his friendship, but at that time it didn't really go any further for me.

Darth apparently had different plans. He would peddle his ten-speed bicycle all the way out to my parents' house. It wasn't a five-minute ride. It was fifteen miles. I was impressed, but I really wasn't ready to be interested.

Darth pushed to put more into our friendship than I was ready to give. When he began showing up regularly, it started to make me uncomfortable. Eventually Darth got his drivers license because he graduated from the bicycle to a motorcycle.

He was over six feet tall, and broad shouldered with a nice butt that held his blue jeans up. I must have been a hard nut to crack because I was still privately pining for Stew. I was also busy with my schoolwork and my part-time job. I went to church every morning before school, three times on Sunday and during the week. I'd also enrolled in modeling school, an exciting new experience. I drove to metropolitan downtown two evenings a week for most of the summer.

Summer was ending, and my next year in high school was swiftly approaching. I'd lost weight, and I was tan from working long hours out of doors. My hair had grown long and blonde and the modeling agency had requested that I be present at one of the drag races to be the appointed trophy girl. I was also required to have an escort for that evening.

Who was an escort I would want to go to the racetrack with? I thought that Stew was unapproachable, and I couldn't think of anyone else, even though I went to school with dozens of guys who flirted with me. I'd finally discouraged Darth to the point that I rarely saw him. He had a new girlfriend who was in my grade, a year behind him in school. I knew her because her entire family went to the same church that our family attended. Sometimes Darth was at church with her. Elise had a long straight hair the color of burnt toast, eyes the shade of stale coffee, a Cindy Crawford beauty mark and eyebrows that needed to be plucked. She was cute and didn't seem to be very serious about much of anything, except Darth.

I made up my mind to go ask Darth if he would be my escort to the speedway races. This was probably the last thing that he was expecting. The trophy girl assignment was scheduled to be one evening during the week before the school year resumed in September. Summer had swept by, and it was late August. I let Darth know the date for the races and we agreed to rendezvous and drive together. Darth knew exactly how to find the Speed Way Track.

I was driven around the track, sitting atop the back seat of a full-sized white convertible Cadillac with fin shaped taillights. The breeze was warm and blowing through my hair. People were clapping, and I was waving the proper wave that I'd been taught at the modeling agency, right up to the stand where the winning driver proudly stood as the overly loud music trumpeted through the overhead speakers. On cue I handed him his trophy. He was at least twice my age and smelled like an ash tray. With one hand he took the trophy with the other arm he grabbed me and kissed me hard and full on my mouth. I could hear the crowd go crazy and all I could think about was how I never wanted to be a trophy girl again.

It was late by the time Darth, and I left the races. The cool summer evening was turning into a great date. At an intersection with a red flashing light, he told me that he really did care for his current girlfriend Elise, and I nodded in understanding. Then he voluntarily ventured toward the idea that he would rather date me. I felt a ripple of excitement when he added that his girlfriend was on vacation with her family that week, and then I felt instantly gloomy that she would be home so soon. He claimed that he cared for her enough that he didn't want to hurt her feelings unnecessarily, unless I was serious about him. I conveniently overlooked the idea of how he was willing to hurt Elise if I gave the answer he was probing for.

He decided that he would tell her he wanted to stop dating her when she came back home. I was beginning to see the shrewd picture. He didn't want to break it off with Elise if I were just stringing him along. Somehow, he made me feel extremely guilty for all the times he'd shown interest in the past year, when I wasn't interested. He was asking me for some type of commitment. I wasn't exactly sure what it was but realizing that Darth wanted a sure thing appealed to me. Being the naïve sophomore girl that I was, I committed to him. I didn't even know exactly what I was committing too, but I jumped in with both feet. Before my junior year in school, we both signed up to share a hall locker together.

In a hurry I had grabbed my purse and Peechee folders from my car, while fumbling with my free hand for the strawberry pink lip gloss in my purse. As I raced across the high-school parking lot digging for makeup, I stopped dead in my tracks as I realized I was surrounded by a circle of female high school thugs. I never imagined that the high school parking lot could be a dangerous place, but I was surrounded by Elise and her cronies.

They were attempting to convince me that I was to give Darth back. I didn't understand what they thought I was supposed to do with him. Those girls wanted me to hand him back over to Elise as if he were a pair of old tennis shoes. Darth had made his own decisions about who he wanted to date. However, I had worried more than once that he was going to change his mind and dump me for Elise. She lived in town which was conveniently closer to him, and he was good friends with her older brother. Her eldest brother was not my type. His Levi jacket smelled like a cigarette butt, making me think that his unhealthy complexion was linked to inhaling too much tobacco. His baby blue bedroom eyes appeared to be perpetually hung-over as they converged beneath swollen pinkish lids. I'd heard from more than one source that his family jewels were bigger than grapefruits, but I had no desire to check it out.

Initially I wondered if Darth hadn't been attracted to Elise because she was handily attached to her bother. In the past year I had frequently seen her with both Darth and her sibling. Regrettably, Elise wasn't taking the loss of Darth's affections well at all. To top it off, I wasn't sleeping with him, and I knew that she had been. The main draw between Darth and her brother seemed to be drinking, community pool hall fights, and running around with beer in the trunk of a Volkswagen bug. I'd also told Darth I wouldn't hang around him if he smoked and I doubted Elise minded the smoking. She had her own smokes or possibly she pilfered them from her brother. I pondered the multitude of reasons that Darth could change his mind and go back to her.

Shortly after school started that year, so did the high school football games. I had never personally participated in extra-curricular activities at school. I worked at my job instead, but I did like going to the football games if I had a date. Darth and I attended all the Friday night games that season and so did Elise. She managed to overdose on some type of illegal drug in hopes that Darth would come running to her rescue. I knew that he still spent some spare time around her because he still hung out with her brother, and she frequently made herself available to tag along. In some ways I felt badly for her. I understood being enthralled with a guy who was not returning the attention. I didn't believe that Darth was still seeing her as a girlfriend, since he declared to me that he wouldn't.

That Sunday morning Darth met me at church. This was working well with my mom. She was still reminding me how marrying within the church was the only way I would find true happiness on earth and beyond. Mom seemed to like Darth a lot and she encouraged me to pursue our relationship if Darth and I went to church together.

Elise found me in front of the Sunday school room doorway and nonchalantly explained to me how she and Darth had slept together the night before. Casually Darth walked up behind me, stuck both of his hands in his pants pockets and leaned his shoulder against the door frame.

He knew what Elise had just said to me, and he didn't deny it. I felt sucker punched but tried to maintain my poker face. He told me it was all true. He explained that he had been drinking with her brother the night before and they'd exceeded their limit. Elise just happened to be available and willing. He claimed it was really me that he wanted. I wanted to believe that it was all her fault. I knew that she had been trying everything to win him back and sex was probably a safe bet. What on earth was I really thinking? I was mentally stretching and trying to convince myself that I was a good girl who could eventually save Darth from himself, of course. But, by embracing martyrdom deeds to mask my insecurities, I was walking onto a future tight rope without a net.

I innocently believed that I knew exactly what Elise was trying to do. She thought her sexual manipulations would make me dump him, and then she could have him back. If I blamed Darth, I would have fallen for Elise's pitiful attempt at reclaiming her relationship with my steady boyfriend. I wasn't going to let a one-nighter ruin the great thing Darth and I had going. I couldn't begin to imagine going back to the way life had been without a boyfriend. When I spent Friday and Saturday nights by myself, since all my girlfriends had dates. Worse yet Sunday afternoons would be spent at home with my parents reading the Bible, as I was not allowed to ride my horse on the Sabbath.

I chided Darth, telling him that I would forgive him this once. After all he was an All-American red-blooded boy. I wasn't going to let an underhanded bimbo that couldn't keep her panties on, ruin my life.

Ultimately, there was absolutely no way for me to know that almost one year later the woman who owned and operated the modeling school agency would approach me to model professionally. She would explain to me that she had connections in New York City where agencies were always searching for fresh new faces. She strongly encouraged me to prepare to leave for a glamorous modeling career and let her handle the details. I couldn't comprehend what my life may have been like if I had gone to New York. I never gave it a second thought, because I had a steady boyfriend. Without thinking it through, my mind was made up. I would stay in high school to be with Darth while I turned down a fabulous opportunity for the illusion of real love with a hormonal teenage boy.

CHAPTER EIGHTEEN

I certainly gave a great deal of thought to what I had been taught at church. Don't do it, don't do it, don't do it. If you do, your eternal life will be ruined or worse yet, you may never attain one. You should not disobey God, and you shouldn't do anything you would not do in front of Jesus which was the primary lesson I learned from my mother about sex.

Years later Darth repeated an old saying to me, and I expect he could have been right. Girls use sex to get love and boys play at love to get sex. What I really wanted more than anything else in my life was to be loved. I wanted to belong and to share special feelings as a couple. I wanted to get married and have a history with that exceptional someone. I was in love with the idea of my version of being in love. I was positive that Darth was that someone. There were probably a hundred and one other teenage boys at high school that could have fit the bill if I would have let them, but I had made up my young mind, and Darth was it.

Darth was sexually experienced, and I wasn't. He was clever about how far to push a screwed up teenage girl who thought she was finding true love with a boy that she thought she could trust. For me sex was an enormous commitment. I intended to only have sex with one guy, the person I would marry.

Nellie and I discussed sex before marriage many times at great length in her bedroom with the door shut. She was facing the same quandary with her boyfriend. Instead of viewing our boyfriends as delinquents with rampant hormones, we viewed them as needing our support, and both of us just knew we could fix them by helping them solve all their adolescent challenges. Meanwhile our boyfriends were surely scheming new angles for getting into our panties.

It worked because Darth and I solidified our relationship. We were together as much as possible. Frequently, I was even with him on Saturday nights until he would drop me off at home and go drinking with his friends. I remembered times that he mentioned puking when he'd get in late on the weekends and his dad would clean up his mess while no one said anything to his mother.

I liked the idea that his mom seemed to really like me. The first time that Darth took me to his house his mother wanted to inspect my teeth. She asked how many years I had worn braces. When I explained that I never had, she was so delighted that she clasped her hands together in anticipation of continuing the conversation. She talked about how her handsome son could marry a girl with perfect teeth. This would be the ideal union for her idyllic eldest son. He'd worn braces, but now his children wouldn't have to.

I thought that I recognized Dodie as the harmless genuinely nice nutcase that she was. I couldn't be a better choice because in addition to be an excellent dental prospect, I was a very nice religious girl. Dodie was ecstatic that I did not drink or smoke. In fact, she was so certain that I was a good girl that she wanted her terrific son to spend all his spare time with me. She was positive that if he were with me, he wouldn't be drinking. Dodie even allowed us to be together in his bedroom as long we didn't play his stereo too loud. While on the single bed in Darth's room, one of us was to keep at least one foot on the floor, that was her only rule. Dodie was easy to like.

She knew that Darth and I had looked at diamond pre-engagement rings at the downtown jewelry store and in several catalogs. Diamonds were expensive, especially for high school kids who worked part time jobs with a budget and a car payment. I had purchased my first car; it shined like an apple and had the new car plastic smell. It was incredibly sporty compared to the old boxy yellow bomber. At seventeen I thought I had the world by the tail with a great committed boyfriend, a pre-engagement ring on my left hand and a new car to drive.

I didn't know that I would eventually be stuck in a substance abuse ruled life where I would constantly be driving my future husband back onto the road of sobriety, finding myself repeating the same strategies over and over, not because what I was doing would work but because my tactics were all I had to work with.

I knew that all of Darth's friends liked to drink and that some of them smoked pot and did various other drugs. Darth explained to me that he no longer did drugs of any type. I preferred to believe what Darth told me. He knew that I didn't approve of the drinking, so he didn't drink when we were together. To my way of thinking, I was not Darth's drinking problem. I was his solution. By insisting that Darth didn't drink with me I thought that I was fighting his problem for him, this of course must make me a terrific girlfriend.

Dodie's children were planned, but she must not have taken into consideration that all four grandparents were alcoholics. At the time I was dating Darth, I had absolutely no information about what an alcoholic was. Dodie's father had a multitude of problems including, but not limited to drinking. Dodie refused to visit or speak to her father.

Dodie's mother was a nice granny with ashen hair, bifocal glasses, and a pasty complexion. Grandma Doyd didn't drive or perhaps she just didn't have an automobile, but Dodie always made certain she was present for birthdays, graduations, barbeques, and holidays. During the gasoline shortages in the early seventies, I had once stayed at her house for a few months. She didn't seem to mind the intrusion as I frequently cooked dinner for her.

During the gasoline crunch Grandma Doyd lived right across the street from a gas station. When I was staying with her, I would set my alarm for 3:00 o'clock AM and park my car in front of the gasoline pump, lock it and return at 8:00 o'clock when the station opened for business. By early morning, the cars in line for the gas stretched several miles down the street. I rotated doing this with my car and Darth's truck. During all this time and years into my marriage I never once saw Grandma Doyd take a swig of alcohol. I didn't know it at the time, but she did drink. She was just a quiet, sweet old lady who closet drank and hid her bottles.

Dick's parents were a different breed of drinkers. Darth took me to his grandparent's house a couple of times before we were married. They were loud, and obnoxious to each other and the family members around them. They both drank heavily on a regular basis and could have cared less about hiding their actions. One of them was buried when Darth and I were still in high school. It was a few years later that we buried the other boozing grandparent.

Darth had issues with his father. His dad had a volatile temper that could rapidly boil to the surface. You never knew where the boiling point was. One afternoon when both Darth and I went to his parents' house together, I went directly to the kitchen to talk to Dodie, while Darth ventured into the living room to talk to his dad.

I don't recall what the two guys were discussing but I could hear Dick raising his voice. When I entered the living room from the kitchen door,

Dick was lounging in his Lazy Boy chair and Darth was standing about three feet in front of it. I could tell that Dick was angry about something, but I didn't know what. I had been standing next to Darth for just a minute when I felt burning sensations bubbling on my hands, arms, and legs. I didn't understand what had caused the searing feeling as I had turned sideways and bent over to pet the family dog. Then I realized that Darth was rubbing his hands and arms. Darth's dad had just thrown his fresh mug of steaming hot coffee on us. My parents didn't drink coffee and as bizarre as they were about some things, I don't think that they would have thrown hot coffee at me. Darth grabbed my hand and pulled me away as we hustled from his parents' house and got in his truck.

Darth would talk about how he was not going to be like his father. He hated his dad's violent temper. From little comments that his mother would make over the years I understood that Dick had always had a fierce and unpredictable disposition. Unfortunately, Dodie hadn't the spine to stand up to him. She preferred the safety of the kitchen sink where she could readily keep herself suitably busy.

One night I was at Darth's house for dinner where meals were always prepared from scratch. That night it was meatloaf, mashed potatoes, and cubed carrots with peas.

It smelled incredible and tasted even better. All the family was busily scooping up their plates when Dick's fist hit the table and everyone's utensils rattled. He demanded to know why Dodie couldn't remember that he had told her to never fix him peas with carrots. Years previously he had rescued a severely injured man from an automobile accident who had a punctured stomach wound. Dick claimed that he could visibly see the peas and carrots the accident victim had ingested for dinner. I knew that I had never personally witnessed an accident victim with their internal organs on display. Though, I was certain that one could not easily recognize chewed and digested peas and carrots in a stomach wound.

Dick's plate of food hit the wall when he stomped away from the table. He sulked off to the family room that hosted a beat-up garage sale chair with his television set and humming air conditioning unit to brood in private. I didn't understand how anybody could get that upset about peas and carrots for dinner. He'd probably been trolling for an excuse to act like an imbecile and the peas and carrots triggered his response. Other than being convenient targets for his temper tantrum, the rest of us were obviously unimportant to him. Never was an apology offered, just a generous portion of potatoes and blame.

Even as a minor, I recognized Dick's immaturity, though Dodie never openly expressed her concerns, she did manage to occasionally get even, without peril. Dick always refused to eat commercially processed canned fruit. I wonder if he ever figured out that Dodie bought processed fruit in tin cans and dumped it into quart size glass canning jars and then stuck the preserves in the fridge. Dodie frequently operated as an under-cover namby-pamby who never had the nerve to tell Dick to stick it.

CHAPTER NINETEEN

That summer difficulties with my own family became even tougher for me to tolerate, and generally, I preferred not to be at home. I felt that I deserved to be treated as an almost adult and in my opinion, I was getting little respect from my parents. I attended school in the evenings, worked full time during the day and spent all my spare time with Darth. I'd even made the difficult decision to sell my horse because I no longer spent quality time riding her. It was an excruciatingly difficult decision to give her up, but I had Darth to be with. That fall I would turn eighteen and even if Darth and I weren't married. I intended to move out of the house as soon as I could afford to do so.

Unable to convince my parents that they sabotaged me with responsibilities regarding my brother when they gave me no authority, I felt that I could not communicate effectively with them about responsibilities, feelings, sex or numerous other topics, including the huge lump that I had in my right groin when I stood up. Maybe it was something I missed three years prior in eighth grade science class when my mother requested that the school board transfer me to the library.

My mother was one of the alarmed parents attending parent/teacher meetings, the purpose of which was to present the materials being covered in sex education class to the concerned adults. Mom arrived home from the presentation fuming about the photograph that was shown of an erect penis. I did not dare to tell her that I had already graduated from seventh grade sex-education class the year before, paying attention to every detail, earning me an A+ in class. I didn't think the erect penis photos were so bad, as I was accustomed to viewing my father watching television in his underwear.

I was keeping solemnly quiet on this issue. My mom could churn and chide all she wanted. She explained to me that I was not to do anything that I wouldn't do in front of Jesus and then she pulled me out of eighth grade science class thinking that she was saving me from sex-education. I never did learn the names of all the skeletal bones being taught that semester in science class. I just knew what erections looked like.

The present lump in my groin, which could not possibly be a bone, was getting bigger. When I would lay down flat on my back it would disappear into my lower abdomen. It was starting to scare me, but it didn't really hurt unless I coughed while I was standing up. I knew how my mom felt about doctors. She didn't like them, she had me frightened of doctor visits and needles. Finally, when I was standing, I showed my huge soft lump to Darth. He knew exactly what it was, a hernia. He said that the guys got checked for them in phys-ed class at the beginning of each school year. He didn't know that girls could get them.

He didn't seem to have a problem with doctors at all. He got on the phone and made an appointment for me to see his family doctor the next morning, and then he drove me to the office visit. The doctor repeated what Darth had said. Then he added that it had to be repaired. For a moment I thought he was going to write me a prescription. Instead, he told me I needed surgery. I couldn't think of anything more terrifying than being cut wide open with sharp scalpels slicing through layers of skin and muscle.

After surgery, the surgeon explained to me that I had the largest hernia he had ever seen, especially for a girl. My parents left for their trip the following day and I stayed at Nellie's house after just two days in the hospital. I tried to go back to school the following week but wasn't up for walking, sitting, and toting heavy books. After the first two classes I ended up needing a ride home. The dog was glad to see me, the house was cold and silent, and I was tired.

My incision had begun to burn and throb. Darth was throbbing too, but not from an incision. We had sex downstairs because I couldn't climb all the way upstairs to my bedroom. I should have said, "No", but did not consider that an option. I thought we had a meaningful relationship requiring me to honor most of Darth's wishes. I'd convinced myself that our physical contact was an act of love and nurturing. If Darth had unfulfilled sexual desire, he would possibly return to his old fling with willing Elise. I was not going to let that happen again and felt a need to perform to keep Darth loyal to our relationship. I had no concept of how sick that idea was.

I had only been out of the hospital for three days. I had stitches and a seeping bandage across my right side. I was completely fatigued and slept like a rock on the sofa when Darth left. It would be six weeks before I could go back to work.

Still, I was earnestly trying to please my mother. I seriously doubted that she would have approved of sex in the back seat of Darth's car at the cemetery or on the sofa. Of course, the very last thing on earth I could do was talk to her about it, so I repeatedly searched the Bible instead. Based on my own interpretations I couldn't find any scriptures that said I was going to Hell for having sex before marriage since I was engaged to the same guy, I was having sex with. I used my own analysis to ease my guilty conscience and our relationship continued to grow, in my perception.

According to church teaching my earthly life needed work. Darth and I couldn't get into the level of heaven my mother desired for us unless he joined our church. I thought it was a lovely romantic notion to marry someone for forever. I was working on this, and my mother was constantly reminding me it was the only way I would ever be genuinely happy. At my request, Darth agreed to take the missionary program lessons. It was a series of privately held teaching to familiarize people with the churches' primary beliefs. These lessons are intended to be taken seriously with careful consideration based on prayer and fasting.

The whole idea is that at the end of the lessons Darth was studying he would recite his testimony that he knew the church was true, and that he desired to be a member. At the end of the last session Darth was asked point blank if he would join the church. "No thanks," he said just like he was turning down a piece of homemade apple pie. I was stunned, and I was petrified. As a teenager there were a lot of things about church I didn't like and questioned. Yet, all I could think was, "Oh no, what will my mother say?" I felt like someone had just sucked the wind out of my chest and I forgot all about the achy incision.

Then, Darth stood up and said, "OK, I'll join." I didn't know what made him change his mind. Possibly he was waiting to see my reaction. I didn't dare to ask; in case he changed his mind. Darth was willing to join the church. My life was now on track and my mother would be pleased with my goals. I was doing everything I had been raised to do, and according to church doctrine we would attain the highest level of heaven united-together.

CHAPTER TWENTY

My junior year of high school was over, and Darth had graduated as a senior. Later that summer he would take the test for his apprenticeship, and if he were accepted his wage level would increase dramatically. I was working on a full-scale basis and going to church three times a day on Sundays. Darth had since been baptized as an official member into our church program and he began to attend his own male meetings.

My stepfather had joined the church prior to marrying my mother when I was six years old. All my stepfather's children had reddish hair and freckles. I barely knew who they were. Why my stepdad's children needed to live with us, they all arrived together the summer after my junior year. This would be tough on my parents because there was no extra room in the house and there certainly wasn't any extra grocery money.

Dad had a large metal shop building that he used to do automotive repairs. He set up two folding cots with army blankets for his boys in the shop. No one had mentioned anything to me, but I knew that Remi wouldn't want to sleep in the shop on a cot with her brothers.

My upstairs bedroom just barely held my bed, dresser and all my teenage stuff, including a small closet full of my home-sewn wardrobe. I willingly volunteered to share my room with Remi. I rearranged my furniture, so we could squeeze an additional twin bed up against the wall. I'd always wanted a sister. Remi didn't like or want to be my sister. Maybe she was shy, but mostly it was an easier adjustment for her brothers. Remi wasn't cheery, nor did she appreciate sharing my bedroom.

I rose early each morning dragging myself out of bed as I raced against the clock to work six days a week. My job was physically taxing which was evident from my hernia surgery. I no longer had my horse chores, but the household chores were always waiting. Vacuuming, dusting, and scrubbing the bathroom took place on a weekly basis. Remi did absolutely nothing. She didn't even get up until the middle of the day, at which time she painted her fingernails and watched the soap operas. By the time, I arrived home from my job she had managed to work herself into a good solid sulk and complained constantly about being bored, but she was not bored enough to vacuum, do laundry, or weed the garden.

Mom laid out her absentee household management plan. I had my regular job, and in addition to that I was to clean house while she was gone. I did a lot of that anyway but while mom and dad were gone on their annual vacation, I was also responsible for doing everyone's laundry, cooking dinner for all five of us kids and making sure that everyone behaved. All three juvenile boys were supposed to load the dishwasher after each evening meal that I prepared for them. One of them was supposed to mow the yard once a week.

The first day went off without a glitch. I came home from work and made a dinner consisting of the four food groups, and everyone ate it. Not one pubescent boy put a single dirty dish into the dishwasher. I did some laundry and drove to town to see Darth. The following evening, I came home from work, cooked dinner, everyone ate. No one cleaned a single dirty plate. I vacuumed and left the house until later. I told all the boys that they needed to uphold their end of the rules and do the dishes. If they didn't, I wouldn't be able to prepare meals again. There weren't any clean dishes, pots or pans left in the cupboards. Remi was still bored and painting her fingernails.

The unkept grass was beginning to bow in the breeze, the garden was withering, the house was a mess and all of Mom's dishes were still dirty on the counter. I gave up. I knew I was going to be held accountable for the disarray and I also knew that it wasn't my fault. I did what I was supposed to, and I couldn't force the rest of them to abide by their assigned tasks. The balance of my evening meals I took at Darth's parents, with Nellie, or at Dairy Queen. I protested by only doing my own laundry. The guys had a drinking party and all of them got drunk. That was a first for my brother. At the end of the two weeks my parents' house was trashed and the yard overgrown.

I usually worked on Saturdays, but I had that day off and Nellie and I planned to go shopping. The largest shopping mall in the state had just opened a short drive from home. When we returned with our bargains, we stopped at Nellie's parents' house enthusiastically modeling our merchandise for her mother. Their phone rang. It was the other mother; she demanded to speak to me.

Mom told me, "You'd better get home right now and clean up this house, but first pick up a gallon of milk." Not knowing what the possible consequences would be, I decided I was not going to adhere to my mother's wishes and run home to clean up after the other children. Then I did another thing I had never done before, I hung up as she proceeded to give me an earful. As far as I was concerned, she had allowed for the mess to be created and she could tell the three delinquent males to clean it up.

I went out with Darth and then home much later. Mom was livid with me. I had never directly disobeyed her before. She even managed to have my dad upset with me. I explained what I thought and then Mom verbally drug Darth into the heated conversation wanting to know what he thought. He'd known about the entire situation for the last two weeks and of course he sided with me. None of this was going over well with my stepdad. It became a real issue when it was insinuated that his kids and my brother were to blame. He basically told Darth he had better leave without delay. I looked at Darth and winked.

Feeling that the circumstances at home would be impossible to deal with, I'd decided I was going to leave home. I would be eighteen in less than two months. I'd been previewing apartments, but I couldn't afford to live by myself in one. However, I was going to take a stand and make a statement, a protest that my mother would hear loud and clear. I'd go spend time with my biological father, and Darth was going to help me. The little wink was my signal to him to pick me up at midnight, where I would be waiting out on the shoulder of the gravel road with my suitcase in hand.

Darth picked me up and took me to Elise's house. I'd never been there before, and Elise had been my arch nemesis the year before. Her parents were on vacation and her older brother was still in town saying it would be all right if I spent the night. Darth had made all the arrangements. He knew how to get into the house and where I could sleep. Her brother was out late drinking with friends, so I had the entire house to myself. In the morning Darth would pick me up and take me to the International Airport. I'd already phoned my biological father and he was expecting me. In the morning, my mother would find me missing and have no idea where I had gone. I thought it served her right.

Later in the morning prior to leaving for the airport, I phoned her at work. She was infuriated with me, but I didn't think her feelings were warranted. I told her where I was going and that I would be back when I was ready to return. She told me all kinds of things that should justify her actions. She didn't understand what she was doing to me when she insisted that I be accountable for the other kids as she let their everyday farm duties slide. I wasn't exactly thrilled to leave Darth, my job and his cousin's upcoming wedding. I was however, going to make my declaration to my folks that I'd had enough of being burdened with their irresponsibility.

I had hardly seen my natural father in the last several years, and he still made a habit of hugging me too hard. I barely knew the stranger he was, but I wanted to make the best of my visit. It was obvious that he still drank like a fish and smoked like a chimney. I thought that his finest talent was his dedication to his job.

We had lived in a quaint farmhouse with a white picket fence when I was incredibly young, where I played in the irrigation ditch and listened to my father cry for a second chance when my mother divorced him. I could still remember the red formica table that sat in the center of the kitchen in the squarely shaped pink house. I was five years old, and my only sibling was two and a half. Mostly, I knew that my father would physically hurt my mother, even though I was too young to understand the consequences of the cruelty.

A lifetime later I would learn that men with typically selfish behaviors often display abusive tendencies toward females. Frequently, they parade an outward appearance of self-confidence which is really a distorted sense of self-importance. Showering their victims with gifts, flattery and apologies, their appearance of confidence is a cover for their own insecurities. Abusers' kind behaviors are meant to lead their victims into denial about the truth, not only can abusers be affectionate they are also spiteful, nasty, and controlling.

Later in the week we saw one of my father's ex-wives walking down the sidewalk in town. I remembered her from the verbal scatter shot my father had thrown at her in the kitchen when I was visiting the summer of my eighth birthday, almost a decade before. The most memorable event of all happened while I was the only child who was not out in the yard playing. The fight was rapidly growing to full scale battle, she probably knew that her marriage was a sham and resented my father for it. Who knows why any of his wives married him, maybe they mistook muscles for manners, but there I was a little kid caught in the cross hairs on the wrong side of the kitchen door. Quickly the fight was escalating as the glass vase sitting on the table got pitched across the room while my father's wife shrieked and cried harder. My only escape route to the door was blocked by my bellowing father. I realized he was still the same man that my mother divorced and left even as he had promised through his tears to change. There I was, trapped in the kitchen with a father whom I loved and a father who could not be trusted with his problems. I was childlike but not childish and I knew without a doubt that I understood just one of the reasons why my mother had chosen to leave him.

The first few days of my leisure visit were pleasant if I ignored my childhood memories. I was totally unaccustomed to having so little to do. I would have preferred going to work but I wasn't ready to return home. I'd paid for my own airfare, and I intended to stick to my plans. At some point my father phoned to talk to my mother, which I refused to do.

Upon returning home the following week, I found Mom on the rickety old back porch doing laundry. I said a polite hello and had no intentions of discussing anything further with her. No doubt, constantly trying to appease my mother made me a better person. Possibly, we could have agreed to disagree and tried to accept one another's opinions. I had tried to talk to her for years and felt that she just didn't want to understand me. I wasn't going to give her another chance now. No matter how hard I tried, I was never perfect enough for her. I relished the idea that she would pitch church standards out the window and raise me as her own daughter instead of a regulated church member.

The following morning, I went to church with the rest of the family. No one mentioned a single word about my trip or the grievances preceding it. Shortly thereafter, the three step kids were gone for good. I was never told exactly why.

Making up my mind that I was not going back to high school that fall, as I didn't want to attend school without Darth, and since I only needed two credits to graduate, I decided to finish high school by going to the local community college two nights a week. Darth and I were still planning on getting married. In our state the female was eligible for marriage without parental consent at age eighteen. The male had to have parental consent or be twenty-one years of age. Darth's parents were adamant that he be twenty-one prior to marriage, which left us three years and two months to wait.

In retrospect, I hadn't thought about a career, just a job. A job served the immediate purpose of my short-term goals of being self-sufficient. Years down the road I would repeatedly wish that I had prepared myself for a career of my choice. If only I'd stuck to college. I wished my parents had promoted that idea as a possibility for my future, rather than encouraging me to become dependent upon a man. What a shame that I had not seen college as an answer to my problems instead of counting on Darth. I did not understand that an education was something that no one could ever take away from me, and what a powerful tool knowledge could be.

Wanting to leave home felt right as rain. I was under the impression that Mom knew I would leave as soon as I could, and she no longer required me to baby-sit my obnoxious sixteen-year-old brother. I still helped with the household chores, but I wasn't home very often except to sleep. Since I no longer went to high school, no one voiced a complaint when I quit going to church seminary in the mornings as I had before school. I was working banker's hours, going to college in the evenings and had my weekends off.

With this turn of events, I had decided that I could handle living at home awhile longer. Darth and I were saving our money for a down payment on our future house. We'd decided that if we could both work and go to school while financially qualifying to purchase a house, his parents would allow us to marry prior to his twenty-first birth date.

He bought me a bigger diamond engagement ring for Christmas that year.

CHAPTER TWENTY-ONE

Steeped in religious beliefs and saddled with a sense of duty, I had fantasized that my future children would never come from a divorced, broken home as I had. They would always know their father and grow up having his undivided attention. They would grow up learning how to honor their commitments, laugh, and face adversities. They would have strong characters and commit to what was right even at a personal cost. I thought that I knew just how this should be. I even had the common sense to know that kids were several years down the road into our future. Darth still had four years of school left. I was in a big rush to get married and own a home, but I did not intend to speed toward motherhood.

We'd been careful with foam and condoms, using both applications at the same time. I'd even been to Planned Parenthood for the exam required to receive birth control pills. I wasn't comfortable taking the pills because they made me feel ill. I kept them in a convenient, easily accessible location so I'd remember to take one every morning. The birth control pills were crammed into a pair of thick, heavy knit socks in my top dresser drawer. This seemed an appropriate hiding place and I didn't think that my mother would be searching through my undie's drawer.

After a good deal of forethought, I made up my mind to go off the pill. That decision was mostly prompted by my guilty feelings. I was still receiving my weekly dose of indoctrinations at church, and I was trying to do the morally correct things. I was perplexed all the time. The virgin part had gone out the window when I was in high school, and Darth stuck with the theory that we were not morally unclean if we were eventually married.

We were becoming brasher about our sexual activities. Once we did it on the sofa at his parents' house while his folks were home late one evening. His father was relaxing in the recliner five feet away intently watching television. Darth and I had the couch to ourselves, and we were laying on our sides stretched from one end to the other. Darth was horizontal behind me and couldn't keep his hands to himself. The television movie was intriguing, holding the rest of the family's rapt attention. We didn't give much thought to our inappropriate behavior since our hormones pulsed beyond our management skills.

Early that spring my mother's birthday was on a Sunday. All Sundays were the same routine at our house, go to church, come home, have dinner, and go to church again. Sexual interaction wasn't preplanned, it just happened. We were upstairs in my room listening to the stereo and waiting for dinner. Dad was in the living room reading the newspaper with his stomach gurgling, and Mom was in the kitchen at the bottom of the stairs cooking dinner. My brother was across the narrow, short hallway in his attic bedroom. He'd painted it bright blood red. The carpet matched the walls and ceiling. I didn't know what he did alone in his room besides shooting his BB gun, which frequently ricocheted bee bees off my single pane bedroom window causing an occasional stray bee-bee to bounce from my forehead.

Darth and I were on my bedroom floor. I was not at ease with this, but Darth didn't seem to mind if we hurried. In our rush to expedite our physical chemistry, we didn't bother with foam or condoms, or thoughts of every cause has an effect. We didn't even have my bedroom door shut tight. I couldn't believe what we were doing, and we weren't getting caught. I cannot even begin to imagine what my parents would have said in addition to, "Don't do it". At that moment there was no possible way that I could have fast forwarded in time to discover that my mother's birthday would be my child's conception date.

The following month, my period didn't start. My abdomen was bloated, and my breasts were tender, and I had painful cramps, but no period. I wasn't sure what to think of this until I started to feel very sick to my stomach. I constantly thought that I was going to throw up. When I told Darth about it, he didn't like it. He seemed to be annoyed with me and for the first time in our relationship he clammed up and pouted. I couldn't tell what he was thinking. I felt as if I was being punished and I was quickly becoming frightened of the circumstances.

I knew that I was in way over my head. This wasn't at all what I had been planning. We needed to call the Realtor and back out of the earnest money we had put down on the perfect house in town with the little yard. I needed help and knew I would never dare to ask my parents, not the parents who tried to pull me out of sex education class to teach me my morals at home. I could never discuss sex in any detail with them. Everything in my life as I knew it was going to change very quickly over the next eight months.

The following day from my desk at work, I snuck a call to the doctor's nurse to check the results of my pregnancy test. It was positive. The reality of this symptom had been sinking in since the day before. This was not what I had intended. I didn't know if the worst part was going to be the embarrassment or the constant morning sickness.

Darth phoned me when he got home from work late that afternoon to check in regarding the pregnancy test. When I told him that it was positive, he said, "Hot dog." I was totally perplexed at his remark as I had no idea what he meant. He probably didn't know what he meant either.

I was at work and not allowed to visit on the phone, so I had to hang up without asking.

Darth was being despondent about the positive pregnancy test results, and it was the first time that he had ever reminded me of his father. He didn't say much of anything for a few days and then he decided that he was going to tell his parents. I had already decided that I would never tell mine. I could deal with his parents knowing but did not feel that I could discuss being pregnant with mine, even though everyone was going to know eventually anyway.

Darth was mad at me. He said that my pregnancy would ruin his life and we were going to have to live in an apartment. I knew we wouldn't have to live in an apartment forever, just for a while. Instead of being angry with me, I felt he should have been upset at himself and shoulder some of the blame. Getting pregnant wasn't solely my fault. He was showing me another warning sign, and this time, it wasn't so easy to ignore. It didn't matter to me because I thought that I had absolutely no way out. I needed Darth to grow up and help me.

He explained to his mother first. He told me her first comment was, "You two should have been married a month ago! Oh, and you know I just love babies." I felt grateful she wasn't making moral judgments about me, and it sounded like she was willing to make the best of our unexpected predicament. Later that day his mother told his father, and I doubt that he got all excited about being a grandpa. I also suspected that he halfway expected this to happen. He had never been concerned about his son's morals. He believed in the All-American, red-blooded boy growing into manhood.

It was Saturday evening at Darth's parents' dining room table and as we collectively set the wedding date for the following weekend. It was a good thing I'd been sewing my wedding dress with seven-inch zippers in the sleeves. For years afterward, I supposed that Dodie thought I had gotten pregnant intentionally, as a reason to get married before Darth turned twenty-one. There had not been any manipulation on my part. That thought had never occurred to me. I didn't think that Dodie dwelt on it for more than a minute. She was trying to make the best of the situation and she was excited about a baby. Then she told me that if I had a girl, she would never speak to me again, but I had other things to worry about, like how was I going to keep my job when I was vomiting at ten-minute intervals?

Experiencing spiritual spasms, I ceremoniously told my parents the following evening at the dinner table that Darth and I were going to get married that coming weekend. I didn't think that they seemed surprised. I tried to calm my jittery nerves by explaining some of the details we had planned for our wedding. I neglected to mention that I was pregnant. I had the impression that both my parents had expected our marriage for some time. There were no objections and very few questions. With only five working days, to put the wedding together we had planned for a few close friends to attend along with our immediate family. I also intended to invite my biological father but stipulated that my stepdad would give me away.

The coming week I went to work and felt severely nauseous most of the time. During my lunch breaks I ordered a small three-tiered lemon-flavored wedding cake with scalloped frosting and real daisies adorning the top tier. Nellie and I went fabric shopping and found a flowing white cotton fabric with a daisy pattern which we trimmed with white satin lace for her gown. Nellie was still in high school and held a part-time job. She would have to sew double time to finish her dress in less than a week. She had mastered the art of procrastination since childhood, so last-minute tasks were natural for her.

I felt fatigued and constantly queasy. I was positive that at any moment I would start puking without notice. I decided all I needed was to get through the week and then I could deal with being pregnant later. Since this was a once in a lifetime affair I splurged and found a reasonable deal on a wedding photographer that I could not afford. Darth's mother asked me about boutonnieres for the guys and the immediate family members. I hadn't even thought about boutonnieres. I'd never planned a wedding before and there wasn't any spare time for making lists. Darth's mother told me that the groom's family would pay for boutonnieres since that was standard wedding etiquette. After which my mother decided that she would pay for the flowers and bouquets.

In addition to all the wedding plans, we needed to find a place to live as a married couple. We rented the apartment that Darth was so apprehensive about. There was a small two-bedroom apartment, with a washer and dryer hook up that was available for occupancy that week. A washer and dryer hook up would be important if we could ever afford those appliances, so I would not have to do diapers at the laundromat. We paid our deposit and signed a six-month lease. We moved in a double bed with a sagging used mattress and squeaky box springs. The relentless urge to vomit never left me, especially when I got a whiff of our donated, threadbare second-hand sofa.

The only lacking detail was the wedding certificate. One of Darth's parents would have to be present at the County Courthouse to sign the consent form. Darth's father was elected by his wife for this chore and drove with us to the clerk's office. Before we entered the doublewide swinging glass doors at the end of the hallway into the room where our wedding certificate would seal our fate, Dick asked me, "Have you considered an abortion?" I was astounded and rocked back on my heels. "An abortion, why would I want to do that, it would be wrong." I didn't understand what he was thinking at all, but I was certain that it wasn't Dodie's idea. After the day at the courthouse Dick never brought the topic up again.

The wedding planning week was almost complete. It was Thursday evening, and I was standing on a table chair in the center of my parents' kitchen. For the first time in years Mom and I both agreed on the length of my dress. Balancing on the wooden chair seat I found myself caught up in the memory of popular classmates and friends who seemed so sure of themselves. I'd always felt so conspicuous at school. I could have died a thousand deaths if I caught someone looking where my knees should be. It was difficult to see my knees. Everyone had knees but me. This made me thankful for the busy overcrowded school hallways where I constantly attempted to hide my old-fashioned hemlines. I thought about my visit to the bishop's office at church where he required teenage girls to kneel on the floor. Upon inspection, their hemlines had to touch the floor, or their parents were summoned for a morals' consultation.

Throughout my youth, my mother had been trying to save me from being a normal teenager who would make mistakes. Her imposed restrictions alienated me to the point that we could not communicate, and I made all types of destructive blunders. Now I was marrying Darth in the church building even though we didn't qualify to marry according to church policies. I promised myself that I was not going to end up divorced like my mother had been, and my child would never come from a broken home.

Friday night was wedding rehearsal and dinner. All I had to do was practice walking down the aisle to music. My stomach was churning, and it wasn't the standard nervous bride butterflies. It was something else and it wasn't the pregnant morning sickness that I'd been experiencing twenty-four hours a day. It was Darth's attitude that was causing my nervousness.

We had barely seen each other all week except for renting the apartment. He was still moody and moping about how my pregnancy was stunting his life's potential. My instincts wanted to kick in. Remote things that I normally paid no attention to were nagging at the edges of my awareness. I started to question the decision I was making. I'd begun to think that I should not marry this guy. It was just a small whisper of a thought. It only lasted a milli-second before the brooms of my denial whisked it away. I convinced myself that reality was something I must rise above.

After wedding rehearsal Darth walked out on me. No explanation, no comment that he would see me at the rehearsal dinner, he simply left. Not only were his actions very embarrassing, but I was also confused. When someone asked where he was all I could say was the truth, he'd left. That was my first grand opening opportunity. I should have left too, and never looked back. Instead, I pretended that nothing was wrong. I went to dinner with everyone else, while busily promoting my own happy façade.

I was the only wedding party member who was pregnant. I had a baby to think about and I couldn't walk away just because I wanted to. I had responsibilities, and I was going to have a child who would need a father. Darth eventually showed up at the restaurant for our celebration dinner. I never did know where he went or why, and he offered no explanation, nor did I think that I was able to demand one.

The following morning was the beginning of my big day. I washed and rolled my hair, so it could dry while I was moving out of my parents' house. I packed all my personal belongings into my car and moved them into the apartment. Supposedly it had been professionally cleaned but I didn't think the cleaning person could have been a professional. The aroma of Pine-Sol left me green around the gills.

I left my parents' house that morning excited to embark on my new life. Mom reminded me not to work too hard, so I wouldn't be tired for my wedding night. She was so weird. Now we could talk about sex, but not in detail. I wasn't worried about being tired. I was more concerned about hurling my lunch while I waltzed my way to the altar.

I was trying to remain composed, get dressed and have a memorable time. Mom appeared in the doorway of the dressing room in a cream colored, knit dress that I'd never seen before. She wore her corsage and I thought that she looked beautiful. I was attempting to pull on my sheer white panty hose without poking runs in them while in the distant background I could her music beginning to play. I assumed that Darth was there in his rented tuxedo.

My stepfather was grinning and waiting outside the dressing room for me. He took my arm and locked it into his elbow while he smiled at me as he patted my wrist with his other hand. Then we walked down the aisle together. I was having difficulty moving my legs in step with the music and I thought about how Mom never liked the way I walked. I felt like I was slogging my way through three feet of standing water. This was the first time in my life I was grateful that my legs were completely hidden by a lengthy hemline.

A thoughtful woman lifted my extended train around the corner and spread it out behind me as I stood facing the pulpit next to Darth. He was smiling at me, and he didn't exit to the left or right. As the music ceased and the audience hushed, the bishop began our vows. This part had not been rehearsed. I presumed it would be the standard wedding ceremony like what I'd watched on television, but all we had to say to each other was the customary "I do." The groom embraced the bride with a wedding kiss, and I was announced to the attending audience as Mrs. Darth Vadies.

(HAPTER TWENTY-TWO

Still feeling woozy from my twenty-four hour a day morning sickness I managed to float on elation and smiles through our reception and cake cutting ritual. It was finally time to make the bride and groom get away. My hatchback was superbly decorated in chartreuse lipstick, lathered shaving cream and multi-colored balloons, while sitting precariously balanced on eight concrete cinder blocks. I suspected both younger brothers had something to do with this. Darth must have anticipated our siblings' artistic abilities as he had already borrowed the keys to his father's four-wheel drive truck.

When we arrived at our apartment complex, I was hoisted over the threshold. What I remember most distinctly was the dingy, musty smell of the place. I hoped it would not always make me feel this nauseous. The bulb in the overhead light of the bedroom was burned out, so I undressed in the dim shadows. Pounds of hard white rice fell from my veil and hair. This continued as I peeled off my panty hose, where I discovered more rice in my underwear.

We eagerly consummated our marriage and then he spent a long time promising me that we would eventually marry in the church temple for all time and eternity. He repeated to me how he genuinely loved me and would always cherish me more than anyone else ever could. He vowed to me that I should never worry as he promised to love me forever right into heaven and the hereafter. I believed him entirely.

Then Darth decided to inform me that I would continue to work at my fulltime job for the bank, regardless of how sick I was. If we were thrifty, we could live off his salary and save all of mine. Every dime that I made would be set aside for a down payment on a future home. This meant there would be no spare money for maternity clothes, movies, or lunch out with girlfriends. I never suspected that ultimately Darth did not want me to spend time with my friends or family. By demanding that I was not allowed to spend any of my own paycheck, he attempted to keep me from pursuing any of my personal activities.

Continually tired, I got up early in the mornings and went to work. I would now start a weekly routine of coming home from work, fixing dinner, and falling exhausted into bed prior to eight o'clock in the evening. I was sick to my stomach all the time. Everything that I ate came rocketing up the back of my throat. I was doing so much retching at work that I thought they were going to fire me. I spent half of my working hours in the downstairs restroom vomiting up bile, even if I didn't eat. When I was at my desk, I was constantly fighting the natural reflex sensation of greasy sludge rolling in my stomach. The constant heartburn leached at the back of my throat and nothing the doctor prescribed changed how ill I felt.

Aside from my continual vomiting and fatigue my doctor thought that I was basically healthy, but I knew how miserable I really was. My stomach was beginning to swell, and breasts were getting larger. I always threw up my anti-nausea medication and all my clothes were becoming uncomfortable around my waist. I bought one pair of cheap white maternity stretch pants at K-mart and two light weight cotton tops that would cover a protruding belly. Eventually, I saved enough money to buy fabric and a pattern to make one maternity outfit. This is what I wore over and over to work and everywhere else that I went, except on weekends when I could wear my blue jeans and hold the waistband closed under my extended belly with a wide rubber band hooked through the hole and fastened around the metal button.

My fatigue was escalating and all I really wanted to do was sleep. Darth didn't like this at all as he felt that he was entitled to sex whenever he wanted, and he claimed that was one of my matrimonial duties to him. He constantly demanded, "You owe me sex whenever I want it. It is the reason I married you." Under my breath I mourned, "Oh, thanks, that makes me feel special." There was sex in the morning when he got up before he rushed off to work, in the evenings when he came home and again when he went to bed.

Attempting to quell my revolting stomach, I eventually verbally protested owing him non-stop sex. I wanted to quit work and rest. Maybe with extra sleep I would stop throwing up and my sex drive would return. Darth didn't agree. One night he forcefully shoved me down onto my pregnant belly where I landed squarely on the corner of the metal bed frame. I cried silently as I sat on the floor. I was at a total loss as to what I could do.

Darth promptly left the apartment. It was Friday night and as he slammed the door all he said was, "I'm leaving." I did not know if that meant for a few hours or for the eternity that he promised to be with me. We'd been married a whole six days. In lingering moments before I drifted off to sleep, I thought about how horrible he was to treat me that way. I felt shocked with fear, confusion, and guilt for bringing Darth's wrath upon me, yet I knew his violent behavior was wrong. I wanted to hold him accountable for his actions but didn't know how. I felt responsible. If I had simply given Darth what he wanted, he wouldn't have acted the way did. Abusing me was a choice that Darth consciously made, but I didn't view it that way. I knew that I would have to be careful not to make him that upset with me again.

No one had ever explained to me that the first indication of violence is usually a single blow and that both partners tend to act as if it is just an isolated incident. I told myself that it would never happen again. I didn't realize that the first act of violence set the playing field for future abusive acts. Darth's threatening behavior was an attempt to establish dominance and control over my verbal defiance of attempting to stand up for myself regarding his insistence that I meet all his sexual burdens.

I thought that Darth had simply lost control of his temper, but he had started a pattern of behavior. It was not a loss of control; it was Darth telling me that I had to be what he expected, when he demanded it. He was reinforcing his own scheme, that he was the person in control. He wanted me to feel helpless. He was breaking down my sense of self-worth while attempting to steal my personal power and freedoms over my own life, but I had no idea of these certainties.

For weeks I heaved so hard, I thought my toenails curled. I don't think the manager at the bank had the heart to fire me, besides they knew that I would be quitting eventually. Eventually the cramping and spotting stopped although the vomiting didn't, and I was beginning to think that it never would. I was sincerely wishing that I had never gotten pregnant. The weeks rolled into months and finally my employment efforts had produced enough money to qualify us for an older fixer house. The total purchase price was sixteen thousand dollars making our monthly payments one hundred and sixty-five bucks. Our budget would be very tight, so we would be counting every single penny. I was in my eight-month, and finally I could quit my job and start making baby clothes.

I gave my two-week written notice at the bank. We loaded all our crappy, second hand smelly furniture into a borrowed garbage trailer and proceeded to move into our new, old home. The two-story house was an early nineteen hundred vintages without much character and a lot of deferred maintenance. The exterior whitewash paint was peeling from the warped clapboard siding and the curling composition roofing had faded from red to dirty brown. Landscaping was non-existent except for an overgrown rhododendron bush under the living room window.

The sellers had promised that they would clean everything after they moved out, so we arrived that weekend with our meager belongings eager to move in, but we couldn't. The variegated green shag carpet was black with oil and smudge. There was spoiling food in the kitchen sink, the bathroom smelled like an outhouse. The double-sided window seat in the dining room was full of stinking soiled diapers, dozens of them. The basement was empty except for ancient, dusty, useless junk.

Darth's parents were there with us to help unload our possessions, but the filth and the stench was intolerable. I sat down on one of the worn-out steps on the front porch and said we would just have to move in later after I'd had a chance to clean house. Our apartment lease was up so we drove all the way back to Grandma Doyd's house and parked the laden trailer in a lean-to shed that provided some cover. We were now down to one vehicle, so Darth would take my car to work and to school and I would be stuck at his grandmothers'.

I craved sleep. I would get up early with Darth and make his breakfast and sack lunch and then go back to bed. I'd sleep straight through the day until about three o'clock in the afternoon at which time I would get up, take a bath, clean the house and start dinner. Darth would come home to indulge in his homemade dinner and head out to class or camp at our wobbly dining room table to concentrate on his studies. I managed to paint the baby's room when I found a gallon of textured paint on sale and used it to cover the cracks in the walls. We shopped for a new piece of remnant carpet, and Darth laid it over new padding because the old stuff stunk so bad neither one of us could inhale. Dodie found a functional crib at a garage sale and donated it to our cause. I made some curtains for the only window, and we were set.

I wasn't puking as often but when I did, it was brutal. The heaves were so severe that they would break the blood vessels in my face and under my chin along my neck. While I was frequently face down in the toilet, Darth would hold my hair back. When he eventually tired of this chore, he made a new household rule that I was not allowed to brush my teeth before going to bed.

We started Lamaze classes on one of the evenings that he didn't attend college. The intense breathing exercises seemed silly to me, but I practiced them anyway. I was very self-conscious that Darth and I were the youngest couple participating in this class. It was obvious to everyone that the other couples were much more financially affluent. I was embarrassed that I didn't have many respectable maternity clothes, but I stuck with the class and Darth always went with me. In my mind I still had difficulties accepting that I was pregnant.

Disbelief had previously set in, but now I felt as if I had a foreign fetus growing out of control inside of me. I'd read about expectant mothers feeling an emotional bond to their unborn child. I didn't understand why I never felt that way, even though I wanted to. I was afraid that my baby didn't like me because of the violent vomiting. I knew how sick it made me and wondered if the baby felt sick also. My stretch marks were increasing, and the baby's delivery date was fast approaching.

At the last Lamaze class, the instructor showed a detailed film of a woman in labor. This wasn't quite the same as I'd seen in the movies while growing up. The film was of close-up views of all the technical stuff, like episiotomies. I was stabbed with visual thoughts where they snip your crotch open with surgical scissors as if the doctor is de-boning a thick steak. This last class scared me right out of my wits. I went home in tears and stayed that way. I went to bed intending to stay pregnant for the rest of my life.

Fall had passed dejectedly, and it was dreary winter weather. The days were dark and gloomy, and I was always stuck at the house. I was home alone almost all the time. All my friends, including Nellie lived an expensive, long distance phone call away. When my mom phoned, she would tell me that if I went to church, I'd learn to be a better mother, and after all, church was the only avenue to everlasting happiness. I wanted to be able to share my feelings of anxiety with her, but I couldn't even tell her that my due date was only a week away.

CHAPTER TWENTY-THREE

Off and on for several weeks, I had severe pains that ran directly across the front of my abdomen. They would begin as shallow ebbs and build until I had to double over from the contractions, and then like the tides of ocean waves the pain would recede. I assumed that this was just another part of the suffering that went along with being pregnant, but on this day, I felt great! I mopped and waxed the kitchen floor, vacuumed, and dusted, washed windows and barely slept. After my house cleaning was accomplished, I prepared an enormous casserole for dinner, and served premium vanilla ice cream I'd purchased on sale for dessert.

After the dishes were washed, dried, and put away. I sat down in our second-hand lazy boy chair where I put my feet up, set a pillow on my lap to serve as a temporary tray and dug into my hot fudge sundae. I'd been craving one with extra thick, sticky chocolate. Then another tidal wave pain struck my middle, and another followed before I could anticipate the second wave, while the baby protested. In the past, the gripping pains had only been singular but then minutes later another double whammy struck.

Darth walked through the living room and wanted to know what I was doing, gasping, hunched over my ice cream. I was surprised that he was paying that much attention to me, and I told him it was just some pains I'd been having for several weeks. He tentatively looked at me, "I think you might be going into labor." "I'm not in labor because my due date isn't until the day after tomorrow," I protested. I huffed and puffed and panted just like the nurse taught me in Lamaze class, after I finished regurgitating the hot fudge sundae along with the contents of my dinner.

The birthing procedure wasn't as scary as I'd imagined once I thought about how I would no longer be pregnant by the end of the following day. I was stationed in a regular hospital room while the attending nurses timed my contractions and monitored all cervical dilation. Without any previous warning signs, I felt the instinctual urge to push. When "pushing" was discussed in our Lamaze class I had specifically questioned how you would know when the time was right. The nurse assured me, "You don't need to worry about it because you'll just know", and now I did. When I expressed my urge to the attending nurse, she summoned another nurse and they wheeled me on my bed to the antiseptic, and brightly lit delivery room.

While I was concentrating on my new surroundings and desperately trying to breathe my way through another painful contraction, I resented having both my legs and arms strapped down to the delivery table. I felt like a trussed-up, fattened turkey spread eagle on the way to the oven. I halfway expected a nurse to artfully arranging a colorful display of vegetables tucked neatly under my rump.

While panting and pondering motherhood my thoughts were interrupted once again by a severe urge to push. Seizing the moment, the doctor and all the attending nurses were excitedly encouraging me. Only his head protruded because his shoulders were stuck and turned inside the birth canal while the baby that I assumed was a boy was wailing away at full-fledged lung capacity. He sounded spitting mad to me. I didn't know if all babies were born mad at their mothers, maybe I couldn't blame him. Being born and squeezed from the inside out couldn't possibly be an enjoyable experience for a baby about to enter the world.

Darth had been in the delivery room with me, telling me to focus on the hands of the clock set high on the wall. At this point, I was tempted to pull his lips over his ears to shut him up. He seemed genuinely pleased about his newborn baby. Darth decided that he was going to leave me to sleep in my semi-private room and drive across town to tell his parents our news.

Left alone in my hospital room at a late hour that night, I thought about the baby. He was exceedingly long with oversized baby feet. All the nurses assured me that he would be a big boy even though his birth weight was only six pounds and six ounces. As a fresh newborn he'd appeared gray, bloody and scrawny. He seemed so unfamiliar to me. I thought that I was supposed to feel a special bond or attachment and I was baffled as to why I didn't. I finally told myself that would come with time and after hungrily consuming a bowl of lime Jell-O and saltine crackers, I slept soundly for a few hours.

The following morning one of the nurses brought my baby to me to breast feed. Breast feeding wasn't going well because Joey didn't want to nurse; he just didn't seem interested. He didn't know that for the last three months I had diligently rubbed my tender nipples with a terrycloth towel after each bath as I'd been instructed to do in Lamaze class, so our nipples would toughen up.

When the nurse checked on both of us, I explained that my son didn't seem to be interested in nursing even though I was certain he must be hungry. She observed us for a few minutes and informed me that I didn't have very good nipples. She did not specify her professional opinion about my nipple problem. I had never in my life questioned my nipples and neither had anyone else. She took the baby and said that she would bottle feed him and I could attempt breast feeding later, leaving me to feel wholly inadequate.

I was to be discharged from the hospital late that afternoon. However, the hospital was going to keep Joey. He was diagnosed with jaundice and would need to be kept under special lighting or possibly given blood transfusions. This was not good news to a first-time mother. The discharging nurse told me to enjoy a few days at home without the baby. She said it would be the only chance that I would get for a decent night's sleep for a dozen years, and I was supposed to remember to pump my breasts every two hours. I'd never heard of such a thing, and I wondered how I was supposed to pump myself. The nurse said they sold breast pumps at all the pharmacies, and they came complete with instructions.

Now that I had put in my nine months of hurling, and spent a long night in labor, worked while I was as sick as a dog to buy a home to have for our family, I was supposed to go home without the baby and enjoy it. I didn't know what kind of emotions I was supposed to feel other than post pregnancy hormones that affected everyone differently.

For the long drive home, I sat on a pillow at Dodie's suggestion. My stitches were sore and raw, and the pillow seemed to be a good idea. I was told to drink plenty of fluids, so I'd produce enough breast milk, but I was afraid to do so because Dodie insisted that urinating on my vaginal stitches would burn for several days. Everyone's conflicting advice left me wondering who knew what they were talking about.

After arriving home Darth went to the drug store to purchase the breast pump. It resembled a miniature rubber trumpet and according to the instructions you stuck it on your breast over your nipple and simultaneously squeezed while the plastic pump sucked like a hungry infant. It worked great and I produced gallons of homemade milk and my nipples functioned perfectly. I joyfully assumed the baby would get the hang of it when he came home from the hospital.

Joey was kept in the hospital that was over an hour drive from our house and we absolutely could not afford cab fare, so while Darth was at work or school, I had no way to go visit him. Regrettably, it would be five days before the hospital would release him to his anxious parents. When he did come home, he was not the least bit interested in my nipples or sucking on them.

I had absolutely no experience with small newborns, and I earnestly wanted to be a good mother, so I tried to cater to his every whim. Dodie told me how important it was for a baby to connect with its mother through breast feeding. All I knew was that my attempts were futile, and Joey cried constantly. Frequently he really did seem mad at me. I mistook his constant bawling as a reflection upon whether I was taking proper care of him. My mother's church friends were phoning to tell me to wait it out and the baby would eventually be hungry enough that he would nurse. The unnerving crying went on for several days, and I was up all hours of the night with a howling, hopeless baby.

One morning I decided that I wasn't going to listen to all the experienced mothers any longer. I bundled Joey up and walked downtown to the nearest drug store. I spent money we didn't have to purchase glass baby bottles I could sterilize and a container of baby formula. I couldn't believe how expensive formula was and I decided it didn't matter. I pushed the stroller straight home, sterilized water and gave that kid exactly what he wanted, milk in a bottle, which he contentedly sucked every two hours on the hour, for an hour, twenty-four hours a day for months. I had not known sleep deprivation could last so long.

I would stand beside Joey's crib while he lay sleeping. He looked innocent and passive in his slumber, and I knew in my heart standing there against the railing of his baby crib that I was stuck with a husband that I didn't understand. Darth was not the person that I thought I had married. I'd seen warning signs, in my naivety, I'd chosen to ignore them along the way, and now I was cemented in a situation I'd created. I did not believe that there was anywhere that I could go and take the baby and survive. As hard as I might try, I could not think of a way that I could go to school, work and support both of us. I made up my mind that I could make our marriage work if I tried hard enough. I could be the perfect wife and mother, no matter what. Darth never once got up in the middle of the night.

If, I did everything just like I was supposed to, Darth would recognize my endeavors and be kind to me. I easily forgot about how he'd thrown me down onto my pregnant belly during the first week of our marriage. I conveniently over-looked how sex was more important to him than my health. I decided that I had made my bed and I would have to sleep in it, literally.

CHAPTER TWENTY-FOUR

Soon I could shed the oversized men's cardigan sweater I had rescued from our grimy basement, finding it wrapped around a rusty exposed pipe for insulation. The pipe was no longer connected to anything except an exterior wall, so I swiped it as an additional article of clothing. It hung loosely on me and buttoned up the front, making it fit perfectly while I had been pregnant. It had also kept me warm in the drafty, old house through the rest of the winter season and into spring. Focusing on the turning point in the weather, I'd begun to feel that my life would improve with the arriving warm sunshine.

Darth was still drinking on the weekends, he generally didn't get drunk drinking beer at home, but he always had to have something to drink in his hand, no matter what he was doing. When he did frequently go out with the guys after work on Fridays, he always drove home reeking of stale beer, peanut hulls, and cigarette smoke. As thoughts careened around in my cranium, I should have understood that Darth did not come from a super-natural origin, he was merely a human feeding his own private beast.

When invited to a co-worker's home for a party, Darth always had too much to drink and then insisted that he was sober enough to drive home. It didn't matter how strongly I objected, he would never give me the car keys even when I would ask him to drive a few blocks, pull over, and switch to the passenger seat where no one from the party could see.

He always refused to put up with my request and continued to drive us home intoxicated. It scared me, but he refused to have it any other way.

If we weren't in the car, Joey constantly cried as if he were enraged. To keep him happy and well hydrated in the summer heat I gave him a daily dose of several baby bottles of home-made juice. I used real cloth diapers because we couldn't afford the disposable kind and I double folded them with all the padding in front. I changed diapers every forty-five minutes all day long, as they were always soaking wet. I was constantly trying to make Joey a happy healthy baby, just as I was constantly trying to please Darth into being a kind husband. Darth tried to maintain his personal happiness by rationalizing his inappropriate behavior. He denied or discounted his appalling acts to minimize the harshness of their effects by blaming me for any wrongdoing. Growing up he was probably the kind of little boy who pulled the legs off bugs one at time, before he squashed them dead.

Darth relentlessly complained that I did not perform sex often enough or adequately. I was tired of the pressure; the more that he forced the issue the harder the act would become for me. Sex could not be given freely upon his demanded request. I really did love him but frequently I didn't understand his motivations to be something other than pure mean selfishness. Often, I was finding that I did not like him as a person. He was supposed to be my friend and partner, instead he was my jailer and taskmaster and I felt I had no choice but to obey.

I tried to focus on the things that I did enjoy. Dad was coming over to drop off some tools for Darth to borrow. We were going to install new Formica on the countertop that weekend, a project the previous owner should have addressed dozens of years before.

Darth was verbally bashing me, and when I objected to his complaints, he slapped me open handed across my face. He had ways of making love and life impossible, but he had never slapped me before. He hit me right across my left cheek hard enough that it snapped my neck backward and left a bright crimson handprint on the side of my face. More than the pain and the insult of the violent action was my mortification at my father seeing a handprint welting on my face.

I struggled to stop crying so when Dad arrived, he would not think that anything was wrong. When Darth stomped out of the kitchen, I immediately escaped to the bathroom where I could apply additional blush to both cheeks in my hurried attempt to hide my reddening face from my father. I removed the barrette from my hair letting it fall forward hiding the handprint. Dad arrived just a few minutes after the ugly slap and didn't seem to notice. I was trying to minimize the impact of the violence with extra makeup. I didn't realize that my denial only let me harbor bitterness, distrust and dread. All I was really doing was making it easier for Darth to continue drinking and battering. If my father did notice a handprint, he never said anything about it. I put on my best smiley face and went about tending to the baby while Dad and Darth discussed tools.

Later that afternoon when Darth had removed the old countertop and cut out the Formica pattern, he solicited my help in laying it. I'd never laid Formica before, so I listened carefully as Darth explained that I would have to stand stooped over the counter with my arms straight out in front of me while he set the rubber cemented formica in place on top of my bare skin. I was to remain in this position until he told me that I could pull my arms out of the way. I argued that the glue was going to stick to me and not the cabinet, but I complied until he verbally allowed me to pull my arms back. I couldn't physically remove my own hands and forearms. Darth latched onto my shoulders and wrenched as we both fell backward while the hide and hair peeled from my arms like layers on an onion. I went to bed that night with salve on my wounds, feeling like Darth was making a point of asserting his dominance over me. The skin on my face was as inflamed as the hide on my arms, while the hurt to my heart remained hidden.

Since I wasn't a drinker, Darth decided to teach me something else he thought I should learn to enjoy. He was certain that if I was stoned, I might find sex more enjoyable. What he was unable to grasp was that I had always liked sex. What I did not like was him constantly pressuring me. He refused to understand that his badgering was not producing the result that he wanted. He came home from work with a bong. He knew how allergic I was to cigarette and campfire smoke and that I had never smoked a cigarette in my life, but Darth believed a bong was the answer to my imperfections. He put ice water in the bottom of the elongated glass tube, so it would cool the smoke without searing my lungs. He insisted that if I would try it a few times I would like it, and if I did not, I wouldn't have to inhale. Instead of banging him on the head with the bong, it was much easier to comply than quarrel with him.

The problem was, having never been stoned, my innocence made the perfect argument for him. How could I possibly know that I wouldn't like it or could argue against using it, if I had never tried it? There was no way I could debate his question. I decided that if I obliged him, then he couldn't continue to use his argument against mine.

Sitting cross-legged on my living room floor with Darth positioned in front of me and the bong placed squarely between my bare feet, I wasn't even sure if Darth's pot would have any affect. Darth knew that I didn't like it when he went out and drank so he told me he would stay home with me if I would smoke some dope with him. Gee, what a fair and worthwhile trade he was offering me. I didn't realize that emotional manipulation is about control. It is not an accident; it is a choice decided by the abuser. Emotional abuse is nothing more than brainwashing, which ultimately leaves the victim perplexed and unable to think clearly of her own accord.

Unknowingly, the victim remains loyal to the abuser secretly hoping that his behavior will change for their best.

After my lungs felt as if they would burst, I was instructed to exhale. Puffing pot worked because I was walking three feet off the kitchen floor when I went to the refrigerator for something to munch on. Whatever I was watching on late night television was hysterically funny. Darth was expecting continual sex and all he got was hilarious comedy. I doubted that being stoned made Darth's sex life any better. If it had made any kind of significant difference, it seems that I would have known it because he had promised that if he were sexually pleased, he would be a better husband to me.

After a few Saturday nights of getting high Darth brought home some hashish, as he boasted about his purchase, he explained to me that this was even better stuff than the pot. On Monday morning, I still felt like I couldn't think clearly. Simple tasks that I would normally accomplish with little effort were difficult. My mind seemed to be in a perpetual haze where cobwebs were clogging my brain. This sensation finally began to diminish after a few weeks. I told Darth that I wouldn't smoke any more pot again, as I had no intention of living my life in a hovering mindless fog. Darth finally gave up on insisting that I get stoned with him and he came home even later after his college classes and work on Fridays.

If we were invited to a party on the weekends, I was generally required to go with him and take the baby. I hated the drinking part of it and never felt like the other wives accepted me, probably because I resented being there. During the week, I was trapped at home by myself with Joey on a full-time basis. Our only vehicle was the Ford Maverick that I'd purchased when I was a junior in high school. Darth used my car to go to work and attend classes.

Nellie still lived far away, and she was working while going to school. On rare occasions, she would drive to our house and as usual, she and I had a great time together, until Darth would come home. He would always find a reason to disapprove of what we were doing. We never did anything wrong, we just enjoyed one another's company and played with Joey. I felt that Darth didn't like Nellie's friendship because he seemed threatened by it, and I couldn't understand why. I did everything that I could to convince him that he was more important to me than Nellie. I felt caught in the middle between the two of them, hiding my righteous indignation from Darth. Nellie wasn't taking his crap as I did. She could leave, and I had nowhere to go, so I stayed when I didn't want to.

When sexually deprived Darth left for work in the mornings, I canned every fruit and every vegetable that I could glean from Mom's Garden and the neighbor's fruit trees. I used the blender to make most of Joey's baby food and I shoveled huge portions into him at every meal. Despite all my efforts, I still didn't think Joey was a content baby. He didn't want his toys and didn't like being outside on a blanket. He wouldn't even try to sit up or roll over. Most of the time he bellowed like a miniature bull, while I would do everything, I could think of to keep him quiet. Nothing seemed to work, except for the second-hand windup swing.

I'd read about postpartum hormonal blues and thought perhaps that was my problem as I was constantly depressed. When alone, which was most of the time, I was frequently in tears. I didn't have anyone to talk to, I was isolated in the house with no vehicle or money, and Darth frequently claimed that his sperm count was backing up.

One evening after dinner before Darth left for class, we had a yelling match. I had tried to explain to him how I had been feeling even though most of the time I didn't dare trust him with my personal fears. I'd been married to him for over a year and that was long enough for me to figure out that if I shared any of my harbored feelings with him, he would wait and at my expense use my concerns to his advantage against me.

Little did I know; that emotional abuse could include exerting verbal pressure, and physically isolating me, while applying ridicule and neglect. There was really nothing else I could blame this on other than myself and the circumstances I attempted to live with, or so I thought. I was out of control emotionally and shamefully I took it out on the baby. During his incessant crying his contorted face would turn reddish purple while his mouth was wide open with horrible sounds spewing from it. Joey reminded me of his Grandpa Vadies when he was bawling at the top of his lungs. I wasn't sure if it was the unrelenting sound or the shape of his inherited Vadies lips that provoked me the most. I could see all the way down his annoying pink throat. I'd had it with the blaring baby and the impossible demanding husband. I knew the life I had dreamed of was never going to exist.

I grabbed the baby and shook him hard. I didn't care what he did if he would just shut up. He screeched worse with each shake and that is when I totally lost it and slapped him. The worst part was I wanted to keep slapping repeatedly until I beat my own existence into oblivion. In my torment, I didn't have time to consider that whom I really wanted to beat to a pulp was Darth. I had just one ounce of what I thought was a sane thought. I took the burp rag off the side of the crib and stuffed it into the squalling mouth that resembled his male relation's pouting lips. Flipping off the light switch as I left the room, I slammed the bedroom door behind me. I laid face down in the shag carpet that still smelled of dirty grease and sobbed until I couldn't cry any longer. I lay in a prone position begging and praying to God to please forgive me, for hurting Joey.

I did not know if I could ever forgive myself because I was so mortified at what I had done. This was the exact opposite of who I wanted to be and who I believed that I was. I did not know who to turn to, so I got out my Dr. Spock book, donated to me from Dodie's garage sale trips. I read every chapter but none of them discussed cranky babies. I was exhausted and shaky and still I'd found no possible solutions for feeling overwhelmed.

Joey pulled the burp rag out of his own mouth and was lying quietly watching the baby chimes that hung over his crib. Upon turning on the overhead light, to my horror I saw the mark I'd left on his cheek. I was stunned that I had committed such a crime against a helpless infant. I sat and cried some more until Darth came home from night class. I tried to explain to him how I felt. I knew it was absurd to whine to Darth about my problems when he was the root of my unhappiness, but I hoped that he would find a way to sympathize, and we could work out our problems together. I told him that I needed to make a change in my life so that this would never happen again.

He was so incensed with me when he looked at Joey's face that he went to bed without speaking to me. I had nowhere else to go so I got into bed, pulled the covers up, and wondered what I was going to do. Darth finally spoke to me from the eerily dark bedroom. He said that if I ever hit Joey again, he'd beat me senseless. Since Darth did things that scared me, his statement genuinely frightened me into keeping silent.

His comment left me feeling afraid, mistrusting, and unsafe, yet I mentally restated my reliance to him as I saw him as being all-powerful and knowing. I understood that Darth had every reason to be infuriated with me. What I didn't understand was his unwillingness to help me. He didn't seem to care about how I was desperately struggling. I vowed that I would find some way to help myself be a better mother. I had no idea what that could be.

CHAPTER TWENTY-FIVE

Joey's constant howling continued. When I tried to explain to someone that I thought he was an angry baby, they looked at me like I was goofy. What could a baby possibly be angry about? I didn't know either, but it sure seemed that way to me. I faithfully took him to the doctor's office for all his checkups and he was always pronounced healthy.

I discovered that the county facility occasionally had a child psychologist on staff. If I could show up on a certain date and wait, she might be able to speak with me. This sounded like a possible answer to my baby problems. I could talk to someone with a degree in child psychology. I thought of her as a celestial being that might shed insight and light on a constantly screaming infant that I couldn't appease.

The clinic did not make appointments, so I kept pushing and navigating the stroller across town. After a few attempts I finally arrived when the heaven-sent shrink was available. I explained to the doctor how well I tried to care for Joey and how nothing I did seemed to work unless I kept him in endless motion. I worried that he was almost a year old and barely crawled. Whenever I laid him on a blanket on the floor with toys spread around him all he did was clench his tiny hands into fists of frenzy and wail at the top of his lungs. I told her that what made matters even worse was that he was driving me crazy.

She said it sounded like he was throwing a temper tantrum and that it was understandable that enough of that behavior would make me want to shake him senseless. The doctor gave me detailed instructions. Whenever Joey exhibited temper tantrum behavior, I was to simply leave the room and not come back until he was quiet. Walking away during tasks wasn't always convenient, but it was very simple to do.

I knew that to keep my sanity I would need to have some time away from the house. I needed to feel like a person with purpose in life, and I hadn't felt that way for months. I wanted to be justified and respected in life as a wife and mother. I thought those feelings were impeded by the two males I'd built my life around.

I decided that a part-time job would be the answer to my issues. Working would take me away from my prison cell within the house. I could communicate with other adults and earn some spending money while I was bolstering my self-esteem. A part-time job would be perfect as it would also allow for quality time with my child. I didn't want to leave him five days a week for the entire day.

The more I contemplated a part-time job the better the idea seemed. While Darth was still at work, I made telephone calls. Modeling was a career I could pursue on a part-time basis that I would really enjoy, and I had two years of training with some experience. Plus, I'd gotten so skinny this would be perfect timing on my part. I was so excited I could hardly wait for Darth to get home, so I could include him in my plans.

"Nothing doing," Darth said, "Nope, no way." He did not like that idea at all, even if it would be advantageous for me and I thought if it would be good for me then it would be beneficial to Joey. Darth said, "You're not worth working part-time because you couldn't begin to make enough money to make your job attempts worth the trouble for me. You can just stay home and stop complaining." Darth's attitude genuinely upset me. I couldn't believe that he could be such an imbecile. I felt like he was being cruel on purpose but there was nothing I could do about it other than argue. Darth was deliberately restricting my ability to work so he could control my freedom, my choices, and finances.

I was not so easily swayed. I knew that I needed to do this. I disputed that even if I only made enough money to pay for the babysitter and the travel expense it would still be worthwhile for me to get out of the house, but Darth wouldn't hear of it. He said that if I was going to work, it would have to be full-time or not at all and that was the only way that he would agree to let me leave the house for a job. This wasn't what I wanted. I wanted Joey to know that he was important to me. I just needed some time out of my rut. My reality remained that I was still trapped in a never-ending loop beyond my emotional resources and Darth could not have cared less.

After agonizing for several days, I finally decided that since I was failing at motherhood anyway, the only thing I could do was comply with Darth's set of rules. I found a full-time babysitter down the street where there were other toddlers. I thought that Joey would probably prefer their company to mine. They would be more entertaining, right away he started doing more crawling and was pulling himself into a standing position.

Our car would be paid for in a few months, so Darth bought a slightly used pickup and I purchased a newspaper to search the want ads for full-time employment. An advertisement for a salesclerk, at an expensive dress shop caught my eye. The job was basically boring, and I frequently had to work weekends. The pay was poor, but it allowed me to earn a few quality outfits at an employee discount that I could eventually wear for a better job.

During this employment, I met a gal who was fun to visit with and as it turned out, she lived a few blocks away from us. She was a personable, attractive girl and we were approximately the same age. I knew instinctively that she really wasn't my type of friend, but we did have a few things in common. Visiting with each other when sales were slow helped to pass the monotonous hours at work, and she liked to come over to our place, and as I soon discovered, she was much more interested in my husband's attentions, than fussing over the baby.

One Saturday morning she was at the house, so I could help her color her hair. We had all been in the backyard when she and Darth had gone inside via the back porch. I'd followed the narrow sidewalk to the front yard looking for our new kitten. A few minutes later I entered the house through the front door where no one noticed me. Quietly crossing the living room, I found she and Darth standing unusually close together silhouetted in the frame of the sunlit kitchen window.

They were talking intimately, enraptured in their own conversation. Their whispering was private between themselves as she stepped back and pulled up her tee-shirt, over her shoulders exposing her braless breasts. I had the distinct feeling that she was immensely proud of her bust line, and of course Darth was very intently staring at her boobs. A few seconds lapsed before they realized that I'd silently entered the room behind them. She noticed the subtle nod of Darth's head in my direction as she turned around, and immediately yanked her shirt back down to her waist where it belonged.

I could tell that they knew that I knew what they were doing. True to form I mentally went straight to denial mode because I simply did not know what else to do, and could not bring myself to accept the betrayal that I had just witnessed my husband participating in. I did not dare to express my disapproval because I believed Darth would find a way to use it as an excuse to exploit his habitual drinking. Lisa mumbled an excuse and left. I asked Darth what they were doing in front of the kitchen sink, and he told me that Lisa had a spider stuck in her shirt and he was trying to find it, per her request. I was naïve, trusting and loving but I wasn't totally dense. I knew hanky-panky when I saw it.

Lisa still acted as if she wanted to be friends at the dress shop, but I knew that she was no friend of mine. Whenever she would phone the house, I had a reason readily available as to why I couldn't talk. I quit the lousy dress shop job and never saw her again. However, I always had a lingering feeling that Darth may have. The next time I searched the help wanted ads I applied for a job at a large corporation. I earned five hundred and fifty dollars a month which would cover babysitting, parking fees, gas expenses, and leave about two hundred a month take home after taxes. In addition to this I started back to school one night a week and attempted to complete all my homework assignments during my lunch hour at the office.

Joey seemed to be doing well at the babysitter's and I was infinitely happier being able to utilize my mind instead of quietly harboring the hopeless feelings I suffered stuck in the house with an intolerable bawling infant. I'd also made a new girlfriend at work. She wasn't gorgeous and busty and all she could talk about was her boyfriend. I felt confident that she wouldn't pull her shirt up in display of her perky bare breasts for my husband's admirations. I thought that life was finally turning around.

Darth and I purchased matching metallic ten-speed bicycles the next summer and attached a baby seat to the back of Darth's fender. After work and dinner, we spent a lot of time peddling around town with Joey buckled securely in his bike seat. Just like the wind-up swing and the stroller, he enjoyed the motion of the bike rides. He was finally walking and learning to talk. I thought that he was doing well and both of us seemed much more agreeable. Darth was excelling in his apprenticeship program and the six-month raises were continuing to increase our financial abilities.

He still pressured me a lot about sex, and I complied as often as I could. I was also keeping a very hectic and demanding schedule. I had to get up before four thirty a.m. each morning to deal with a baby and drive to work on time. Sometimes I had classes twice a week and that kept me out late. There were always piles of soiled diapers to be laundered and housework to be done. I never sat down and when I did, I was generally bushed. It was a rare moment if I wasn't attempting to accomplish a task. If I wasn't moving, I was generally in bed, and I could never understand why Darth was never tired.

The less that I saw of Nellie the better Darth liked it, so as a couple we were spending many weekends with Jane and Mike, the new flat chested girlfriend that I worked with at the massive corporate office. Jane and Mike were engaged to be married the following summer and Darth seemed to enjoy his social time around both. Mike liked his booze too. I did not particularly care for the indulgent drinking, but I did enjoy both Jane and Mike's friendship. We had a lot of fun together as couples, we went camping and bike riding and spent leisurely time at the beach when one of Joey's grandmothers would baby-sit. Darth and Mike drank hard when all of us were together, but Mike allowed the somewhat sober Jane to drive him home.

That fall we put our sixteen-thousand-dollar house up for sale and made a ten-thousand-dollar profit. We purchased a brand new fifteen hundred square foot rambler in a new housing development closer to where Darth worked. This meant I would be driving further to downtown for my corporate job. Getting up even earlier was not an option but another requirement.

I was excited about the newly constructed house. It was the first time I had ever lived in a brand-new home. Things looked prettier on the outside for me, but the inside was still tremendously difficult. I thought that Darth's drinking was escalating. In addition to drinking with Mike, Darth always had beer handy for the neighbors who lived across the paved running path directly behind us. He always had a cold beer stocked in the refrigerator for himself, and he'd found a new readily willing drinking partner.

A journeyman employed at the same construction company as Darth. Will was old enough to be Darth's father and his wife Barbie was probably ten years older than William. Darth always wanted to have them over for barbeques or they were inviting us to their place. There were ample rounds of before dinner drinks, drinks with dinner and flaming after dinner drinks. Will, Barbie and Darth never had a problem with enthusiastic consumption and Darth always insisted on driving home. I was positive I was going to die in a drunken car crash with Darth at the wheel.

Finally, I had the perfect excuse not to accept another dinner invitation at Will and Barbie's place. Darth had gotten so drunk at our last dinner, that two minutes after he drove us home, he passed out on the bed. I could smell the alcohol all the way down the hall. He reeked of it and moaned something about being sick. I hated gagging and retching and did not want to have a thing to do with vomit or the reeking, stinking Darth. I took a large mixing bowl out of the cupboard and balanced it on top of his chest. Intentionally leaving the bedroom light on, I went to bed in the spare room next to Joey's.

The next morning, I swiped Darth's expensive hard liquor from the cabinet over the top of the refrigerator and proceeded to pour it down the kitchen drain. I watched as the rich golden liquid flowed in lustrous swirls as the poison fluid disappeared. I knew I still wasn't ready to admit that alcohol was bigger than I was. I hoped Darth would love me more than a bottle of booze. I managed to dump half the bottle of rum down the garbage disposal before Darth appeared. Embattled over the half empty liquor bottle, I burst into threats promising him that this was it. He had to choose me, or the brew and he couldn't continue to have it both ways.

I managed to panic him without him breaking his empty fifth over my head. For the moment he decided what I secretly hoped for, as I'd devoutly meant what I'd threatened. Instead of drinking the following weekend Darth and I mutually decided to purchase a new car. The Maverick was five years old and would make a good trade in and I could afford to make a car payment on my salary since I'd just received a hefty, well-earned raise.

I had always wanted a Camaro or a Mustang. They had been my dream cars since I'd been old enough to drive. We went car shopping, and test drove a brand-new Camaro and I was sold. Darth didn't like my hasty decision and wanted me to test drive a Datsun 280-Z. I'd never driven one and I knew they were way cool, but I also knew that the Datsun cost almost twice as much as the Camaro. As usual I complied with what Darth wanted to do and we went on a Datsun Z-car test drive.

The Z-car was sleek, with gleaming hood under which the powerful engine purred like a giant feline. I'd never driven anything like it. It made the Camaro seem like a tractor in comparison. I was in smitten with the feeling the Z-car inspired. Darth was right. When I agreed with him, he immediately switched gears and said I should have the Camaro. I never understood why he did that to me. He would try to convince me of something and then when I was convinced, he would insist upon returning to my original decision after I'd changed my mind.

Only this time I was not changing my mind. I liked the sporty Z-car with the elongated hood that hid the tremendous dose of horsepower. What an awesome machine, it had my name written all over it. I picked shimmering silver that shone like a well-polished starship. Darth drove it home and tried to figure out why I should drive his truck to work, and he could drive the car even though he insisted that I was the one who had to pay for it. That night Darth wanted to celebrate. According to him, he was not going to drink anymore, and he thought it was actually a good idea because without hard liquor, his sex life would probably improve.

He would frequently ask if he could tie me up for sex, which was one request I would never agree to. Deep down, I didn't trust him enough to be at his total mercy. I could never be certain what he would do to me. I remembered our last summer in the old two-story house. It was a hot humid August night, and I had the windows in the house wide open with our only electric fan blowing in Joey's room. Darth had been drinking from his stockpiled beer that night and he'd been annoyed with me for several months because I wouldn't have anal sex with him. He was not deterred as he insisted that if I loved him, I would be delighted to oblige him.

Darth let his groin do his thinking on this night of last August, he held me face down and forced himself in me from behind. He would not stop pumping, forcing himself into my rectum and pinning me down against my will with his two hundred and thirty-five-pound frame. He insisted that if I would just let him, I would find out how much I could enjoy it. According to him, he knew this to be a fact because he'd read about it in Hustler Magazine. When he penetrated and pushed, it hurt beyond my imagination. I was screaming in a voice that I didn't recognize, and I'd never heard escape from my own throat.

Our headboard was stationed up against the wall with the only window and it was wide open, six feet from the neighbor's open kitchen windows. I was positive that someone was going to hear my monstrous screams as Darth rammed and plunged again. In excruciating pain and terror, I realized he wasn't going to quit. I couldn't muffle my horrific screams of pain from his penetration. Finally, from drinking one too many beers that day he vomited and rolled over, easing off me as I was still squirming to free myself from his grip.

I should have known that even in marriage forced sexual acts are considered rape, and aside from murder, rape is considered the worst violation of someone's body. Rape is about control, not sex. Control is a need to subdue the victim and that control is frequently premeditated.

I simply did not know what abuse and battering were. If I had, I could have gone to the library and researched those topics with my library card. Instead, I thought that Darth's emotional and physical violations could not be helped because of his inherited volatile temper that I believed was provoked by his drinking. It seemed to me that the constant liquor intake caused the abusive behavior, but alcohol does not cause mistreatment nor does the victim cause the mistreatment. Abuse is purely the conscious choice of the abuser in his own selfish need to control his situations. Alcohol and drugs merely fuel the abusive flame.

Somewhere in a lowly and infrequently visited corner of my mind, I was beginning to wonder, if what Darth repeatedly claimed about me was true. He frequently stated he was a perfectly normal male and that there must be a deep-seated problem in my inner core.

CHAPTER TWENTY-SIX

Darth had given up his alcoholic intake for almost a week, and his resentment had turned vulgar. There was a gaping hole the size of his work boot in the bottom of the bathroom door at the end of the hallway. Earlier in the week there had been a hole the size of his fist in the sheetrock by the front entry. Tonight, he slugged three new holes in our bedroom wall, each gaping offense resembling the knuckles of his right fist.

With malice, he claimed that he was not getting enough sex, so it was not his fault that he was frustrated. He told me that it was my fault that his balls could turn blue and if left unattended they would harden and drop off like miniature bowling balls. I'd never seen blue testicles before, not even in seventh grade sex education class. I was obviously dumber than he'd thought, and I couldn't possibly love him because I was not effectively performing sexual acts as necessary. He wanted more sex the same way that I had endured going to church when I was younger. The more I went the better it was supposed to be for me. If I, did it often enough it could save me right into everlasting eternity.

With apprehension, I told him he could have sex with himself as often as he liked, after he finished repairing the wall in the bedroom. He purchased tongue and groove knotty pine wood strips to hide the damage, which was easier than repairing the sheetrock with spackle finish and paint. I evacuated the bedroom with my pillow and spent an uncomfortable night on the sofa listening to Darth saw and hammer.

Shortly after the wall punching exercise, Darth had a new idea. He'd go get a vasectomy. I questioned his plan, but he insisted that he had given it prudent consideration and he was determined to go through with the outpatient surgery. He understood that I was careful not to get pregnant again. My doctor had prescribed every type of birth control pill that existed and all of them made me feel ill. I'd tried the IUD method and spent months hemorrhaging. Finally, at my doctor's insistence he removed the IUD which left us with the option of condoms or foam, both of which Darth felt he shouldn't have to bother with since he was a married man. Of course, abstinence was out of the question. Therefore, I was careful and watched the calendar on a weekly basis. After previously puking my brains out for nine months and being miserable with a baby who cried nonstop, I was not eager to have another; and I didn't trust Darth.

Recollections pulsed through my head, and I thought maybe someday, if Darth ever quit his drinking, I would consider having another baby. Darth thought he was solving all his problems with a vasectomy. I wouldn't have to worry about getting pregnant again, and he could haphazardly have all the sex he craved. That way I would not be driving him to drink.

He went through with it. I halfway expected that he would change his mind at the last minute like he generally did with a harebrained excuse, but he came home on Friday night walking awkwardly with a couple of stitches in his scrotum. It was a gorgeous warm evening, so I suggested a bike ride for Joey. After biking around the housing development Darth was sorry that he hadn't backed out of peddling. His macho ego had gotten the upper-hand and now he was waddling like a duck. Buoyed from the bike ride, I volunteered sex that night when we flopped into bed, and he passed on the offered opportunity.

While Dearth was waddling, I had driven my glossy Z-car with spoke wire rims to work for about four months. I'd gotten a speeding ticket on my way home that afternoon. Without realizing it, I was going 45 miles an hour in a 35 mile an hour zone on the frontage road. The car went fast easily as it glided on the pavement and hugged the road so efficiently that it always felt as if I was driving slower than I really was. The ticket was the only speeding ticket that I had ever gotten in any car. Darth used it as his reason to get rid of the car. Yet, he drove it over a hundred miles an hour every chance he got. He did not like the fact that I enjoyed driving the sports car. What he liked even less was the attention I unintentionally attracted while I was driving it.

One evening during dinner, he insisted that we sell it. I disagreed. I didn't want to sell it and I was paying for it, and it had been his idea to buy it in the first place. Secondly, we'd had it for less than half a year. I knew with depreciation that we couldn't sell it for what we owed on it, and I knew Darth was smart enough to figure that out. He badgered me about selling it every few days and I always shook my head and proceeded with my household chores.

We had been in our new home for about sixteen months, just long enough to complete the landscaping. I didn't really want to move but I was tempted when Darth decided that we should purchase a chunk of acreage and build a house. This got my attention because I knew that if we had property, I could eventually get another horse. We made the decision that we would start looking for land around the area where we had grownup.

This was leverage power for Darth because he knew that I would love to have another horse. He charmingly told me if I would sell my car, I could purchase a horse and keep it on my parents' property until we found our build-able acreage. I was loath to sell the car and he knew it, but I finally conceded, handed him the keys and said, "Trade it in."

In the third grade, I had sold all my valuables carting them door to door from one neighbor's house to another. I was positive that if I could supply the funds, mom would allow a pony. My mother's reaction was not what I had hoped for. It goes without further explanation that a pony did not come home to live in my backyard. Mom knew we couldn't afford a pony just like Darth knew it was an unwise financial move to sell the Z-car. We had to hand over a couple thousand dollars more than the price of the new car, so the dealer would take our trade-in because we were upside down on its current value. Darth informed me that I could only have one type of new car and it had to be an economical undersized Datsun. Driving the little bitty Datsun was like driving an empty tin can on wheels. The only thing that I liked about it was the gear knob. It was imitation wood.

Darth thought that I should be delighted about it because he allowed me to choose the color. The upside was we were going to move to the country eventually, and I'd been promised another horse.

The elderly, know-it-all Jewish woman who managed the dress shop where I had originally worked for a few months when Joey was just a baby had remained a friend of ours. Dinner one night a week at her house was a general practice for several months and then she announced that she would like for all of us to meet her son and daughter-in-law for a barbeque at their home. We were instructed to bring our bathing suits and arrive Saturday afternoon.

From stories that she told, I knew that her son was a successful businessman, lived in an upscale neighborhood and enjoyed entertaining. I privately thought Peter was loud and opinionated. He had his mother's pebble shaped dark eyes but there was no kindness apparent in them. Both Peter and Darth ardently enjoyed their liquor and storytelling abilities. I thought their egos should have collided head on, but I think they were always too sauced to know it.

Pete's mother had told me about the automotive business that Pete owned and one of the things that he specialized in was promotional advertising. Supposedly he used models for all types of promotions and one of them was a Turtle Wax campaign. Pete's mother suggested that I should inquire about a modeling job for one of his upcoming promos. This sounded good to me. We could always use extra money toward our property purchase in the country. Peter had set an appointment with me to meet him at a downtown restaurant for lunch one business day to discuss the modeling promotional.

At this point, I had known his mother for several months and had been to Pete's home with the rest of my family on many occasions. A few times Pete and his wife, who I thought was too nice to be married to him, along with his daughter who was a few years older than Joey, had been to our home. Pete's wife was rather quiet, and I didn't think that it was mere shyness as her mother-in-law had explained. I had an inkling that Peter preferred her this way. Her opinions weren't important to him, and she'd learned to keep them to herself, yet she had an infectious smile on the rare chance that she did laugh.

Our luncheon appointment went well, and Peter brought me up to speed on how the promotional functioned, and what was expected of the models. He told me that he had a convention coming up that I could work at, and he wanted me to meet with him the following week in his office to discuss the details. Darth knew all about this plan and was supportive of me making some extra money.

I had driving directions to his office, and he invited me to come over on my lunch break. As I parked my car, I saw it wasn't an office building; it was an old house that had previously been converted to tenant space. The place felt sinister when I opened the squeaky wooden front door. Hesitating, I ignored my apprehension. I expected there to be people scurrying about doing their office duties or at least a secretary typing behind a desk, but Peter was the only person present. He smiled and graciously invited me back to his office. This room was a bedroom that had been converted into an office. When I inquired, he said that his partner had gone to lunch. His office was equipped with a plain but spacious desk. The tasteless lamp was dimly lit, and a military type of chair sat directly in front of the desk. It was obvious that Peter lacked his mother's decorating abilities.

Peter leaned backward in his distinguished leather chair. I presumed this gesture was supposed to punctuate his importance and make him appear taller than he really was. He proceeded to tell me about the model that he and his partner used at the last promotional. He descriptively explained how she stood next to a new car and handed out pamphlets while wearing nothing but feathers. The feathers were meticulously applied with surgical glue while she stood naked. I was wordlessly questioning why anyone would promote Turtle Wax with a two-legged imitation human owl. I would have expected a turtle complete in a shell costume.

I could not quite picture standing naked in gummy glue while technicians applied feathers to all my body parts, but I politely listened to Peter brag as he puffed along on a cigar accentuated with a gush of self-importance. He proceeded to tell me about how it was imperative that the models who worked for him always do exactly as he instructed. When, how and wherever he gave critical instruction, he wanted to know if I could do my job exactly as I was told. Well, I thought so. I did that every day at work. I always endeavored to be efficient, thorough, and responsible about my job. Peter thought this was good but wasn't sure if I really understood what he meant. I was beginning to get uncomfortable, and I was wishing that his partner who went to lunch would come back to the office and knock on the door with an unimportant interruption.

Peter explained that he had a test that he gave to all the models to make certain that they would indeed follow his important instructions to the letter. However, prior to doing the test he wanted to see what I looked like.

He knew what I looked like; he was looking straight at me. Nevertheless, he said he wanted to see what type of body build I was. At this point I was trying to think of how I could get out of his office without appearing panicky. He told me to stand up and take my dress off and turn around. He said it was important for the costume that I would wear.

I told myself that it was no big deal. I had on underwear, nylons, and a practical one-piece beige nylon slip. I stood up and took my dress off and then he said the slip had to go too, because I would be wearing a swimsuit and they needed to decide if it would be a two piece. I figured I had on underwear, and it wasn't that much different from the two-piece swimsuit that I wore at his house when both families were swimming and splashing in his pool.

Now that all I had on was my underwear, Peter complained about my choice of underclothing. He wanted to know why I had worn such plain, ordinary undergarments to my interview. I was astounded. I told him, "This is the only kind of panties and bras that I own and always wear." Ned proceeded to tell me, "No one wears plain underwear to these interviews because they know what they are being interviewed for." In my own dumbfounded way, I was beginning to understand that this interview was not at all what I had anticipated.

Then Peter, told me that we were being videoed. "I always video my interviews," he said as he pointed a finger to the corner over the closet. Sure, enough there was a video camera with a red blinking light. I did not know how I was going to get out of the room, and I was afraid that if I ran, he would pounce on me, like a paw licking cougar waiting for the frightened deer to veer and take flight. Then he said, "We still have to do the test." Peter's test was not questioning on paper with handwritten answers.

Peter told me to come around the back of the desk and kneel in front of him. I was instructed to unzip his pants, so he could wag his wiener. I was scared and equally repulsed at the same time and determined that I wasn't going to show it. If he thought that he was going to force me into oral sex, I was going to bite it off, spit it at him and then run. I was worrying about the location of my purse and keys. When I knelt in front of him, I was eye level with his beer gut.

I felt tremors in my hands and was determined I would not shake. His jelly belly hung over his belt buckle which protected the top of his zipper. I pretended to have exaggerated difficulty with his belt buckle due to his three-martini lunch gut. On purpose, I couldn't even begin to find the top of his zipper. I fussed and fudged and finally looked him straight in the eye and said, "If you want me to follow every single instruction you'll have to suck in your paunch."

Intentionally, I humiliated him into ordering me to stop. Subconsciously knowing that this was the turning point where I either took control or relinquished it, I stopped but I stayed on my knees and democratically asked him, "Are you sure? I don't want to blow the test."

Then Peter the Prick, told me, "Get up and get dressed. I don't think we can use you for the model because you have a figure like a boy." Sweat trickled down my spine but it didn't matter because I'd managed to turn the tables on this egocentric pervert, and he wanted me to leave. I stayed friends with his mother from a distance. I didn't tell her about the office episode because I decided that it would be hurtful to her even if she would possibly believe me. Then I elected not to tell Darth. I didn't know what he would think but I was afraid that he would find a way to use it to his advantage. Not telling him made me feel underhanded, as it was the only secret that I had ever kept from him.

CHAPTER TWENTY-SEVEN

The next time Joey wet his pants after sitting on his potty seat I carefully lifted him into the tub setting him down feet first and let him stand there while I turned on the faucet. I washed him off front and back from the waist down and talked the whole time about how this good cleansing would make him squeaky clean. Then I let him play with his uncomfortable wet clothes on for a few minutes. The second time I washed him off in the tub I did the same thing only I used cold water. That was the end of it, and he finally learned how to piddle standing up when the kids at the new daycare showed him how.

Darth's mother thought I was mean and unusual, but the situation worked out great and I was thankful for an idea I would have never thought of on my own. In the meantime, we had continued our ongoing search for build-able acreage. We finally found four and half acres that were located about two minutes from my parents' place where I had grown up. I was ecstatic about this because I knew there were places to trail ride and I would be geographically closer to Nellie.

Our house was on the market for only three days. This wasn't what we had expected. We were thinking it would take about six months while calculating that the new house would be mostly completed by that time. However, one of the subcontractors put the brown master bathroom linoleum in the blue and white hall bath. The kitchen sink wasn't what I had ordered, and the appliances were the wrong color. Darth didn't like the living room carpet I chose, and the builder was three months behind schedule.

Most of our furnishings were in storage in Dad's shop or the old barn and we had placed a queen-sized mattress directly onto the plywood subflooring in the unfinished attic at my folks. There was only one window and during this very dry, and extra warm September weather it was torture to live in the hot attic. I doubt Darth was happy living at my parents' as it limited his drinking opportunities. He would never dream of stocking beer in my mother's refrigerator. To my knowledge he had basically been on restrained non-drinking behavior at my parents' house, and I liked that a lot. The attic was over the kitchen, and I was very self-conscious about any noise that we made before my parents went to bed. Unable to remember what we were discussing, while both lying on the mattress in the unbearable heat, Darth reached over and punched me smack in the stomach, knocking the wind out of me; I thought I was going to be sick.

What could I do? I saw myself as a victim, not a prize fighter. Slugging him back probably would have worked in the third grade but not at twenty-three. I struggled with my innate need to reconcile with him but didn't feel that I had done anything wrong. While I was still gasping for air Darth got up and yanked on his pants. He didn't look back or speak to me as he went down the stairs to the kitchen and left through the back-porch door. A moment later I heard him start his truck in the driveway and leave. My parents had gone to bed, but I was certain that they had heard him leave. He didn't come back until the following evening after work. I had no idea where he went or what he did. When my mother asked about why Darth left late at night, I made up a phony partially believable remark. I didn't understand the excuse, nor did I understand the violence.

Perhaps I should have changed my current perception of our relationship where I wished that Darth would change his behavior and stop drinking. I had always blamed his rotten behavior on his alcoholic in-take. It had never occurred to me that he had his own private problems and weaknesses which he tried to escape with a bottle. Another option I never considered was a resolution for me that the marriage I desired would never be possible. Maybe, I was looking at our relationship through a distorted lens, without realizing my part in our dysfunctional cycles.

My tender stomach had ached all day and I thought about that as we sat around the oak dinner table at my parent's house where I was presented with gifts, and birthday cake. Most of the gifts were from Darth. Halfheartedly I acted as if I was grateful, but the memory of being slugged from the night before was still fresh in my mind.

While I was helping Mom clear the dirty dishes from the table, she whispered to me that I did not seem very appreciative of Darth's gifts. She told me that I should act like I was thankful. The galling thing was I knew that she had absolutely no idea of what he had done to me the night before. He never did apologize. I was simply expected to get over it.

Initially, I did not recognize Darth's behavior for what it really was because batterers can possess endearing personalities and be well liked by their associates and friends. It is rare that an abuser would exhibit violent or mean behavior to anyone other than his own personal victim. Intentionally exhibiting different behavior in public or around other family members, and friends. Most abusers have grown up under the domination of an abusive parent. The abused child will even claim that they will never repeat abuse in their adult relationships, yet eventually they can easily resort to the foul actions.

Focusing on Joey, I searched ads and inspected different ponies until we found a gentle, well-trained pony. I was basically concerned about safety, and this pony was small which meant it was a short drop to the ground. After work, I was rushing home, so Joey and I could groom the new pony before dark. I was heading home on the freeway going into the "S" curves. The six-lane freeway was a main thoroughfare that always slowed at the curves. Today brilliant sunshine glared through my windshield as I approached the curves in the far-left lane. The old white beater Ford pickup with the crooked rusty bumper in front of me had its right turn signal blinking. I began to slow down waiting for him to drift into the center lane. Suddenly, I realized that he wasn't switching lanes; he was trying to stop. I could see a Cadillac in front of him with both brake lights flared. There was smoke coming off the truck's tires. His left brake light must not be working as he kept pumping his brake.

I braked hard as my pulse accelerated. I did manage to stop completely and was amazed my tires didn't skid. There was approximately two feet between my front bumper and the back of the beater Ford when my pulse sprinted into action again. I had a memory flash of the tailgating car behind me. I glanced up at my rear-view mirror to see the midsize car rapidly closing in. It was tilted sideways at a twenty-five-degree angle as it skidded toward me. Smoke was searing from all four tires. I could see the face of the idiot who had been tailgating me. His eyes were the size of flying saucers, and his open mouth was screaming, "Oh shi…..."

I did not hear the impact as much as I felt it. I thought my head was going to pop from the stem of my neck when it slammed backward against the headrest on the bucket seat. I felt the seat belt shoulder strap snatch me hard across my side as my head snapped forward with full force. My knees and shins were scrunched into the dashboard on impact. There was the tiniest moment of relief and then to my astonishment the same impact happened again, this time my front end hit the back of the crooked bumper of the beater Ford truck.

My legs throbbed, and I couldn't move my head. I could already sense the splitting headache gnawing at the trunk of my neck and consuming me with each passing second. Then something that I had not even begun to fathom happened. I felt a solid slamming again from the right-hand side of my vehicle. It was the same car that had rear ended me. It was spinning out of control and had just broadsided my crumpled car. I remember thinking that I would hate tailgaters for the rest of my life.

I could not move. My legs were imbedded on the dash and my neck wouldn't turn. Surely, someone would come and help me. The guy in the beater Ford was standing on the left-hand side of the shoulder of the freeway talking to the stupid woman in the Cadillac who had come to a complete stop in the S curves because the gleaming sun had been in her eyes. No one had hit her, so she drove off merrily on her way, completely oblivious to the injuries she had caused. The guy in the truck decided his bumper had been crooked to start with and he didn't much care. He told me the front of my car looked totaled and he drove off.

Rush hour traffic was backing up behind me in all three lanes. I was positive that a cop would appear and assist me. Instead, the tailgating driver walked up to my window and tried to talk to me through the glass. I knew that I needed to write down the license plate number and copy down his insurance information, but I was straining to release my death grip from the steering wheel.

When I managed to partially roll down the window as the tailgating lunatic stooped forward to speak to me, over the top of the window, I could see his pupils were dilated. He had a glazed appearance while proceeding to tell me that he was driving his girlfriend's car, and that when she found out that he'd wrecked it she was going to kill him. I told him that if I could move my legs, I'd save her the trouble and kill him myself. My threat was sufficient to convince him to show me his driver's license. I copied down all the pertinent information in barely legible writing as the sky darkened on that January day, and freezing cold darkness set in as I shook uncontrollably.

I was not certain if I was shaking because of the plummeting temperature or shock from the accident. I had a severe headache that was escalating and major pains in my neck. Traffic was backing up so far that I couldn't see the end of the stationary string of headlights in my rear-view mirror. A semi-truck was inching past me with his window down. He was yelling something at me. Dusk had transformed to darkness and still no sirens, no police cars, and no ambulance.

The maniac that hit me was standing on the shoulder leaning against the metal guard rail smoking a cigarette. Some guys had helped him push his car to the side of the freeway. More drivers yelled at me to move my car. I was stunned when I turned the key and it started. I put it in first gear and eased back into traffic. My hands shook with such force that I couldn't drive safely so I took the first exit that appeared. My car still ran, but I had no lights, and it didn't steer worth a darn. I had just taken an unfamiliar exit. Now I was completely lost.

Pulling into the nearest parking lot without any head or tail- lights, I got out checking the damage. I was amazed that it ran and that I was still alive. When I entered Radio Shack, I asked the clerk if I could use the telephone. He hesitated until I explained that I'd been in a traffic accident, and I needed to phone my husband. I tried Darth at home, but to no avail. When I phoned the shop where he worked the secretary told me that he had already left. I was beginning to feel like I was going to puke in public, as my head swam in lopsided circles.

I phoned my parents at home, and I began to cry as I tried to explain the situation over the phone to Mom. She wanted to know where I was, and I didn't know. The clerk who had let me use the phone had just walked back into the store from inspecting my vehicle. I put him on the phone to give my parents directions. I found a chair to sit down and tried not to be sick. I had to hold my head up with both of my hands. I couldn't position my neck so that it didn't hurt. Expelling a pent-up breath, I wasn't aware I'd been holding, I wished that I was home in bed and could just drift into endless sleep.

Both parents arrived in about an hour. Dad thought that the car was totaled but said that he would drive it home and I could ride with Mom. She talked about taking me directly to the hospital and I refused. I wanted to go home and have Darth take me. I'd decided that I wasn't going to bleed to death, and I didn't think that it was an emergency for me to go directly to the hospital. I thought what I really wanted was Darth.

When he did arrive home, he looked at the car before he came in the house. He stomped through the door, annoyed that the car was wrecked. Over the years, I had grown accustomed to never knowing what type of reaction he would have, but I assumed that he would naturally be worried about me. Instead, he was upset with me until I explained to him that it wasn't my fault. With that he softened his tone. Once he knew that I had been rear-ended, he was pleased that his insurance company was off the hook. All I wanted was to lie down, and drift away to stop the intense pain from pulsing through my neck up into my temples. Darth told my folks that he would take me to the hospital, so Joey went home with them for dinner.

The emergency room nurse wasted no time having a doctor examine me. He immediately ordered x-rays and an orderly wheeled me away down the hall strapped into a neck brace. The doctor was stunned that I had a concussion, yet no visible head injury. He was also certain that my spleen had been ruptured by the shoulder harness seat belt. X-rays revealed that all I had was a sever whiplash. I was given a stiffer neck brace, pain killers, muscle relaxers and sent home to ice the bulging bruises on my legs. The attending physician told me that I would have sustained less damage if my neck had been broken, provided it would not have paralyzed me.

It was almost midnight, nearly eight hours since the accident. I hadn't eaten or rested and the pain in my head and neck had continued to intensify. I didn't feel like I could make the half hour ride home as every delicate movement sent pain reverberating in various directions. I asked Darth if we could go to his parents' house for a rest break and something to eat. I knew his dad would still be up. Darth shrugged and said, "Sorry, but you don't get to go anywhere for sympathy." I didn't understand him at all and just tried to hold my head still for the drive home.

The following morning, I was completely wasted. I couldn't see straight or think about even trying to turn my head. The very slightest movement sent shooting spears of pain up and down every muscle in the front and back of my neck. Darth insisted that I was just being a baby about a little wreck and wanted me to go into town with him to his parents' house where he wouldn't stop the night before. I imagined that he'd forgotten about the possibility that Dodie might give me a slight dose of sympathy.

By the time I was ready to leave, all I wanted was to go back to bed. I couldn't take the movement of bouncing through potholes in his pickup. I made it about two miles from the house and insisted on being taken home. I thought that Joey was worried about me, but I didn't think Darth was. I had no idea what a healing process I would endure over the years to recover from the injury. I had never been through this type of physical trauma before. It would prove to be a lengthy and impossible ordeal for me.

Darth and Joey dropped me off back at the house and did not bother to come inside. I shed my leather jacket onto the back of the family room sofa and gingerly lay down with my shoes still on. I had to hold onto my head to lean backward even though I was wearing the neck brace I'd been instructed to use. Pain exploded with the slightest movement as I tried to find a comfortable position on the sofa with too many pillows in my way.

CHAPTER TWENTY-EIGHT

The following week, mornings started with physical therapy and proceeded daily through the end of the week, and back again each afternoon for repeated sessions. I wore the neck brace constantly because I literally could not hold my head up. The ligaments in my neck had been hyper extended during the three consecutive impacts. I had tried returning to my job, but I simply couldn't spend eight hours a day sitting upright and functioning behind a desk.

The healing process progressed so slowly. The worst part was the unbearable headaches. I took pain killers and muscle relaxers and went to physical therapy. I spent hours laying upside down on the bed with my head hooked into a harness attached to a pulley weighted with a bag full of sand for traction. I couldn't work, I couldn't ride, and I felt that my life was dismal and useless. I felt completely handicapped, the crux of my situation was that I looked alright. I was not in a wheelchair, I did not have a cast or stitches, and there was no apparent profuse bleeding. Everyone seemed to think that I should be myself.

Darth claimed that I was faking my injury. I couldn't believe he was so insensitive. If he knew me at all he knew what a hard-responsible worker I was. I may have been guilty of a lot of things, but laziness was not one of them. I repeatedly tried to explain that faking my injury didn't make any sense. I much preferred working and riding to being in physical therapy and doped up on painkillers while spending several hours each day lying upside down with my neck hooked to a weighted bag.

Darth was skeptical that I had motives. He stood behind his theory that I had intentionally caused the car accident just to screw up his sex life. This was his excuse to go out repeatedly after dinner and not return home until the middle of the night. I began phoning the friends whose houses he claimed to be visiting only to discover that he really wasn't there and had not been there previously. I didn't know where he went or who he was with. When I would question him on his whereabouts, he would become ill tempered and accuse me of things I had never even thought of doing. He was a master at switching the blame to me. I didn't believe his excuses, nor could I force the truth from him.

I was mortified, and so miserable in my own right that I could not comprehend that Darth could possibly be, unhappier than I was. There was nothing physically wrong with him, he suffered from no injuries, and was free to come and go as he damn-well pleased. I eventually concluded that all I could do was concentrate on healing my injuries, caring for Joey, and keeping the household routinely functioning.

It was mid-summer, and I was still in my neck brace, so Mom would come over occasionally to help Joey with his pony. Mom had some horse experience from her childhood, and she was a lot bigger than the pony. Peewee had different ideas about who was boss and proceeded to run all the way back to the barn after he'd dumped Joey in the dust. Joey lost all interest in caring for his pony and did not want to ride him again, so Peewee took a trip across the street to the neighbor's farm where their young daughter enjoyed him.

While I was struggling, to literally keep my head up, Darth decided to quit his job. I was aghast. He was finally making full journeymen wages, and we had a huge house payment, and I had a bad neck. I had absolutely no idea what was going to happen with my career or when I would be fully recovered from the whiplash. Now of all times, Darth wanted to quit his job. Not only were his wages more than I could ever hope to earn, but we really needed the full medical coverage provided by his employer. Darth had not consulted me about his decision, and he was forcing me to be the reliable bread winner when I was not physically able.

Darth wanted to go into the construction business with Will the co-worker who was old enough to be his father. Darth could be a real jerk, but I had never known him to be this stupid. He and Will had one whole construction job lined up that would last a couple of weeks at the most. No benefits, no regular pay and here I was with my neck in a brace. Darth wasn't looking for a better career choice; he was looking for an excuse to spend more time with Will, his drinking collaborator. Darth claimed Will needed him because he was lonely. Barbie and Will were now divorced. As far as I knew she was still alive even though she had previously thought in her drunken stupors that Will was trying to murder her. This situation was absurdly convenient for Darth. Now he could push me to work more hours because we would need the money. He would switch pay dates on me so that I constantly struggled to balance the household budget. He would not come home until late, and he always smelled like brewery yeast.

Finally, a year and a half later I received a small settlement for my neck and back injuries. It turned out that the idiot driver who hit me had been driving with no insurance and the car he was driving did indeed belong to his girlfriend. However, she had not been current on paying her insurance premiums, so her policy had been cancelled the day before her boyfriend rear-ended me. This left my insurance policy. There was a small clause unbeknownst to me that said if I were hit by an uninsured motorist my coverage was limited to only fifteen thousand dollars.

I had to sue my auto insurance company to get them to pay my coverage. After deducting my legal fees, I was left with just over eighty-six hundred dollars. Prior to receiving the check Darth informed me that it was his money and that he intended to take it and deposit it into our joint savings account. For the uninsured coverage payment to be deposited to our account was not an issue for me, so I decided that it wasn't worth further bickering.

After Darth quit his journeyman's job, he developed an attitude about me pulling my own weight. He demanded that I earn a certain amount of money, so I could pay what he calculated was my share of the household bills. He had the house payment, groceries and electric bill split into percentages and I was expected to pay my fair share. He would, however, agree that I could take a few hundred dollars from the insurance settlement.

I purchased a new bicycle for Joey. I was hopeful that he could pursue the bike with more enthusiasm than the pony. I purchased an expensive leather covered Bible for Darth and had his name embossed on the cover in bold gold letters; perhaps scripture could save him. For myself I bought an inexpensive dress from J.C. Penney's. Darth deposited eight thousand three hundred dollars into the joint savings account.

The orthopedic physician was not doing much to help me recover from my injuries except prescribing more drugs. These made me moody and irritable, and I was tired of trying to fix a broken arm with a band aid. One doctor referred me to a shrink who specialized in hypnosis. Twice a week I would lie on his office couch, and he would talk me through relaxation and breathing techniques to relieve pain and stress. My frustrations wanted to erupt like an active volcano gravitating toward a tectonic shift yet, expanding my lungs with air through deep breathing was supposed to calm me. I wanted to scream obscenities about my absurd husband.

Mom suggested a chiropractor. She was not big on doctors, but she had a church friend who liked a certain chiropractor. I went for adjustments twice a day for six days a week. As time progressed, I went once a day and then every other day. I was getting better. There was less pain, fewer headaches, better range of motion and I cold hold my head up without a brace. I was so drained from my physical problems that I felt like it had been a thousand years since the accident. I had finally quit my corporate job and filed for unemployment to cover my percentage of the household expenses.

Darth cornered me one day in the kitchen. He had a nasty habit of doing this. He was insisting that I not be allowed to continue my visits to the chiropractor's office. Darth referred to the chiropractor as my "quack-o-practor" and claimed that I should no longer participate in my treatments because he said I was addicted to them. I had grown accustomed to Darth's irrational tantrums. I admitted to myself that I was fearful in ways I didn't begin to understand or want to recognize. Even worse I didn't begin to know what to do about it. As an enabler, I tended to ignore important warning signs of physical danger. Emotional abuse generally precedes most physical battering, but it was impossible for me to know when any type of abuse, be it financial, physical, emotional, or sexual abuse could spew into dangerous or deadly behavior.

Unconsciously, I was waiting. I finally realized I had been waiting for an exceptionally long time. At the outset I had waited to be rescued, when that didn't work, I waited for Darth to have a crisis of his conscience and treat me with respect but that wasn't ever going to happen. Aside from being a sufferer for a cause, which was really nothing more than a willing sacrificial victim, I was angry. I was incensed about the injustice of dealing with Darth, and I was constantly puzzled by it. I decided to teach myself to think tactically. If I could stop sabotaging myself in a relationship where the abuser constantly premeditated my ambush, I could forge ahead.

Easier said than done, but I knew I needed to be a thinker, not an emotional bobble head. I was tired of being the bearer of good things and the keeper of crazy peace in dysfunctional insanity.

PART THREE

FINAL STAGES

CHAPTER TWENTY-NINE

At age twenty-nine, I sat in present tense, pondering my memories with trepidation in my internal search to understand why my life had gone wrong. With current day clarity I realized that I had so little time, and so many bad feelings. With unfaltering resolution, I decided that every new day would provide me with a fresh opportunity. Acting on my thoughts, I wrote my parents and I told them I was afraid. I knew this would frighten them, but I didn't know how to begin explaining that my life had gotten way out of hand. I had filed for divorce, and I was uncertain how Darth would react.

Approximately a week after I mailed the letter, my folks phoned from somewhere in New Mexico. They were temporarily working part-time as Park Rangers in a forest service campground, and they were hurriedly preparing to depart the following morning. This news and quick response were liberating relief for me. With my parents present Darth would not be as comfortable appearing and leaving in an alcohol sodden state with no courtesy call to capture and disappear with Joey whenever he pleased. Best of all, I wouldn't be all by myself with a nine-year-old who seemed to be devoid of feelings for me while aggravating the situation because he wouldn't communicate. I imagined it was my punishment, and that he liked to torture me just because he could. Just as Darth always insinuated, I felt woefully lacking in the motherhood department.

A few days later when the front doorbell rang, it was not the parents I had been expecting. It was a tall, dark-haired stranger appearing to be

Dick Tracy, asking me, if I was me. I said I was, and he handed me a thick envelope of paperwork and told me, "You've been served". Whatever, exactly that meant. It was surely the revelation of the tip of the iceberg.

I delivered the paperwork to my attorney's office where he explained to me that Darth was suing me for full custody of Joey. My chest seized. In my opinion this was one of the worst things that Darth could do, maneuvering Joey into the middle of the battlefield that was about to detonate. Darth did not need custody. I'd never forbidden him from seeing his son and in my divorce suit I had been willing to fully share custody. I felt that he didn't have any right to show up without warning and take Joey whenever he wanted. It was wrong of Darth to drink and do drugs and drive. I knew Joey didn't see it that way, so I tried to tread lightly on those matters.

Frequently, one or two of the employees from the main shop in town would arrive in the mornings at the home shop to construct commercial grade cabinets. In the past I had known all our employees and had been instrumental in hiring them. One morning while Danny was moving the ski boat, he informed me that Darth had sold it and he was to take the boat over to the main shop. He also mentioned that Darth was selling other equipment as well.

Darth would liquidate as many assets as he could. That way I wouldn't be able to collect my legal share of the assets and/or he would have money to support his expensive cocaine habit. Initially when I'd broached this subject with my attorney, he'd guaranteed me that I shouldn't fret my pretty head about Darth selling off assets. He told me that someone as smart as Darth would not act like a hoodlum, especially since my attorney had served restraining orders on Darth's attorney since the process server could never locate Darth.

The restraining orders expressly prohibited Darth or any other shareholders from selling company assets or company stock. I was positive that Darth's father and brother were riding lookout for him at the shop complex or Darth would have been available to receive his legally ordered restraining papers. As my attorney explained, it really didn't matter because the orders had been properly served on Darth's attorney in lieu of Darth. The restraining documents would serve to protect all my assets until the divorce was finalized and our community property was legally divvied up.

Sporadically, I would receive telephone calls from Darth regarding a few of these matters. Some of his calls sounded as if he wanted to wage a war. He would make threats about how I would have nothing left and he was going to take our son and I would never receive visiting rights. When his conversations would escalate to yelling about what a naughty Bitch I was, I would simply hang up and pull the phone cord from the wall-jack to stop his further attempts at mentally mugging me. Other calls from Darth were more difficult to deal with emotionally. Occasionally he would phone to tell me just how much he sincerely loved me. He would explain that if I would reconcile with him, he would treat me like an exalted princess.

During these psychologically taxing phone calls, I would concentrate on flipping my emotional light switch to the off position. I would purposefully and precisely explain to Darth that such matters were not open for discussion until after he had gone to treatment for his multiple addictions. He would verbally counter that life was not worth living without me, and he would promise to go to treatment if I reconciled with him. I had explained to him that his actions spoke the truth to me far clearer than his words and I would be watching what he did. Instead of listening to his retort I reminded myself that Darth always denied or minimized the depth of his problems, as he continued to deny the severity of the consequences.

The calls were difficult for me, just as Darth intended them to be. I felt as if there was nothing left of myself. I wanted so badly to believe Darth, but I had learned to say exactly what I meant and stick to it no matter what Darth pretended to promise. He'd broken a thousand promises to me over the years and I wasn't going to volunteer for his deceptions anymore. Instead, I would only believe his actions. Actions always spoke the truth, especially if I watched and waited. All my heart wanted to amplify the words of salvation that Darth spoke, but Al-Anon and past experiences with my addict had taught me to adhere to watching for the truth.

I had learned that practicing denial was a mechanism that enables people to give up more of the things that are profoundly important in their lives, for an imitation and fleeting sense of security. Denial is the foundation that provides the comforting delusion that everything will be all right. I did not want my entire belief system to be altered by the influence of continual denial. Unlike Darth, I was no longer willing to let my perception of the truth become distorted by denial.

The court scheduled hearing date for the custody suit that Darth had instigated was approaching and I needed to prepare mentally for the challenge. I knew that I would need more reinforcement than I could get from Al-Anon meetings. I decided to inquire from some of the women at Al-Anon if they knew of a therapist who specialized in abusive addicts. Two different women in the support group both recommended the same counselor, so I decided that I would phone the following day. I had to wait two weeks to get an appointment, but I was in.

The following evening on our way to the local AA meeting, I was talking to Joey about what I had been studying at my Al-Anon meetings. I explained that not every situation worked the same for each individually addicted person or their family. Our group had been discussing taking what you liked from the meetings and leaving the rest. Joey seemed to be listening intently for a few minutes when he said, "Mom, I understand what they taught us kids at last week's meeting." "That's great kiddo, what did they teach you?"

He was quiet for a minute and then he explained to me, "I understand that Dad is an alcoholic and I know I could become one too, because it's a hereditary disease." We furthered the discussion by talking about all four of Darth's grandparents, two of whom had died as alcoholics when Joey was just a baby and the two remaining maternal grandparents who had been divorced for years. Joey's divorced great grandpa lived a lonely life in a filthy boarding house where he was alienated by his own daughters.

For a moment, I felt an enormous triumph. It was so important for Joey to understand how alcoholism worked and someone besides me was telling him and he was getting it. This was fantastic! I worried that Joey thought his father couldn't possibly be an alcoholic because Joey loved him. It would be impossible for Joey to understand alcoholism without being educated with the facts. If he didn't understand addiction, how could he identify truths. It would be easier for Joey to invent reasons, other than alcoholism, for his father's crazy-making behavior.

Recalling statistics, I reminded myself that eighty-five percent of all women who leave an addict or are left by one eventually join or remarry another addict or abuser. I had to re-read this information several times before I was willing to believe it could be true. If I had an eighty-five percent chance of remarrying another addict, there was no point in booting the one I already had. There was no logical reason to trade another name and face for the same type of behavior. I was not about to make that mistake. If I broke apart a family to start over with another addict, then I should just put myself out of my misery now. Or I could keep the addict I was already miserably married to. At least I recognized his schemes. I didn't care what I had to put myself through. I was going to be in the miniscule fifteen percentile that did not repeat her co-dependency mistakes.

While I was assessing my situation the phone rang, it was Darth's mother. I hadn't seen Dodie for several months since I'd requested my in-law's assistance in prodding Darth into treatment. I'd attempted to talk to her a few times on the phone, but she had made it clear to me that the divorce situation I had implemented was far too upsetting for her to deal with and she simply couldn't talk to me anymore. I'd honored her request and no longer phoned her. I felt that her culpability to Darth's actions were just another denial phase where she was suppressing the facts until they wouldn't be so hurtful, but I still felt slighted that she could so easily shut me out of her life. I had been a member of her family for a dozen years. She and I could continue to have a relationship, especially since I was the mother of her only grandchild. She had not spoken to me or initiated any type of further contact, and I was surprised that she phoned.

She did not ask me how I was or what I was doing. She simply wanted to know where Joey was. I thought that was a strange question. I knew that she knew it was a school day. I told her that Joey was at school, and he had caught the bus a couple of hours earlier. For some reason I sensed that she didn't believe me, but I couldn't understand why. I had just hung up the phone when it rang again, and it was Darth's father asking, "Where is Joey?"

I gave Dick the same answer I had given Dodie and then I inquired, "Why are you phoning to ask where Joey is, when you know that he would be in school?" Dick claimed he was just making sure. I thought about how Joey was in the fifth grade and this was the first time that his grandfather had ever phoned to make sure that his grandson had gone to school.

This time when I hung up the receiver, I stood perched next to the phone contemplating what was going on. Darth had to be up to something, but what? I put my hand on the receiver to call the school and check on Joey and it startled me when it unexpectedly rang beneath my touch. This time it was Darth's brother asking the same questions. Darth's younger brother and I had always been on good terms. He was a sweet guy that I had been fond of since before Darth and I had married. Maybe, he would tell me what was going on. He evasively claimed, "I've got to go because I'm at work", but he thought Darth might be planning to leave with Joey, and he hung up excluding any details.

I immediately called the elementary school where I had struggled to adjust as a fifth grader when my parents moved to the country, and I had been elated at the idea of owning my first horse. I talked to the same school secretary that assisted the principal when I was in attendance there. "Oh yes, Mrs. Vadies, Joey's teacher's attendance chart shows him in class this morning and we were just going to phone you." When I inquired as to why she explained that a woman she had never spoken with before had called to tell the school that she would be arriving shortly to pick up Joey for his father to take him to a doctor's appointment.

I explained in exact terms that Joey did not have a doctor's appointment and that I wanted her to go and physically check to see if my son was in class or not. She scolded, "The recess bell just rang, and I'll have one of the assistant teachers survey the playground for Joey." As I paced back and forth across the kitchen floor, the secretary came back on the line to inform me that Joey was outside playing kickball with the other kids. I told the school secretary that no one was to leave with Joey, and I'd be there in two minutes to pick him up.

I imagined all the things that could go wrong and then I tried to visualize successful resolutions to them as I sped to the elementary school to rescue my son from his father's devious designs. I knew that Joey was not going to like me butting in on his father's misguided plans. Joey had been talking about the farmhouse his father had purchased for them to live in together. Darth had automatically concluded that the court would award full custody to him based on the premise that he was such a wonderful daddy that he purchased a secondary house in the country in the same school district where Joey had gone to school all his life. I assumed this was supposed to imply that the judge would allow Darth to take the child completely away from his mother. Of course, this transition wasn't going to be difficult for a fifth grader because he could live full-time with his alcoholic father in an expensive home located within the boundaries of his elementary school district where he knew all his classmates. Or Joey could keep living with his non-alcoholic mother in the same circumstances.

Darth spent little time performing his working obligations at our business, making it easy for him to find time for developing new fiascoes. I knew exactly where the house was located, it was an attractive rambler built on six acres which sat on a corner lot on the main road junction about five miles from our own residence. It was surrounded by other country acreages and kitty corner was the only business for miles, a tavern which had been there ever since I was a kid.

The stories I heard indicated that Darth had given a sizeable down payment and the owner was carrying a note for the principle, and interest. I wondered how long Darth would stay there before he stopped making his monthly installments and lost his down payment with the owner pulling the contract. I also wondered if Darth was running our construction business into the ground. I didn't think that his father and brother would idly stand by and watch their investment go down the tubes along with their full-time employment. I had no idea if they were planning to stop Darth's escapades? I also wondered who the woman was that Darth was sending to take Joey to the bogus doctor's appointment. It was a demented plot, but I suspected that Joey was very willing to participate.

I parked next to the front entry in the bus turn-around and marched directly to the principal's office. I had previously instructed the school secretary to go to the playground and have Joey waiting in the principal's office for my arrival. There he sat, with sunken shoulders, on the bench in the waiting room. I couldn't think of any possible way to remove him from the muddle his father was creating, and I knew that both males wholeheartedly blamed me for their separation.

When I asked Joey whom he was waiting for, he despondently cried that I had ruined everything. I'd intentionally foiled all his father's plans since today his father was going to take him to live in his new house and they didn't need my permission because they could do whatever they wanted. In my heart I knew that this child really believed everything that his father told him. I didn't know how Darth explained away his drinking and the new house to Joey, but I'm certain that no matter what story Darth concocted, Joey desperately wanted to believe it.

Joey needed to feel safe and secure and no words in the world that I could say to him seemed to stick. I'd been trying to instill in Joey's tender mind that drinking was the root of our family's problems. I was also hopeful that he could draw his own conclusions about why he shouldn't drink when he grew up. I knew my words to him could not prevent his future alcoholism when he attained adulthood. I wanted the bits of knowledge that I could share with him to eventually be useful tools for him. I wanted him to choose not to drink because of his knowledge. But how could the information and experiences we were learning together at AA be sufficient for him to identify drinking as a problem prior to it becoming a dependency?

Joey was fuming all the way home and when we arrived; he stomped off to his room and slammed the door. I asked Mom and Dad to watch him because I was afraid that he was going to run away to his father. I phoned my attorney and explained what had transpired that morning and told him that I knew what Darth was trying to do but I didn't know what I could do to counteract it. My licensed legal advisor thought my parents should leave town and take Joey with them.

I was flabbergasted. My attorney could not possibly understand the ramifications of what he was proposing. Not only would Darth be infuriated but Joey was already as mad as he could be. I understood what my attorney wanted to do but Joey would never understand it in a million years. Darth had already created so much damaged trust between my child and me that I didn't know how long it would take for Joey to recognize the truth. The poor kid was already despondent where I was concerned. I argued at length with my attorney and finally he told me that if I let Joey stay, Darth would likely take him again and never bring him back.

There was no arguing with that assumption. I knew that my attorney was being realistic, and I was trying to deny the true nature of the circumstances to make life easier for Joey. My legal representative also added that since it was entirely his idea, based on his legal advice, I should also leave town and the actions couldn't be held against me during the custody suit. I couldn't argue a better option, so I conceded. I explained the request to Mom and Dad. Both agreed that they would take Joey out of town for a few days, and no one was to know their location. They could phone me from the road while camping with Joey. Over the years he had been camping on several occasions with them and I knew that they would make the trip as fun for him as possible. I packed some clothes for him, and all three of them crowded into the cab of their truck for departure.

Even though my pending divorce and financial distress had put an end to my horse show schedule, it had not stopped me from riding and continuing to train my horse. Perhaps a horse show was a good idea. It would be a welcome distraction from my commiserating. The regional show hosted five breed categories in which every individual horse could be shown in a variety of classes in both Western and English disciplines. I carefully selected a few classes and submitted my entry forms. Halfway through the first day of showing one of the world class trainers approached me and suggested that I should come and ride at her barn, so she could coach me on to world titles. Later that afternoon another distinguished trainer approached me and inquired if I would like to sell my horse for a lot of money.

There was no way that I was going to sell my gelding that made me feel as if I'd ridden out of my life and into a folklore legend. By the end of the second and final day of showing I'd managed to shove Darth to the back of my consciousness. We'd won the Quarter horse highpoint award, the Palomino highpoint award and the over-all award for all five breeds. We'd claimed the winner's sliver tray and embossed polar fleece horse blanket. It was a memorable weekend.

Late that evening my friends helped me unload my horse in front of the barn. I checked all the boarder's horses to be certain that the chores had been finished properly while I was gone, and I went to bed. I managed to pull my boots off, and I skipped the much-needed shower as I was exhausted. The waterbed felt comfy even if the house was abandoned and far too quiet. I wondered where my parents were camping with Joey. I knew that they would phone me in the morning.

CHAPTER THIRTY

The phone rang twice at the head of the bed before I remembered who I was and where I was. It startled me into opening my tired eyes before I realized that it was probably Mom reporting in. There was sun peeking through the slats on the bedroom window seat which meant I should get out of bed and go feed the barn full of hungry horses.

I answered with a groggy, "hello" while I reminisced enjoyable thoughts of the horse show victories. The voice was male, agitated and reverberated over the line devoid of any warm pleasantries. It was Darth. He wanted to know where his son was. He growled that he had been phoning constantly all weekend and I had not been home to answer his calls as he thought I should. Not wanting to rouse him further, I very coolly explained to him that Joey was camping for the weekend with my parents and since he was gone camping, I went to a horse show with friends.

In a tirade, deranged Darth began to wail into the phone that his son had not gone camping and that I had better put him on the phone. I could tell Darth was coiling like a venomous snake ready to strike. Darth knew that Joey would not have chosen fishing and camping over moving into the new farmhouse with his beloved daddy. I told Darth that Joey really had gone camping with my parents and he'd be home in a few days. Darth told me that if I did not put his son on the line that second, I would be deeply sorry. I knew that Darth felt righteous in his rage. My stomach twisted with sour bile and burnt grease, even though I had not eaten.

A pang of dreadfulness rippled to my awaking consciousness, in my sleeping stupor I assumed that Darth was either at his new farmhouse or at the office working. It dawned on my slumbering brain that he could be anywhere because he was possibly on his satellite phone. As he pursued chaotic verbiage, I had the distinct feeling that he was closer to the house than I realized. He could even be watching. I was now in an upright position. I racked the telephone handset as I swung my legs over the edge of the bed. I didn't stop to pee. I didn't put my contacts in or brush my teeth. I grabbed my robe as I ran past the closet, down the hall and directly into the attached garage, tugging on my cowboy boots with each stride, I felt wiggle room around my toes and realized that I had forgotten my socks. I knew you could not negotiate with a bully, and from Darth's point of view, I'd just kicked him in the nutts.

My truck was parked backward facing the automatic garage door. In the truck behind the driver's seat was my hefty wooden club, in the ash try was my charge card and in the ignition were my keys. For a single instant I congratulated myself for being paranoid enough to start parking in this fashion, perhaps worry had not been a misuse of my imagination. I pulled out of the garage before the door was completely aligned in the upright position. I thought I had hit the bottom of the garage door with the top of the cab roof on the way out. I had a few seconds to think about which way I was going to turn when I met the end of the driveway. For some reason I opted to go right, in the opposite direction of the shop and office. I floored the gas peddle and thanked God for my gas guzzling V-8. I did not know where I was going or where I would hide, but I had figured out that life was rarely a result of random forces colliding.

It occurred to me that I could go to Kathy's house. She was just a minute away and I knew I needed to get off the main road in case Darth was coming toward me. I didn't really consider Kathy to be a girlfriend, but I let her 4-H club ride in my arena free of charge in the wintertime.

Her house sat privately in a cul-de-sac, and I didn't think that Darth knew where she lived. I was hopeful that she would understand my explanation and be home, so I could use her bathroom before my bladder bulged beyond its limits.

Kathy was home, and she let me hide my truck in her garage, use her bathroom and then her telephone. Her two daughters accepted that I appeared unannounced in their living room wearing my robe and cowboy boots, smelling like a horse show and unable to see properly. I was certain it gave them something to talk about on the school bus. I hoped no one noticed a hint of halitosis. Kathy's girls caught their school bus and I phoned Nellie to tell her what had just happened as I explained where I was and gave her the telephone number. I sat stifled on the sofa, not sure how long I should wait before returning home. I wondered if I was over-reacting. After all, it was not unlike Darth to shout sanctimonious threat to get what he wanted.

My meandering thoughts were interrupted by a phone ringing. It was Nellie asking to speak with me. I could not recall ever hearing her sound so disconcerted. She didn't want me to go back to my house. She said that Darth had just phoned her demanding to know where I was, vehemently telling her when he found me, he was going to strip my guts out, after he cleaved my head in half. Nellie thought that Darth meant it. He was livid that I had taken his son from him to go camping. I knew that Darth did not care that Joey was camping with my folks. He was angry because his premeditated arrangement to take Joey from school for a phony doctor's appointment had backfired, and I'd ruined his plans to harbor our child while I retained custody during the divorce proceedings. I wondered if he knew that his mother, his father, and his brother had all warned me with their inquiring phone calls.

Did Darth think that I was just going to keep rolling over and allowing him to do whatever he pleased? Darth was beginning to make mistakes. He was underestimating me. His problems had progressed to the point where I was no longer preoccupied with his behavior. I had progressed to the point where I mentally declared that I would no longer be the co-alcoholic partner in his disease. I now recognized co-dependency for the deviant devil it was, and I was finished being his enabler.

I understood Nellie's fear because I had learned to recognize escalating moods, violent actions, and unrelenting threats from Darth. I knew it would be easy for him to gain access to Nellie. She only lived thirty minutes away. What bothered her most was that she had an infant son to think about and she was afraid Darth would harm her child to force her into revealing my location. Nellie worried that Darth would possibly confiscate her child to get his own son back. I felt so guilty. I was causing problems for the people that I cared about the most and it was not their fault.

I phoned my attorney's office to let him know what was happening and to ask what he recommend I do. He apologized to me that he had not taken me seriously when I had initially tried to tell him about what kind of animal Darth was. He told me he was going to have Darth served with a restraining order that would prohibit him from setting foot on our property or getting anywhere near me in a public place. I decided that the attorney still did not get it. Darth wouldn't respect a restraining order. He would prove to my attorney and everyone else involved that he could do whatever he wanted.

My lawyer reassured me that if Darth came onto the property all I had to do was phone the police and they'd arrive to nab him. I laughed out loud at that. I lived a half an hour out of town and none of my neighbors lived within screaming distance. Mr. Lawyer was silent for a moment and then he said, "The next time Darth phones you, you tell him that if he ever wants to see his son again, he has to make himself present at his attorney's office to be served with the accumulating restraining orders, and if he does not, you will never bring his son home." I responded with, "Great, now I've really declared war." My lawyer continued, "Oh and Rylee, don't you dare go home alone. I want one of your girlfriends to be with you at all times."

No problem, now Darth is so livid that he is threatening a potential witness and claiming that he is going to murder me and to top it off, I cannot go home without a baby-sitter. I would have to inconvenience my friends some more. I phoned Nellie and told her exactly what my attorney's instructions had been. We both thought Darth would be phoning her back soon. I started making phone calls to girlfriends who could drop all their own plans on moment's notice and take turns staying with me. Kathy volunteered to come home with me and stay long enough for me to do chores and take a shower. I had to admit that knowing someone would be in the house with me made me feel safer and less vulnerable, emotionally, and physically.

I was glad my father had left his revolver with me when he and Mom took Joey on the hideaway camping expedition. I thought about my attorney's last phone comment where he tried to make a joke about how I should not worry, he had never had a client die on him. One of my most frightening thoughts was that my situation was beginning to feel very normal to me and I knew that it shouldn't.

Kathy and I were going out her front door when the phone rang again. Darth had just called Nellie with additional repetitive threats. He insisted that I was a real bitch and deserved to die for it. Nellie thought that Darth had listened when she relayed my attorney's message. He had crossly disconnected his phone. Hard telling where he was.

Kathy and I pulled into my empty garage and went straight back to the barn to feed and turn the horses out. When we walked back up the driveway past the original shop building, one of the cabinetmakers was working. Our employee stated that Darth had just searched the house and the barn, and he had left with his car tires squealing and gravel flying. Kathy spent the morning waiting with me for the next friend to arrive on the sitting schedule.

The home line phone rang. I considered just letting it ring but I thought that it might be my parents so when I answered I was surprised that it was Lydia across the street. Ever since the molestation problems with her eldest son, she and I had not been in as much contact with one another. Lydia was phoning to see if I was all right. I said that a girlfriend was visiting, and another was coming over later. I inquired why she wondered. She had been standing at her kitchen sink doing dishes, when she saw Darth's car come barreling out of our driveway at breakneck speed. She watched the car fishtail back and forth down the street sending a plume of dust over the road. She had also seen me leave in a hurry earlier that morning. She said that I pulled out of the driveway about thirty seconds before Darth pulled in from the opposite direction and she knew it was normally too early for me to be going somewhere. If I had hesitated long enough to use the bathroom, I would have met Darth's vehicle head-on in our single lane driveway with no way past him.

My attorney phoned me later that afternoon to inform me that Darth had appeared at his lawyer's office and all the necessary paperwork had been legally served on him. My anxious inner voice told me that was great, so the next time my parents phoned I could tell them to bring Joey home. Then in the next sentence the attorney announced that he wanted my folks to keep Joey out of town for an indefinite duration. He did not trust Darth and he wanted to be on the safe side. I knew that this was going to make Joey awfully unhappy, and it put my parents in an awkward position.

It also left me alone in our vastly quiet country house. My attorney also mentioned that he was under the impression that Darth's lawyer was becoming annoyed with him. That was probably an understatement.

Later, I discovered that Darth had come into the house when I was gone to the horse show and absconded with all our handguns. I was relieved I had hidden the one that my father had left for me. That night I would start sleeping with it loaded under the pillow in our sloshing waterbed.

CHAPTER THRITY-ONE

As the week came to an end, I had not seen or heard from Darth again. There'd been no additional calls to Nellie, threatening to dismember me, so my attorney ordered that my team of sitters could return to their normal schedules, leaving me free to attend the appointment that I'd planned with the shrink. Pulling into the parking lot of his office complex I thought about how I'd never imagined that one day I would be in the throes of a bitter divorce, seeking professional advice on how to methodically deal with a live human grenade. So much for growing old and rocking my grandchildren on the front porch while Nellie and I strolled down memory lane making humorous jokes about our men. Perhaps I really was off my rocker as I told myself that frustration was a normal emotion, that my attitude toward handling frustration would determine whether frustration was a momentary inconvenience or an all-consuming creature.

The waiting room was full of overstuffed chairs and the coffee tables were piled high with last month's magazines. The secretary's desk was vacant, and there appeared to be four different consultation rooms. While I nervously waited, I flipped through pages of ancient memories of the boys that I'd gone to high school with, especially the ones who had obvious crushes on me. I hadn't given them the time of day. They were too nice.

Well, that was just one of my mistakes, so I sat suspended with determination that Darth was not going to continue to destroy my life. I had done a decent job of resolving myself to the reality that there was nothing that I could personally do to stop Darth from obliterating his own. Anyone looking from the outside in would certainly agree that Darth had achieved the All-American Dream. He had a child who adored him, parents who held him in high regard, a custom-built home on acreage, his education, a successful profitable business he'd built almost single handedly from the ground up and a blonde wife who had been supportive and committed to him and his family. I thought most people went through life trying to attain the same things, and we'd accomplished these worthwhile goals while we were a dysfunctional couple still in our twenties.

Invited into the doctor's office, I wearily sat down as I noticed the expensive cherry wood furniture, the blinds that were slanted over the window and the table lamps that were dimly lit in the poshly decorated office. I chose the chair in front of the desk rather than the couch. I sat with my purse in my lap clinging to it as if it were a life preserver that could add buoyancy to my failings. I felt completely, emotionally spent. If only I could find checks and balances in the accounting register of my life. The therapist was probably in his early forties. He appeared to be tall even though he was reclining behind his desk. His dark hair had just a touch of gray in his sideburns and his chin hosted a five o'clock shadow at two in the afternoon. His piercing baby blues looked like I felt, drained of all human feeling.

He seemed genuine enough when he asked me to explain why I had made an appointment to see him. He easily accepted what I was telling him about my circumstances. He looked directly at me and said, "You're right, and there isn't anything else that you can do, other than save yourself." That consideration had always seemed selfish to me, and it had taken years for my preconceived ideas to shift directly to my own safety. The doctor stated, "Sooner or later Darth will most likely end up dead and you should prepare for that now." I tried to comprehend those words, "Darth will probably end up dead", and I had difficulty breathing because I felt as if I had been sucker punched. How dead were we talking about here? From my studies I knew that eventual death due to addiction was a statistical likelihood. I just couldn't quiet comprehend it. Death didn't figure into the All-American Dream at all.

The therapist told me what I needed to do to prepare for the custody hearing. He was familiar with the exact procedures. I would be present at court with the judge ordering both Darth and I to attend a pre-determined number of mediation appointments without our attorneys' present. The mediation counselor would be appointed by the county in which I had filed for divorce. There would be several meetings during the following two months with mandatory attendance for both of us. Joey would not be required to attend. The intent of the mediation meetings was for Darth and me to settle on an acceptable custody agreement between us. I wondered if they would prescribe medications to induce logic for Darth.

I explained to the therapist that I was willing to share joint custody with the father. However, I was not willing to share joint custody with an addict who was irresponsible and dangerously out of control. The doctor agreed and told me to have all the details ironed out in my head before the first mediation and then stand my ground. He warned me that I would probably experience strong tendencies to back down when I had to deal with Darth face to face at the meetings. I promised that I wouldn't backslide. He looked at me intently and told me that he understood how difficult my position was. He said he knew because he had been a rampant addict at one time and destroyed his own family. His wife and children never forgave him. He was now sober and clean, and he tried to assist others. I left my appointment understanding his hollow regret-filled eyes and somber attitude.

Driving straight home I settled into my desk chair and proceeded to make my list. It was simple and straightforward. It was the only way I would agree to share custody with an addict. My request required Darth to admit himself for treatment for one month in a standard treatment center that specialized in addictions. After completing his required treatment, he would have to work his program by joining AA and attending their meetings at least twice a week or more. He would also have to continue counseling from the treatment center as an outpatient. Finally, he would have to stay clean. He would have to prove to me that he could remain drug and alcohol free for one year. At that point we could re-evaluate and if he could prove himself as recovering, I would give him full custody, and adhere to simple visiting rights for myself. I was willing to abide with this scenario if I could grant a sound and healthy father to my son. I believed that was more important for Joey at this juncture than living full time with his mom.

I arrived ten minutes early to the upstairs waiting room in the designated county building for our scheduled mediation appointment. There, sat Darth. I guessed that in his twisted way he'd decided that if he beat me to the meeting it would give him the upper hand. He did not know that neatly folded in my purse was my yellow slip of lined paper with my custody requirements. We were mutually ushered into a room with a grey painted metal desk, fully equipped with a bureaucratic government functionary employee. This mediator man sat with his wire rim glasses, a balding head, and a plump midsection. He appeared to be a wholly average person in every respect. I started to worry. If the book was like the cover, Darth was going to walk all over this guy. My plan was already in trouble.

Mediator Man introduced himself to us, explained how the system was mandated and then directed his next question to me, "What will it take to resolve this custody issue?" I did not say anything. I simply removed my neatly folded yellow sheet of paper from my purse and handed it over to him. He appeared to be reading it with careful consideration and then he asked Darth the same question.

Darth didn't have a list on a sheet of paper. Predictably he puffed up his chest, held his chin with the scar in a condescending manner and proceeded to tell the mediator about how he loved his son more than I did. He was an excellent father while I remained a dreadfully incompetent mother. I was not a fit parent, so Darth had moved out of our home and purchased his own. He had carefully planned to relocate in the same school district where his special son had gone to school all his young life. He insisted that his son should live solely with him. When the mediator asked Darth why, Darth proceeded to explain all my shortcomings and his multiple successes.

The nerdy looking mediator was not amused and continued to listen quietly while Darth repeated what a grand guy he was. I frequently felt a strong urge to defend the lies that Darth talked about me, but I didn't. I decided that silence would be my best policy. I believed that if Darth were given a shovel, he would do a good job of digging his own hole, so I mentally handed over the biggest shovel I could imagine and kept my mouth shut. When Darth had concluded his account, the mediator studied him for a moment and told him that he thought my request was excellent and that he whole heartedly agreed with it. I could barely contain myself or my seat in my chair. I wanted to hug this man and repent of all my rude thoughts about government employees.

Our mediator handed Darth my handwritten request and all three of us were silent while Darth sat seething and reading. He wadded it up and threw it on the stained, dingy linoleum floor, stood up with indignation and declared that my request was an outrage. He snarled that he would never agree to something so blatantly idiotic and that I had absolutely no proof that he was any kind of addict. And didn't we know that he had friends in high places and family members that would testify to what a stupid, misbehaving wench I was.

The mild-mannered mediator man calmly told Darth to sit down. He spoke slowly and deliberately when he told Darth that I didn't have to prove anything, because Darth's actions were doing a fine job of establishing the truth. I wondered who had trained this guy. I was blown away. This man was a blessing disguised as a court appointed geeky go-between.

I sat adhered to my chair, not daring to move a muscle as Darth stomped out the door. He slammed it so hard that the sheetrock on the dingy walls crumbled. Mr. Mediator looked at me and told me to stick to my guns, no matter what. I wondered if he knew I slept with one.

I had to focus on positive reinforcements for my circumstances. I frequently repeated to myself an analogy for the word "FEAR". The F was for "false", the E was for "expectations", the A was for "appearing" and the R was for "real". Many of the things that I feared the most were merely, "false expectations appearing real". To fill my head with positive invigorating feelings, I decided college classes would be an excellent resource. The local community college was inexpensive, so I signed up for the two classes. One was focused on rehabilitating displaced homemakers.

I resented those words, "displaced homemakers", but the course was mainly designed to find out how we would excel in the business world regarding pursuing a new career. Turns out I was rated as an excellent prospect for a military career or an executive banker. Theoretically a drill sergeant or an administrative superior would probably be major control freaks, I could easily adapt, no doubt. I'd been trying to control Darth's life for years.

The secondary course was on stress management, certainly something that I qualified for. During one of the classes, we were instructed to write a list of reasons addressing why we would be "OK". This attempt was exceedingly difficult because I didn't think anything in my life was ever going to be "OK" again, until I broke down the items that concerned me the most into small categories and realized that I could approach each problem in a single step. I referred to them as baby steps. When the problems seemed insurmountable to me, I took one tiny step at a time, after which I could take another baby step. Over time I proved to myself that I could attain anything that I set my mind to if I basically started somewhere and kept on going. My subconscious mind believed everything that I told it, good or bad, and it worked relentlessly to accomplish my goals. Leaps and bounds might have been impossible or overwhelming, but the baby steps were doable. In simple steps I was trying to preserve and banish worry from my mind. Worrying was a misuse of my imagination. Worrying was a non-productive emotion. Worrying could create failure.

Initially when Darth had learned that I had filed for divorce he had promised me that he would keep the house payments current. He knew that I could make the barn business pay for itself but there was no way I could cover the household bills and mortgage payment too. I had believed Darth's statement about him providing the house payments because I wanted to believe he was decent enough to keep a roof over Joey's head. True to form, he hadn't made a single house payment, nor had he made the temporary child and alimony payments that the court had ordered him to disburse monthly prior to the final settlement. I'd already accrued attorney's fees that were miles beyond my means. I could occasionally visit the addiction therapist and my insurance would pay for most of those office visits. I did not know how long it would be before Darth would think about canceling our medical insurance which was provided through the company. Of course, the court system had ordered him to keep it current, but I knew if he instructed his secretary to stop the monthly installments, she would.

My parents were still at large with Joey. My attorney had warned Darth's counsel that his son was not coming home anytime soon. If Darth could behave himself, attend his custody mediations, refrain from violent threats, and pay his child support, my attorney would have Joey home soon. Maybe this was the reason that Darth had been so scarce, he did not want to pay up.

He had not been at the house that I had known of, but he did continue with his incessant phone calls. Sometimes I wouldn't hear from him for several days and other times he would phone in multiple successions. I would eventually take the phone off the hook. I had spent so many years believing everything that he told me until he expected that I would routinely keep listening. During various calls, he would tell me he was sorry that he had not previously realized that he could not replace me with other women. He verbally claimed he was sorry, but I was certain he was indisputably sorry for himself. Poor Darth, he couldn't find another woman who was as special to him as I had been. I had responded to his sniveling apologies by saying, "Oooo or Awhh", and he had proceeded with his line of rubbish.

Drugs and drinking frightened me. I think that I had always respected how they could destroy people, mentally and physically. Perhaps Darth had never thought about chemicals altering his mind, but I had come to the decision that the problem with addiction is similar for all addicts. I anticipated that user's brains functioned somewhat like a hard drive in a computer, with masses of microchips and complicated wires. Every time that the addict uses, one or more wires in the hard drive reconnects to a different wire. A few wires here and there get rerouted, and the computer really doesn't know the difference. A little more chemical altering of the brain and more wires reconnect to different fuses. So, there are a few minor glitches, but nothing terribly severe, just inconvenient hiccups.

The potential addict starts to tell himself that he is only using twice a week, just for fun. Or sometimes it is only beer, and of course he can stop whenever he wants. A little more time passes with more chemical alterations to the wires and microchips. A few more fuses blow while conductors deflect to other support systems in the hard drive brain components. At some point in the process the computer goes oops, and the enter key means backspace. Well, that is still all right with the potential addict. He has an easy solution, he can use the backspace key to hit enter, and he can still control his functions. No problem.

However, his unimportant hot wire and microchips continue to change and redirect every day, even if he does not constant drink. Wires are secretly transferring and spiraling out of control with no one knowing the difference while they involuntarily reprogram and soon none of the keyboard buttons work the way they would have under warranty. Somewhere around this time the cravings have kicked in. By the time the drinker's computer brain knows that it has a problem, it is too late. The problem is there, and nothing can make it go away. So, when the chemically altered mind recognizes that it has a problem, the hard drive is too skewered to accomplish the task that it wants, which is to quit. Even if the addict never touches alcohol or drugs again, he is still skewered, he still craves, and he is still addicted. Once an addict, always an addict. That is a fact. Personally, I was always too scared of drugs and booze to take chances, unfortunately Darth never was.

I asked Darth exactly how he thought the repercussions could be any different. His deliberate and frequently irresponsible choices had led him down this road. I told him that it was never too late to change what kind of father he could be to his son. If he would just get into a treatment program, he could make the crucial changes. He always countered that he could only do that if I reconciled with him first. I wondered if I should reconcile with him but in all honesty, I really preferred my life without him it was much saner than being ruthlessly held under his hardened thumb.

One evening when Mom phoned from a campground in another state, I told her about my last conversation with Darth. She said one of the wisest things she ever told me. "You can always remarry him at some point down the road if you want, but for now do not turn back on your decisions." That bit of advice gave my heart an option it occasionally needed, and let my mind work the way it should. I wanted to get out of the destructive relationship. I was going to finish what I had started for the same reasons I had initiated the divorce in the first place. I was going to take my life back.

Mom also told me that an unidentifiable person had been making telephone calls and asking questions of several of her relatives. It sounded like a private detective was searching for Joey. Darth had access to substantial funds. I'd suspected that he might hire a detective. I also felt guilty about what I was putting my parents through. I knew it wasn't a picnic for them when Joey was disagreeable, just because he could be. When I'd packed his suitcase weeks ago, I had included his Al-Anon book for kids. I'd given my mother specific instructions about how I felt that it was crucial for him to read one page a day. I thought that he needed to be better prepared to deal with an addicted father.

I was going to lose the house to the bank, so I had decided that I should put it on the real estate market. My attorney agreed but instructed me that I could not do so without Darth's consent and signature. After the determined Realtor tracked down Darth to authorize the listing agreement, the house and boarding facilities went on the market for one hundred thousand dollars less than the current appraised price. The property was a bargain at the asking price, but the problem was the property was considered unconventional with the horse facility and huge shop housing office space. It would be difficult to sell since most people didn't need a fifteen-stall barn or the workshop that was in the front pasture.

Instead of worrying, I decided to concentrate on my upcoming vacation. Vacations had not been a common practice in my married life, but I had a boarder that I had become friends with, and she wanted to include me in their annual family vacation. I had to admit that a week-long horseback riding getaway sounded like fun.

CHAPTER THIRTY-TWO

Mediations continued for over six weeks. The meetings generally started the same way with each visit. Both Darth and I were suitably seated in front of the military issue, metal desk fully equipped with the mild-mannered mediator man. I was quiet while Darth began as cool, calm, and collected. He never ended that way.

Darth dug his hole deeper and deeper with the imaginary shovel I happily provided. While I wondered what it was like to have the money to purchase the new clothes that he wore each week, I was trying to comprehend that I would eventually be a divorced displaced homemaker. Darth had mentioned several times that he was coming over to pick up his things, as a subtle statement that he was out of my plans and my life, I took it upon myself to toss Darth's closet full of clothes into a messy heap in the center of driveway. If he wanted back into the house there was nothing left for him inside. He never did gather his pile of attire. I eventually boxed them and stowed them away in the cabinet making shop, so I didn't have to drive over them.

At our last mediation appointment, the mediator shared his thoughts with me. We didn't have to talk in front of Darth because Darth hadn't bothered to show up for all the mandatory meetings that he had initiated. The bottom line according to Mediator Man was that Darth needed treatment along with anger management classes.

Unfortunately, this was not good news for Joey. It meant that my attorney was going to keep Joey out of town until we had finished upcoming court dates. Instead of paying bills, I had sent the barn income to my parents, and they paid the remaining balance on a motor scooter for him. Dad thought that Joey would enjoy learning to ride a scooter and it would give him something fun to do. It thought it was an excellent idea and I knew that Dad would purchase an appropriately sized scooter for him. I was pleased that my parents were able to cope with the circumstances I had drawn them into. Mom still thought that someone was searching for them, so they frequently moved to campgrounds in different states.

To help me, my brother had offered me a job in another state, selling roof cleaning and preserving treatments. This certainly had not been a consideration in my displaced homemaker college course. My brother had generously offered to pay me the regular sales commissions plus his profit after the deduction of his overhead expenses on each job. Roofs didn't appeal to me in the slightest, not to mention that I was terrified of heights and experienced terrible vertigo. Working in southern Arizona would locate me over a thousand miles away from Darth and that idea offered immense appeal. My other consideration was my neck injuries from the car accident five years prior.

My neck was fickle at best. If I kept up on my exercises, my chiropractic visits and the weekly deep tissue work I could keep turning my head and riding. The very worst thing that I could do to my neck was to re-injure it or sit for long periods at a desk. If I took the job my brother offered, I could break up my work regimen into daily segments and be home when Joey would get out of school in the late afternoons. I was seriously giving consideration for southern Arizona where the sun shone bright and splendid.

Meanwhile during the following court date, I found I was not emotionally prepared for Darth's attorney. She was a no-nonsense, dour looking woman with a vengeance, hidden under her frumpy appearance in long skirts and sensible flat shoes. She did an outstanding job of portraying me as an unreasonable woman with an unhealthy attitude, hell bent on destroying her husband, her household, her husband's business and most certainly her husband's precious relationship with his son.

The frumpy female battle ax was on a legal assignment to stop me from gaining any type of custody or moving to where I could get a job that suited my given needs. It did not seem to matter to her that Darth had not paid his temporary child support or alimony. He had not made the required house payments. He had finally cancelled the medical insurance. Darth had not completed the required mediation hearings and as far as I knew he had continued to sell company equipment and assets.

He did a fine job of silently sitting with his ankles crossed, and his feet poking out in front of him as he slouched with an attitude in his court chair. His expensive new cowboy boots were obvious and so was the smirk on his conniving face. I assumed that his arrogance offered him comfort, until reality would tear down his walls and then his smugness probably would not be enough.

The court dates were accomplishing nothing other than driving my legal fees to the moon. I felt as if I was at the end of my rope, and it was being drawn tighter. I was given to private fits of rage and outrage at what Darth was getting away with. I felt as if my flesh had disintegrated, as muscle and sinew sluiced from my bones. All that continued to hold me together was merely lose, spongy skin that could easily rupture. I needed to implement something new I had learned in stress management class.

Setting a time limit for aggravation was a tool I could readily use. I was permitted to feel any way I wanted. I could be as miserable as I wanted. However, I was only allowed to feel this way once a day and it had to be at the same given time each day. It could only last for as long as I had previously set the time allotment for. In other words, at noon each day I could bawl like a baby or beat a pillow with my fists, but I could only do it at noon and for a limited time of fifteen minutes or less. The advantage of this self-discipline is that when I found my thoughts wandering to despair, grief, or disdain I would coach myself that it was already past noon, and I would have to wait until tomorrow at my predetermined time to start feeling sorry for myself again.

The house was officially put onto the real estate market, and I knew that I would have to vacate. I planned to take the huggable terrier and the cat with me. I intended to keep my Palomino gelding even if it meant crawling over crushed glass. The other horses would have to be sold. The stallion had become so studdy and out of hand that I was afraid to ride him. I decided he might be easier to sell as a gelding, so I fixed that too.

Mentally and physically, I was preparing to evacuate the house and barn. I knew that I was not going to have any choice. Better to be packed and prepared. The gal that had approached me about temporarily renting the place had some minor horse experience. She was a bookkeeper for a friend of mine whose husband ran a horse facility as a hobby. The bookkeeper and her family would live in my house after I had moved to go to work in Arizona. She and her family would continue to run the horse barn. They would live-in the house rent free and forward the barn boarding income directly to me. I believed this would be a plausible option as it would give my boarders additional time to find new boarding facilities. It would also give me some income while I got started in a new life and job.

When I broached the rental subject with my lawyer, he informed me that I would have to obtain Darth's permission and it would have to be in writing. I didn't think that Darth would sign anything unless he got the proceeds from it. My attorney would send the rental agreement to his attorney. I would concentrate on using my fears for the fuel that I would need to get myself into a new life no matter how overwhelmed I was. Darth could take everything from me, but I would no longer participate in life as his puppet. If I could draw breath, I was no longer willing to sacrifice myself to him.

As far as fuel went, I did not have funds for gasoline. However, there was an underground tank full of it on the far side of the driveway parking lot. I had not used a drop of it because the business purchased it for fueling company trucks. Not knowing the shelf life of gasoline, I decided that I still technically owned the business, so I could use the company gas. I had not seen any of the company employees stop to fuel trucks so if I used it sparingly it would last the rest of the summer.

While packing boxes I did not posses the heart to throw away our wedding album. Unannounced, I delivered the photos to Dick and Dodie's house and dumped them unceremoniously on their front porch. I thought it was symbolic of the way they had abandoned me. I packed the rest of my family photo albums into a box thinking that someday it would be appropriate to pass them on to Joey.

CHAPTER THIRTY-THREE

My brother met me at the airport. The concrete buildings were long, low, and flat with heat waves rippling off their roofs. It was an intense dry heat that felt invigorating. My brother's place was a magnificent white colonial house with multiple pillars and balconies, complimented by a circular drive. Expensive vehicles were parked in a uniform row in front of the four-car garage. The house stood four stories tall with a glistening pool in the back yard accommodated by kennels full of attack trained German Shepherds. This was so unlike the home where I had lived.

I rose the next morning to brilliant skies and blue hues engulfed in sunshine. I pretended it was the only sensation I knew. Then I thought about my plans. I needed to find a place to live when I moved later that fall. My brother was a busy guy, and he wasn't exactly the coddling type. Later I wouldn't be seeing much of him. He handed me the keys to a gleaming new white convertible Corvette along with a city map and told me, "Good luck".

I would take any luck I could get and a drive in a new Vette. I bought a newspaper and started reading the rental adds. I spent a couple of days making phone calls and appointments for viewing rental properties. Arizona drivers were impatient overzealous tailgaters, and I couldn't believe how expensive rental houses were. I detested the way the rentals expelled a noxious odor that smelled of secondhand smoke, oven cleaner and carpet deodorizer. It was July of 1986 and I had been so jolted from my fractured life, that everywhere I went felt completely foreign to me, and I didn't understand how I was supposed to adapt.

It was even more difficult to find a place that I could afford to board my horse. There was a large outdoor arena with level footing but absolutely no pastures for turn out. The stalls were older with attached narrow paddocks where my horse could get into the inviting sun if he were tired of his stall. The boarding facility provided the hay, but I would have to purchase compacted shavings in plastic bags if I wanted to put uneconomical bedding in his stall and the barn did not allow me to clean my horse's stall to save on fees.

The household rental I settled on, was situated in an apartment complex. I chose it for its location, halfway between my brother's home and the boarding facility. The small kitchen opened onto a miniature patio with unkempt flowerbeds. The dinky patio had a rotten wood fence that I hoped would provide a secure outdoor area for our small Boston Terrier. A large grassy common area behind the complex was centered with a shimmering tiled swimming pool. I chose that for Joey's entertainment as it was heated, and I had an unrealistic idea that he would swim in it. The rent was more than double what my house payment had been on our acreage.

I was not depending on my brother for moral support. I decided that I should take moral support with me. My buffed boarder, gym queen friend was a young single woman who had just sold her horse and wanted to live on her own. She was excited about the notion of living in Arizona where she could explore unlimited opportunities of working out. It was pre-agreed that she would be responsible for one third of the rent and grocery funds. I didn't consider her to be a live-in nanny, just a friend, and if she could occasionally help, that would be appreciated. She was also horse savvy and expressed some interest in spending time with my horse. Mostly,

I wanted and needed an understanding human body around to confide in and to shoulder part of the financial burden.

The apartment owner's wife claimed her husband was a demanding businessman who had purchased the rental unit as an investment. She was dark skinned with swaying black glossy hair and a round red dot in the center of her forehead. She complained about cleaning the carpets and cabinets because she had a pregnant belly the size of a carnival balloon. I had the distinct impression she was wealthy, lazy and a power whiner. Except for the pregnant part I silently wished my only problems were like hers. I was planning to move in September.

Back home again, I spent a few hours each day packing boxes. I was getting an early start and I thought it would help to face the fact that I was going to leave everything I knew as my life. Darth and his attorney's office had not cooperated in signing the proposed lease agreement on our home. I knew he would not, but my attorney insisted that we had to have his legal authorization for me to move forward with my plans. I instructed my attorney to send me the prepared paperwork and I would go get the stupid signature myself.

It was early evening with plenty of daylight when I pulled into the enclosure of Darth's new house. Scattered about the front was a variety of brand-new toddler's toys, lots of them. The pink tricycle had plastic steamers with fancy white handlebars. A large dolly lay face down in the border of flowers. Various other toys gave the impression that at least one child lived or played here often. I supposed Darth provided these toys for his new girlfriend's children. I had heard rumors there was a woman living with him.

I wondered how it would make Joey feel if he knew his father had replaced Joey's slot for attendance at school with someone else's kids.

How I yearned for Joey to recognize the truth about his father. Not seeing Darth's Mercedes, I thought it may have been parked in the attached garage. I did not see any activity in the yard, and all the shades were drawn tight on the windows. I grabbed the envelope containing the rental papers and walked up the sidewalk to the front door. I rang the bell not really expecting an answer. I was looking for a secure spot to leave the envelope where it would be noticed when without warning the front door creaked open a few inches.

Handing the envelope to the woman peering from behind the door, I asked if she would please give it to Darth. She nodded her head in acceptance, so she must have understood English. There was a little girl about two years old standing with one tiny arm wrapped around the woman's knee and I thought I could hear another infant somewhere in the background of the dimly lit house. I tried not to stare.

I had expected Darth to shack up with a healthy, well-kept athletic woman. The poor frail female in front of me, halfway hidden behind the doorjamb looked terrible. Her complexion was pale; there were deep, dark circles under her eyes that she did not try to cover with makeup. Her fingernails were chewed to the nubs and her hands appeared to be rough and dirty. Her clothes were soiled and wrinkled and the small child clinging to her knee was even filthier. The shacked-up woman had stringy oily hair, and a few faded freckles smattered her cheeks. She must have been at least eight and half months pregnant. She was incredibly thin, and I didn't think that she looked healthy enough to survive giving birth. I did not imagine that Darth's vasectomy had been reversed so it could not possibly be his baby.

I was so stunned by her appearance that I pulled onto the shoulder of the road after exiting the drive. I did not feel like I could handle driving until I had regained my composure. What was wrong with me? Why had I expected the other woman to be like myself? I was afraid my own reality still was not lucid enough to recognize Darth for who he had really become. He was living with another addict. I reminded myself that Darth didn't have relationships, he had conquests.

I felt anxious all the way home, my sweaty palms slipped on the steering wheel. I tried to concentrate on my upcoming vacation with Gretchen and her family. I barely knew her husband and her kids. I knew that her children's grandparents would be there, and her divorced brother-in-law was bringing his teenage kids along with their friends. I was going on a real bonifide family vacation without my own family.

During the trip to the rented vacation house, Gretchen gave me the lowdown on her brother-in-law, Rod. She painted an attractive picture about a man who was her husband's younger brother. He was a divorced dad of five years with two teenage kids. His sixteen-year-old son was a kid who drove his mother nuts, had a driver's license and all the typical teenage problems, including acne. His daughter was slightly reserved and must have resembled her mother, did well in school and was three years older than Joey. Rod was an entire decade older than me. I was attracted to that idea as I had a preconceived notion that an older man would be more stable and responsible, even if he did have a few wrinkles. Then Gretchen mentioned that he was a trial lawyer. I thought that I had a minimal tolerance for lawyers plaguing my life. At least this one could not send me a bill.

The mornings were casual. We got up whenever we felt like it. Gretchen and I always went riding before the afternoon heat hit, and the kids would take off with the guys to hike, golf or swim. The grandparents did dishes and puttered. While Gretchen and I rode our horses, we discussed girl matters and verbally dissected Rod and his potential motivation to have a relationship.

He seemed nice enough and it was obvious he was a devoted dad. After many stories I concluded that Rod's ex-wife was a terribly busy gal, she had boyfriends while she had a husband. She and Rod had married in college, and she had been pregnant at the time. Apparently, it was very painful to Rod when he learned that she had been cheating on him. I certainly understood what that felt like. He had wanted to mend the fences between them. Instead, she had requested a divorce. I also sensed a substantial brick wall with extra mortar that Rod had built around himself as an emotional barricade. I pondered if another woman could ever mend trust broken by an ex-wife.

It sounded like Rod, and I had some common ground, but I was not interested in commiserating. In the meantime, I had a child and horse to support and an ex-husband to escape. I didn't think that scenario made for a grounded situation.

Living for a week with an ordinary family was surprisingly interesting to me. There was no fighting. Disagreements were settled with simple conversations. I was watching for incidents of manipulation, but there were none. I did not detect anyone selfishly using the other for personal gain. No one seemed to own anyone and there was no drinking. No one got angry and threw food across the room during dinner and I wondered why I constantly caught myself holding my breath whenever one of the adult males would begin a conversation. I realized that these must be normal people. What I had grown to recognize, as normal behavior in my own life, was not normal at all.

In the afternoons when we girls would sunbathe on the deck, Rod generally appeared. He was the only male who wanted to lounge in the with the females. Then he took advantage of an opportunity to ask me to go bicycling with him. It had been years since I had ridden a ten-speed bike. Now I was peddling about with a gentleman and really enjoying myself. I tried to ignore the nagging of my constantly aching foot. The one that was swollen twice its normal size because earlier in the week Gretchen's gelding had stepped on it.

That night after dinner Rod requested his brother, Gretchen, and I to go to the nearest nightclub that advertised a live band. I was not enthused but decided to be a good sport and agreed anyway. I knew my swollen foot was going to make me pay. I thought about resting it in Rod's lap, but figured he would protest, so I elevated it on the chair next to me. Later that night, before heading to bed I asked Gretchen's hubby for some aspirin and then laid awake all night because I was wired by the caffeine in the Excedrin. I might have been a little wired by Rod, too.

Mid-week he left early in the morning to return to his law firm. He had a court date that required his attendance. I thought that I missed him a tad that afternoon when we sunbathed on the deck without him. He returned that evening just after we had finished a spaghetti dinner. He walked through the front door with his suit jacket slung over his shoulder, and a trace of fatigue under his eyes. They were an intent, yet gentle pale blue and looked directly at me as if he had returned home victorious. I wondered what he was really thinking and questioned my imagination. He wanted to go for another bike ride in the dark. I gladly tossed the ice bag off my foot and skipped with a gimp out the door.

The following night the adults had elected to go out for dinner. Gretchen had forewarned me that they usually did this for one special night out and it was a dress up occasion. She said that she would take a dress, so I should pack one too. After showering and doing my hair, I dressed and headed down the stairs where everyone was gathering for the car ride to town. I glimpsed Gretchen at the base of the stairs in the living room. Dang her, she had on tight, white jeans with pegged legs and a brown shirt.

The traitor, we had agreed on dresses for the night out on the town. Here I was descending the stairs in a very feminine summer dress in a sheer pink and purple swirled floral print with a fitted waist. To make matters worse I wore opaque lavender hose with matching patent leather pumps and purse. I felt like a flowering spectacle, compared to Gretchen.

Gretchen's husband stopped talking in mid-sentence and stared, Gretchen conveniently acted astonished, and Rod's teenage son whistled, while Rod looked at me like I was the next best thing to sliced bread. I wanted to shrink into the woodwork. Instead, I opted to make the most of it and I smiled like I was living in an enchanted fable.

Rod was hoping that he, his daughter, and I would go for a white-water rafting trip the next day. There were a couple of good-sized rubber rafts and a line up of waiting rafters adorned in life saving floatation devices. Everyone was seated and instructed on how to row, how to duck and why and where we should wave at the photographer stationed along a rock outcropping. I was chosen by the tour guide instructor to sit at the back of the raft next to him while he called out the rowing instructions. I had a blast. Rod had to duck and row.

The day that I had surprisingly begun to dread had arrived. It was time to leave, the week was up. I thought I could have continued to live this way forever. All of us were busily packing our bags in preparation for our departure when Rod entered the tiny room that I had shared in the rented house with Gretchen's youngest son, my designated eight-year-old roommate. Rod seemed a bit nervous to me. Being a successful trial attorney, I doubted that he was anxious very often. He claimed that he had really enjoyed the time we had spent getting acquainted. He realized that I had a full plate ahead of me the following month. He knew that I had an important court hearing for custody and that I intended to move as soon as possible. However, once I was settled in Arizona, he wanted us to take a trip to Disneyland and include Joey for the weekend.

He gave me a heart-melting hug and left with his kids and suitcase. Most likely, I drove Gretchen nuts on the drive home, pulling the horse trailer, since I did not stop talking about Rod. Perhaps my impromptu vacation could be the prelude to something spectacular.

The following week was the final court hearing for Darth to take Joey from me.

CHAPTER THIRTY-FOUR

Darth did not sign the proposed rental agreement and return it to me in the self-addressed envelope. Big surprise. There were no evident signs that he had been in the house during the week that I was gone with Gretchen's family. Dry goods from the kitchen cabinets and laundry room supplies were still in the cardboard boxes where I had arranged them. My mind was not yet capable of comprehending the devastation of the situation, other than forcing myself to pack possessions into brown corrugated boxes.

Two days later, I was in the same courtroom as before. I sat at the table with my attorney and directly to my right sat Darth with his legal mouthpiece. I wondered if she cost more than my attorney. I didn't know how I was ever going to pay the escalating bill. The judge requested that Darth take the stand, after his attorney moved that Darth's mother and any other witnesses be removed from the room. I thought this was wrong and that my attorney should have argued it. I felt that Darth's mother needed to be present to hear testimony about her son. It would give her a better understanding of how Darth was trying to manipulate the legal system and divorce proceedings. She was there because she had been subpoenaed. My attorney intended to put her on the witness stand to testify under oath about why she had phoned me the morning just after Joey had left for school and she had acted frightened about where Joey was.

Nellie was sitting in the courtroom next to Dodie. She had not been subpoenaed because she had willingly agreed to testify about Darth's murderous threats. I knew that my lawyer had also attempted to subpoena

Darth's father and brother, but the process server had not been able to accomplish the task. Dick and his youngest son had hidden behind closed doors. Even if it meant having no family at all, I knew that I no longer wanted to play in the Vadies' family charade. I had grown to believe that they were all infected with denial.

None of the witnesses' need be in attendance during further negotiations and would be called only as needed from the hallway for their individual testimonies. Darth took the stand. His lawyer asked him all kinds of questions about his business and the new home he had purchased. She neglected to ask him about who else lived there and how much time he spent at his tavern drinking and doing drugs. She inquired about what type of activities he liked to do with Joey and why he was such an outstanding father. He sniffled and swiped at his eyes when he expounded on how much he missed his son. He could not live without him. Darth of course, loved his son more than all the rest of us ever could. I silently tried to pinch my memories off from the stem of my brain. I could hardly believe that I had been so ignorant; to think Darth was a man I could change, when the only thing worth changing would have been my way of thinking.

Next Darth's attorney questioned me about my future, I explained to her that I needed to get a job because the house payments were in default. Of course, she never allowed me to finish a sentence before she interrupted me with another question. She even asked me about my drinking problem. I tried not to let this woman rattle my cage. I pretended that she was just doing her job and I knew that my lawyer was going to ask me some of the same questions. When he approached the bench, we discussed exactly what I was doing and why. Move and get a job so I could support myself. Darth's attorney objected and said that I should not be allowed to leave the state.

My attorney finished his questions and sat down behind the table with his thick file and notepad. I hesitated a moment and the judge said I could step down. I tried to silently mouth some words to my lawyer, and he shook his head at me. I could not believe it. We had covered this important material in his office prior to going to the courtroom. I wanted to talk to the judge about my custody requirements for Darth. This was it. The judge was going to make a ruling today and I wanted him to know my foremost concerns. Ignoring my expensive attorney, I turned and asked his Honor if I could talk to him about custody rights. This man in an authoritive black robe was intimidating to me. I knew that he wielded all the power and I needed him to know what I thought. The judge nodded for me to proceed.

In a brief sentence I explained to the judge that my intent had never been to take the child from the father. My only intent was for my child to have a healthy and safe father. I had come to court prepared and I handed the judge my slip of paper. The previous evening, I had written out my requirements, the exact same requirements that I had given to the mild-mannered mediator man.

My veneer was not going to crack. Neither was my determination. My Chinese fortune cookie said, "If you fight with pig, you cannot win. You get dirty, and pig like it." I was willing to give the pig full custody if he would go to treatment and honor his rehabilitation program for one year. When the judge finished reading my handwritten script, he intently studied me over the tops of his reading glasses, and I jumped on that opportunity to simply tell him that this had also been my exact request during custody mediations.

Glancing to my left, I looked directly at Darth. Sheer hatred was spewing like sharp metal spears from his eye sockets. The judge handed my paper to Darth's attorney, she was unspoken as she read, and then she passed it to Darth. He knew what it was going to say. He didn't give it the courtesy of a reading. History was repeating itself. Darth was going to start shoveling again. He crumpled the sincerely written request into a worthless wad and with immense disdain tossed it onto the floor. Then he stood up and told the judge he did not have to take my crap.

His attorney's mouth was wide open, only it was wordless as the entire room waited for verbal bombardment, there was none. The judge with all his clout and disciplinary demeanor told Darth to sit down and close his trap. Darth turned his back to the judge and stomped out of court. Maybe the swinging door hit him in the butt on the way out. The judge looked sternly at Ms. Attorney and told her; her client was in contempt of court. Then he looked at me and said my request was granted and until Darth decided to cooperate and enter a treatment program, I would have full and legal custody of Joey and I could move to any state I wanted.

The appointed hearing was now over. I was disappointed that Nellie and Dodie would not testify, but I was somewhat absorbed by my custody triumph. As I rose to leave the witness chair, Darth's attorney asked the judge if Darth could be given legal visitation rights to be enacted prior to my leaving the state. At this point Joey had been "camping" with my folks for over four months. His Honor sat back down and peered over his platform at me. He told me that prior to my moving he wanted Darth to have three days of visitations with his son. The court would allow Darth to visit for two-hour increments for three consecutive days.

Nodding in acceptance, I handed the judge another piece of paper. Plainly written in alphabetical order were five different names and addresses of people that I trusted who had already given me permission to deliver Joey to their residences should Darth be allowed visitation rights. All five of my choices were people that Darth had known for years, except for Kathy, who Darth had known as an acquaintance when she brought her daughters to ride at our barn. I doubted that he considered her to be a friend of his.

I explained to the judge that I was willing to comply with the visitation order. I also expressed my concern about Darth running away with our son. I stated that anyone on the list would accommodate Darth's visits and he would have privacy with his son in their homes. The judge agreed and ordered it into the record, and then he handed my list to Darth's attorney and told her to comply. I reveled in my slight success and would worry less about what Darth would do during visitations. I also felt that my lawyer should credit my account since he had neglected to cover this ground during the actual custody hearing. I was grateful to my ex-addict therapist who specialized in these matters. It had been his idea for me to prepare the list of potential peace keeping troops to watch over Joey while his dad visited.

CHAPTER THIRTY-FIVE

I was picking up Joey. Finally, he was coming home. There were so many things that I wanted to share with him and so much that I was afraid he would be unwilling to discuss, and unable to accept. I did not know how I was going to protect him, because I knew I could not.

There he was, crowded in people at Gate C-21, nine years old and looking around as if he was not sure which direction to go It was apparent that Mom had been feeding him, he was not chubby, but he looked good. He was not as thin, and he had a tan that made him look like a wholesome kid. I had missed him a lot and I could not believe how uncomfortable it was when I finally saw him again.

I wanted to squeeze and hug him but did not think that he would accept such affections from me. All I dared to do was get my arm around him. Sour uncertainty wanted to cling to my heart. I smiled reassuringly at him. I did not know if I was failing. He acted as if I were profoundly boring. For starters, I tried to initiate easy conversation with him before jumping into the tough stuff and the moving far away schedule. As we drove home, I told him about what I had been doing all summer and tried to ask a lot of questions about his adventures with his grandparents. I was learning to frame my questions so that they required more than a one syllable answer. I really wanted him to talk to me.

During our drive home, I explained to him about the mediation hearings and the court dates. I explained further details about custody, and what legal custody meant. I also tried to make it clear that I had agreed for his father to have custody, but first his father would have to give up all dinking and drugs. Joey was not saying much but I knew he was a smart kid.

As I spoke, I tried to be ever so careful not to degrade his father. I sincerely wished that I could inoculate Joey against the grief his father could inflict. I felt if Darth genuinely loved his son, he would willingly admit himself to rehabilitation. However, I was certain that the son loved the father and I assumed that it was important for him to think that his dad loved him back. I told myself that in the years to come Joey would eventually recognize his father for who he really was, the master manipulator who never thought twice about the people he used for his own selfish benefit. Darth was an expert at organizing lies and half-truths to serve his own interest, as he had little remorse about whom he hurt.

As I continued, I explained to Joey that the court ordered three visits from his dad, for three continuous days, to begin the following afternoon, and that Darth had chosen Kathy's house to visit with him. I did not know why Darth had chosen Kathy's, maybe it was because he did not really know her, and it caused less embarrassment for him, but I kept that question to myself. Kathy had promised me that Darth and Joey would have privacy in the living room to discuss whatever they chose. I really did not think this was a good idea but knew that I had no legal grounds to question their confidences. However, Joey was not allowed to leave the property with his father or to get into a vehicle with him. Those were the judge's rules and if his father did not abide by them there would not be visitation rights in the future.

At home that evening we nonchalantly picked at our dinner while I tried to remain upbeat. Our Boston Terrier was delighted to have her young master back and they both settled into old habits of sleeping in

I Kissed the Bully - Would You?

the bed together. That night I prayed that Darth would show up for the scheduled appointments that his attorney had requested on his behalf, after his outburst in the courtroom. I had received the allotted time segments for Darth's arrival from his lawyer and shared them with Kathy. I knew Joey had been so betrayed and disappointed. I thought it was crucial that Darth honor his requests and do right by his son. Then again, I did not think it should be unrealistic for me to expect the worst. When I checked on Joey late that night he appeared to be sleeping soundly. Packed moving boxes were stacked around his room. I tossed and turned all night.

Kathy understood the courts obligatory rules and she promised to phone the police if there was any problem. I expected Darth to take Joey and run, but he did not. He didn't show up on time either. His son who trusted him waited for several hours on Kathy's front porch steps until Darth finally arrived. After Kathy's call I picked Joey up to bring him home. I was not sure what I expected, but I did not want what I got. The little boy, who had been somewhat responsive to me the day before, was now totally clammed-up. Joey was infected, by his father's visit, and he was not talking. He refused his dinner and went to bed in his self-inflicted silence. I was sure that I was as dejected as he was. Only two more visits to go.

On the second day, we followed the same pre-approved procedure and Darth showed up late again, and this time he left early and did not use all his allotted time. Kathy kept these tabs and filled me in when she phoned for me to pick up Joey. On the last and third day Joey waited the entire afternoon for his daddy. His father did not come to visit him and did not even phone to talk to him. The hopeful little boy sat dejected on the porch steps and waited and waited, yet no loving father appeared. The father who claimed to love Joey more than the rest of us, never even bothered to materialize, before Joey moved far away the following day.

Darth's maneuver did not surprise me at all. I had expected it, but I still wanted to skin him alive. I imagined de-barking a human tree. I would never have any way of knowing what Darth was telling Joey. The poor kid was not about to share it with me, probably because he instinctively knew I would not approve of hogwash. What I did know was that Darth was continuing the lifelong assault he had started years ago when Joey was an infant. Darth was doing a fine job of poisoning his son's mind. Joey was in a full-blown funk and there was not a thing I could say to make him feel better. I tried to add stability to Joey's wounded feelings by acknowledging the broken promises he was experiencing with his father. I was certain that he was angry and hurt, and those were certainly valid feelings. I tried to convince Joey that his father was not breaking promises because he did not care about him, but because he was lost in his addictions. Just possibly, Joey was beginning to recognize that Darth really was not the dutiful father he claimed to be, even though Joey would never admit this aloud. Darth's preoccupation with drinking and drugs had become his number one priority in life.

Not wanting to completely withdraw from the relationship that I had with my mother-in-law, I had tried to talk to her earlier that spring. After I had initially filed for divorce and requested my in-law's assistance in getting help for Darth, Dodie had told me that she could no longer endure contact with me as the situation was too stressful and upsetting for her. In my mind, I had thought her to be strictly spineless, and then honored her request. However, I had received an invitational phone call from her that she and Grandpa would like to see Joey before I moved away with him. I felt uncomfortable with her request, but responsible to oblige her. The following day, Joey and I went to say goodbye to his father's parents.

Dick, the underhanded, corporate thieving grandpa acted as if our farewell meeting was normal. Given his childhood with his alcoholic parents, maybe this was normal to him. It was probably normal for Dodie also. For Joey's benefit I tried to be pleasant and cordial. What I really wanted was to shake them so hard their teeth would rattle out of their heads. They could have helped me; they could have helped Joey and all they did was cower on the sidelines. I thought they were a pathetic, feckless family, including the uncle who was such a nice kid when I met his father in high school.

Standing by myself, I tried to let them have their private time. I was surprised at how quickly they all said their goodbyes. Perhaps they thought I would not make it in Arizona, and I would be back soon. Most likely Darth had fed them a cock-a-bull story about how he was winning the custody battle and I would be forced by the long arm of the law to bring Joey back on his terms. I decided Darth's family was asleep at the wheel.

Dodie was trying to pull the situation together into a pleasant farewell as if it were just a regular daily occurrence. She smiled at me and told me that I looked beautiful. I thought about it and said I didn't have another choice and I meant it in many ways. When Dick stopped talking to Joey and they were ready to leave, Dodie said that she wished me well. I stood my ground about three feet in front of them. Dodie, Dick and their youngest son stood shoulder to shoulder on the sideline. I wanted to make a summation in simple terms that I thought they could all understand, and I opened my big mouth.

"Ya know, of all these years that I've been a part of this family, each of you has done a fabulous job of persuading me that I'm the person with the problems and that I've even caused your problems. But that is not true. Your entire family has been paddling their canoe in a circle because I have been the only person in the canoe who had both my oars in the water." The no brainer for me was that I could divorce Darth, but no matter what his family did, they were still his closest relations and I felt sorry for the entire, pitiful lot of them. No one made a comment; instead, they all stared at me with slack jaws as if I had evolved from a different species. I wanted to throw rocks at them but knew it would be pointless.

The following morning, I made my second trek to the airport. This time I was picking up my brother. He would drive the U-Haul and I would drive my rig with the horse trailer. The U-Haul would pull Vonnie's Honda packed full of her personal belongings and gym clothes. I had packed feed, tack, and boxes of trophies into the horse trailer compartments, leaving just enough room for loading my horse and the cat carrier. I did not know what I was going to do with all the trophies, but I stubbornly felt that I should not have to leave them behind along with the rest of my life. I was relieved to have my brother at the house for the departure day. I had been worried about what Darth would have planned. I did not think that he would confront my brother while we were loading the ugly orange moving van, but I had been concerned that he would arrive and upset Joey.

Every item I owned was in a taped up brown box. In my attempt to be fair, I had arranged for articles that belonged to Darth to be put into the cabinetmaking shop, leaving his gun case full of rifles, his grandfather's antique library table along with half of our furniture stored next to new custom cabinets waiting to be installed. I left the pool table upstairs as it was too heavy to move. His and Joey's motorcycles were left in their original positions in the garage collecting dust.

I did not have signed rental papers, so I was not going to receive any rent on the house. The family that was moving in agreed verbally to pay their own electric bills and do the barn chores. The new tenant who was not really a tenant promised to send me the board checks at the beginning of each month.

Vonnie arrived after the last parcel was loaded in the moving van so we could attach the towing device to her car. My brother started the van to let it warm up and Nellie arrived to say goodbye even though we both preferred not to think of it that way. I pretended that it was just an interruption. The entire debacle was so wrong that neither of us could really comprehend what was happening. Joey, Vonnie and the Boston Terrier climbed into my truck, and I loaded my horse into the trailer. We stuck the yowling, part-Burmese cat in the carrier and put him in the tack compartment of the trailer so we wouldn't have to listen to him. I left the new patio furniture on the patio and drove away, forever. Everything that I was and had worked toward my entire life had just been dumped into the trash heap of my personal history.

CHAPTER THIRTY-SIX

Our caravan reached the state line by the ashen light of nightfall. I located the county fairgrounds keeper and paid for a stall for my horse. I snuck the cat carrier and a litter box, along with our terrier into our hotel room. Joey decided that he wanted to stay with my brother, instead of with us girls and other mammals. I was delighted. I needed a break from his surliness. I knew he was emotionally wounded, I was feeling just as crippled in my own feelings, but I put a smile on my face. I was determined not to freefall into despair. In its place I faked guts and gumption.

By early afternoon, we were in the blistering desert. It appeared treacherous and desolate mile after sweltering mile. We traveled down the deserted highway until we reached a gas station with a ghost town tavern. While my brother was fueling the U-Haul, I walked over to the tavern to purchase a bag of ice. I filled my horse's five-gallon bucket with ice water and gave him a drink. I made sure all the windows and vents were open on the trailer and then I moved the yowling cat into the air-conditioned truck with us. To cool my horse, I poured the remaining ice water over his back, and we hit the road again.

The engine temperature gauge had been steadily rising, so I eventually turned off the air-conditioning to lessen the load on the towing truck. Gee, it was hot. I worried that our tires were melting. Later I discovered the combination of heat and steep grades had warped the discs on the brakes. It was a good thing I had new tires. I had purchased one tire at a time. One per month over the summer because it was the only way I could afford to pay for them. I wondered how hot my brother was in the U-Haul, as he did not have air-conditioning. At some point in the desert, I finally passed him. I didn't think it was a good idea for us to separate but I was worried about my horse in the heat generating trailer.

Before I could get all the necessary items unpacked, it was time to enroll Joey in school. The Arizona school enrollment system was completely different from any previous program that I had dealt with. I could choose whichever district I wanted, regardless of where we lived. The problem was all Arizona residents knew this ahead of time and placed their enrollment preferences the year before. School was not going to be walking distance for Joey. He would have to ride the bus for an hour and a half each way, every day, and that was after I drove him to the bus stop because it was six miles from the apartment.

Joey was in a bad mood, and it escalated with his school situation. Most of the kids were Hispanic and he didn't know how to speak Spanish, nor did he want to be there in the first place. On the third day of school, he caught the wrong bus from the stop where I dropped him. It was a city-bus not his school bus. He rode the city-bus the entire day, all around town until it dropped him back off at the pickup point. At least he had the common sense to remain on the same bus.

He had outgrown his school clothes from the previous year, and he needed new shoes, a new winter coat and prescription glasses, and I had zero money left. I had spent the last of my money on the rent deposit when I had signed the apartment lease. I only had that money because Darth and I had received a tax return check. Instead of forging Darth's name and signing my own on the back of the tax refund check, I had taken it to the bank and asked the Branch Manager if she would cash it, if half of it were deposited into Darth's private account. Now, I wished I had forged Darth's name and kept it all, especially since he had not paid any of his child support. I unboxed the canned goods, so we could eat. I saved most of the good stuff for Joey and ate crackers. I still had to buy feed for my horse.

My brother wanted me to start attending his and mom's religion again. This statement naturally made me feel that to one degree or another my brother's love was based on a condition. Most of my relatives had never understood my love for my horses, but I was beginning to understand it. That love, and affection was never conditional. My horse was the same horse every day, and I always knew what to expect of him. It was a totally honest relationship, and it was always unreserved, even when one of us screwed up. My brother continued with, "You should do what you know is right." In other words, go to their church. So, here we were at the religion issue again. I knew that my relatives meant well. I did not want to insult them, but I did not agree with their religious opinions. I thought that they were certainly entitled to their own beliefs, but I was weary of them not being willing to accept that I was entitled to mine. Not all our values were the same and I was not eager to change mine, just to be included. It bothered me when I felt as if my brother had helped me in a partial effort to get me to attend his church. I decided I was going to be on my own emotionally.

I told my brother that I would be ready to start training for my new job on Monday. I had absolutely no idea what that entailed. He said that he was going to pay one of his sales reps to train me and the guy would be giving me a call. Tom was a fun, personable guy, and it did not seem to me like he was working while he was training me. He took me with him while he knocked on neighborhood doors asking homeowners if he could do a free inspection of their cedar shake roofs. This did not seem so bad. It was slightly intimidating to me, but Tom seemed thoroughly entertained by it. As we walked from neighborhood door to door, he kept a running list on a spiral notepad of each address. Approximately one third of the owners were not home, the other third said they were not interested, and the rest agreed to have their roofs inspected, especially if they did not have to climb up there themselves.

After knocking on doors and asking permission, we advanced to the next step, presenting the findings from the actual roof inspections. Now we were driving around and stopping at our list of addresses with report forms Tom had prepared after he climbed and inspected their roofs. I quietly listened while Tom made his presentation to the homeowners. It seemed that at least half, if not more of these people wanted to have the cleaning and preserving procedure applied to their roof.

The following morning Tom and I left in his truck with his extension ladder and list of homeowners who had said, "Yes" to an inspection the night before. Most of them were not home during the day so after ringing the doorbell, we went straight onto the roof. How high is up? I hated heights and always had. Heights made my knees wobble and my stomach slosh. I felt ill if I looked down. I was positive that gravity would release me, and I would float beyond the atmosphere. Tom taught me how to walk on roofs, where to step and where to climb wearing the studded spikes strapped under my tennis shoes. I learned how to estimate the size of the roof, how many repairs to anticipate and if the shake shingles were still in a restorable condition so they would stand up to the pressurized cleaning system. I was quickly becoming an expert on something that I did not want to know anything about. A week later I was considered professionally trained and would be left to my own demise.

All I had to do was attend the monthly sales meetings with the other staff, sell roof cleaning and preserving jobs and I could make ends meet. Each evening about five thirty I hit the streets with my paperwork and notebook pad. I knocked on complete stranger's doors until I had about a dozen roof inspections to perform the next day.

The following morning, I took the aluminum ladder I had charged on my credit card and did my cedar shake roof inspections. Most of them were two stories, while some of them were four different levels. Wrapping a bungee cord around the rungs so the ladder wouldn't overextend, I yanked it from the first roof level to the next until I had completed a thorough inspection and knew exactly where to estimate the charges and repairs. I tried not to think about what Darth had done to me when I climbed beyond the first level on the roof. At that point I usually crawled on my belly across the rough splintered shingles. I didn't dare to get hurt as I had no medical insurance. I thought it was amazing what a person would do to earn rent money.

I would conclude my days by taking care of my horse, going for a ride, and running to the school bus stop to pick up Joey. I would continue to attempt conversations with him, and we would eat dinner together while he sat in front of the television mostly ignoring me. After Joey's dinner, I was off again to knock on strangers' doors and present roof inspection reports. Then I would attempt an unconvincing job of closing the presentation by obtaining a down payment check from the homeowner, followed by a signature on the dotted line. I would return home around nine thirty p.m. and try to spend time with Joey before he went to bed, usually we took the crazy terrier out for a walk together. Every night his question was the same, "Mom, how many jobs did you sell?" He knew we really needed the money and every night I had to answer, "None."

Here we were, in another state and I could not give up. The rent would be due again, we needed groceries and each month the board fee for my horse was due. I had a son, myself, a cat, a dog, and a horse to feed and shelter. I constantly found myself sliding on a slippery slope toward my private pity party. I tried to only cry in private. I was determined to get the hang of this. Then, two weeks later, daylight savings changed. I was walking and knocking in the dark.

I did not think this was a safe idea, but I had no choice. If I were frightened by someone or a pack of males, I would stop and stand at a front door entrance and wait until they were gone. Sometimes I could jog to where my truck was parked for safety and self-assurance. Worse than not being able to close a sale was looking into the windows at the families, together with one another. Since it was dark out, I could usually see into their homes. Watching families together was harder for me than climbing up to the fourth level roof tops and crawling like a lizard on my belly.

The first of the month all my bills were due, and I had no money. I had not sold a single roof job and I was even working on the weekends. I think Joey thought I was a total flop. As soon as I had been trained, I trained Vonnie to the best of my ability and she had not sold a single roof job either. My brother had been so successful at it that I asked him if he could coach me. He said to keep trying and I'd figure it out. The following week it worked. I sold a job and then another. I ignored the husband homeowner who pinched my butt when his wife was not looking, and I sold them a job too. I bought groceries and some frozen yogurt. Joey smiled once. Now if Vonnie could just pay her third of the rent.

We were not in the clear, but we had not starved to death either. I was trying to pace myself. I felt pacing myself was better than the awful drifting sensation of living in the nothingness that I felt. I frequently felt as if I were lost at sea in the giant ocean of hopelessness and fear. I repeated to my brain that I could see land in sight. I wrote to Nellie. I could not afford to call her. She decided that it was all right to give her my phone number since she had not seen Darth for a few months. Beforehand I had given her little contact information, so if he captured and tortured her, she would know nothing. She was an emotional grounding rod for me.

I had several conversations with Joey where I explained in detail to him why I did not dare to let anyone know where we were. I made it clear to him that he was never to leave with his father. I did promise him repeatedly that when his father received treatment for his addictions, I would be the first one to take Joey to visit him. Then a letter came. I knew that Dodie did not get our address from me. Joey had given our contact information to her. I gave him quarters to call her from the pay phone across the street in the parking lot. From that location he could call her collect, and only the payphone telephone number would be printed on her monthly phone bill, but I always asked him not to tell where we were, and he always promised me that he didn't. I never felt that my request was right, just justified, but now I knew Joey could not be trusted and that he would lie to me about what he had done.

Reading Dodie's letter, she explained how she had asked Joey for our address, so she could write. She guaranteed me that she would not tell her son where his son was. I didn't know whom to believe anymore and it did not matter now, since she had the address anyway. I certainly could not afford to move again, I still had not paid the gas bill I had charged for the last moving trip. As I read her letter, I was hopeful that I would find her volunteering to give financial help for Joey's clothing and food. She had ample stockpiles of money and surely, she knew that we had none.

Instead of an offer for assistance, Dodie proceeded to complain about a lump that had been removed from her breast. I could not believe this woman. She still had a husband; he still had the business that used to be mine, she had her job, her paycheck, and her house. She continued to live where she had grown up and she could keep her lifelong friends. She was not hiding and trying to bring up an irate boy by herself with no money. I did not even begin to know how to deal with Joey's anger. When he was a baby and pitched temper tantrum, I had been instructed to simply vacate the room. Now the only thing that I could conjure up was to tell Joey that his father still loved him, his dad was just sick and not thinking clearly. I was lying to Joey, but I said it anyway for his sake. Grandma Dodie did not express any concern about Joey's welfare or school clothes.

CHAPTER THIRTY-SEVEN

Submerged in my private thoughts, climbing over rooftops, or running errands, I thought about Rod. I savored the memories I had from my week of vacation with Gretchen's family. I carried my recollections in a pocket of my mind like sugar sweetened candy that I could roll over on the tip of my tongue. I wondered if he really would contact me. He said he would after I moved to Arizona. I wanted to think he really meant it.

As the week passed, Vonnie talked me into going to a nightclub with her. She wanted to go dancing and she could care less that she didn't have a date. I had no interest in going dancing. It sounded like fun, but I simply did not want to mingle with strangers of the opposite sex. Joey was invited out to a movie with a schoolmate, so with much apprehension, I went with Vonnie. I felt like I was in high school again. Making my feet move felt as if I were trying to drive my truck with the emergency brake on. The dance floor was enormous and the live band with disco lighting was too loud. There were a billion people, some normal and others a bit deranged. There was a wide range of age groups, and everyone appeared to be having a good time, including Vonnie.

I meandered about with a plastic cup of diet Seven-Up in my hand; it held me adrift in the commotion like a floatation device. I didn't know anyone and tried to appear as if I were enjoying myself. Then my concocted fears began to take form, as guys were asking me to dance. I just wasn't up for dancing with a stranger. I didn't want anyone to touch me. I didn't want to make small talk or answer frivolous questions. I didn't want to be single, and I didn't want to date. I kept glancing at my watch. Twenty minutes had passed, and twenty-three diversely different men had asked me to dance. To his credit one of them had asked me three times. I felt absurd that I was single, and all alone in a dance club telling inquiring guys that "no" I didn't want to dance with them.

At last, I left. I didn't care, I'd been married to the same man for almost twelve years, and I'd just turned thirty-one, or thirty-onederful as I referred to myself. I just wanted to go home and be in my safe bed with flannel sheets, mindlessly lost in an entertaining Ann Rule true crime novel. Her books made my life seem more acceptable. The next morning, I phoned Gretchen for Rod's address. I sent him a simple card that said if he could hop a plane, I could find the airport. The day after I mailed the card, I received a large manila envelope in the mail. It had Rod's return address on it. Surely my invitational card had crossed postal paths with his envelope. So much for timing. I couldn't imagine why he would be sending me an oversized envelope, but I was pretty sure it was going to make my day.

I had forgotten all about the photographer who had balanced on the edge of the rock precipice where we had rafted the river together. There was the proof in a 8x10" photo. Later that week I received a note from Rod with a flight scheduled for Friday night two weeks into the month. Those two weeks drudged by slowly. When it was finally the "Friday", I refused to get in a rush to do my hair and find the airport. I'd purchased a city map and thought that I could drive directly to the airport with no difficulty. I did, but it was the wrong airport.

Now I was late. If Rod's flight were on time, he would be de-planeing as I wheeled around the wrong parking lot. I dodged to another parking spot and ran to the gateway. All types of people were walking toward me. I felt terrible. I was afraid Rod would think I had stood him up. I was not even sure if I could remember exactly what he looked like. I watched faces and heads bobbing toward me.

There he was! I remembered him now. He recognized me, and I was scared all over again. All I wanted to do was back track. I could not believe I had agreed to this. Now I had a date for an entire weekend, not just one dance. Rod was carrying an overnight bag and he gave me a hearty hug with one free arm. He smelled incredible and the hug felt better than I remembered. From his touch, magnetism hummed between us, as I sensed a direct pull on the power line to my fragile heart wires. I suggested something to eat, and he voted for popcorn. A cloudless sky buffered overhead so we opted for the drive-in theatre. We got lost and talked all the way. He bought movie tickets and popcorn and we never shut up.

I was housesitting for my brother that week, so I dumped Rod there. He could have the spare bedroom and I would go back home. I made sure the attack dogs were in their kennels and told Rod I'd see him in the morning, later in the morning. It was already four o'clock A.M. To drive home under the influence of no sleep, I tried to level my emotions with a peanut butter cookie, making mental justifications that peanuts were full of protein. I was hoping that Rod might be as nourishing for me as peanuts.

The following morning, we drove to a boardwalk and spent a glorious day doing absolutely nothing but having fun. I'd never wasted away a day like this before. I kept waiting for Rod to be angry with me over something he could blow out of proportion, but he never was. He seemed to be content indulging himself with me. That evening we took Joey to a haunted house theme park and the following day we invited one of his school friends with us to play miniature golf.

For the return trip, I knew where the airport was, and I wished the weekend would never end. While I sat with Rod waiting for his flight announcement, he asked me if I would come and visit him. I couldn't think of a reason not to, other than I couldn't afford a ticket, but my pride wouldn't allow me to admit that to Rod, so I agreed. When I checked I discovered that I could purchase an advance round trip weekend ticket for fifty bucks. I thought it was the bargain of the century.

It was a shocker that Joey seemed to like Rod. There was not any reason for him not to, other than his obstinate loyalties to his addicted father. I sensed Joey was burdened with his secret hopes that I would reconcile with his dad, but I knew for certain that I never would. One of the nicest things about Rod's visit was Joey's improved attitude. He seemed like a real boy instead of the curt and ornery imp that was inhibiting his body.

Then, Darth showed up. I did not know he was coming, but Joey did. Joey had been phoning his father from the phone booth in the Safeway parking lot across the street. Joey had discovered that he could place collect long distance calls and his father would accept the charges if he were home. I knew that Joey made these calls, and he repeatedly promised me that he wouldn't tell his father where we were living. I did not believe that it would be morally right for me to deny him conversations with his dad even though I knew that Darth was spewing lies and unkept promises to him via the telephone. I was afraid of what his father would do if Joey had unsupervised time with him. Depending on his mood, who knew what Darth was capable of, and I could not risk what he would do with a trusting little boy.

I insisted that our living location be kept from his father who was supposed to be hundreds and hundreds of miles from the state line. I had a hunch that Joey recognized that his father was an alcoholic who did drugs; however, I was fearful that Joey believed that his father's problems were just a lack of willpower and overrated self-indulgence on Darth's part. Joey probably figured that he had seen enough to understand alcoholism and how it could impair your life and thought to himself that he would always be different from his dad. I possessed hopefulness, but I was not certain about Joey's future adulthood.

A thousand miles was not far enough, and a pre-arranged meeting took place that I did not know about until afterward. Joey told me he would be across the street in the parking lot phone booth calling his father. I had no idea that this afternoon Joey was speaking face to face with Darth just fifty yards from the apartment front door.

Joey reported this to me when he returned home from the nearby phone booth. He was elated and excited that he'd seen his father, but those emotions were superimposed over something darker. I wanted to know what he and his father had discussed. Joey told me in a matter-of-fact tone that his father was on a road trip with his live-in heroin addicted girlfriend. When I asked Joey where his dad and the girlfriend were going, I thought he would tell me they were heading home. Clumsily, I thought they had driven all this way to see Joey and I bet that is what Joey had thought too.

They were not going back home; they were continuing further south. Both were going to a preplanned destination to sell the girlfriend's newborn baby. The purchaser was waiting for them, and they wanted the money. I had been astounded that Darth had driven all the way to where Joey lived. He had certainly had the perfect opportunity to take Joey and run, but he did not because he and his significant other had a baby to sell.

Thinking about it, I was glad for the baby and Darth's talent of bilking an adoption agreement. I felt that was why Darth did not take Joey with him. Now I knew why Joey was so glum. His dad had left him behind and stayed with the girlfriend that had a baby that was worth more money than Joey's feelings. Joey threw himself straight into a slump that I couldn't cajole him out of and worse yet, I now knew that I couldn't trust him either.

Joey's moods deepened and darkened, and he became even more impossible to deal with than he had been. Given my own emotional rawness I began to question if I could continue my motherhood pledge to stand by him. I hated Darth every moment that I sat on the edge of Joey's bed and tried to convince him that he would not always feel this forlorn. I did my darndest to connect to an almost ten-year-old. To repeatedly explain away his father's actions, I offered that maybe, someday his dad would choose to live a life that could include his son. I perjured myself when I tried to convince him that his dad really did love him, that his father was sick with a disease. I lied about it over and over and thought that lying to spare Joey's pain was the only thing that I could do at the time. He needed to have hope, but at some point, he needed to understand the painful unvarnished truth. I believed that Joey would have to learn to accept the hard truths about his father on his own terms. I didn't know what else I could say to a very lonely, withdrawn and unhappy boy.

After Joey cried himself to sleep, I went outside to the truck. I got in on the driver's side and locked the doors. I looked out the windshield at the clear crisp starlit sky and wondered about other places I had never been. I reminisced about my last years in high school with Darth. He'd been my friend when the other teenagers called me names in the school hallways. I had thought that he cared about me and then I had foolishly believed he loved me because I wanted him to. I thought he had been the answer to all my prayers. I had wanted his love for all the wrong reasons. I looked to him to make me happy. Instead of looking outside of myself, I should have looked within. Within me was the one person I could trust. I'd been young and naïve, and I probably still was.

Enmeshed in my moment with my hands resting on the steering wheel I decided I was going to change some things. I could not change my past and I would have to diligently work not to repeat my mistakes, but I could be in command of myself. I was going to bury my feelings of

Darth. I wanted to silence him forever into eternal nothingness. In my imagination I would extract my feelings from him. He would always be banned from my future.

Letting out a cleansing breath I purposefully took another and reminded myself that the mighty oak was once a little nut that stood her ground. Tomorrow I had roofs to climb and inspections to complete. While Joey was in school, I went to the barn to ride only to discover my horse was sick. He had an abnormally high fever and was kicking at his under belly. It was colic. It wasn't just a stomachache because his neck and throat were swollen. I called the vet which meant another bill I couldn't afford. The vet agreed my horse was sick, it was caused by strangles. I thought that was impossible because he'd been vaccinated against strangles. Strangles was like strep throat in a human; only if it spread to the horse's digestive tract it could kill him. The vet sold me the required amount of water-soluble penicillin tablets to dissolve into his grain and then lanced the swollen glands in his neck. They oozed running yellowish puss.

Joey had been looking forward to the trip that Rod, good to his word, had promised for Disneyland. I knew that I could not leave my sick horse. I would have to spend weeks doctoring him, and I didn't want to disappoint Joey, but we would have to stay home. Rod understood completely and then it didn't matter anyway, because Joey was down, super sick with the flu.

CHAPTER THIRTY-EIGHT

Several weeks later, I flew north to Los Angeles International Airport. I was elated and full of anticipation, yet I felt weirdly peculiar. I was semi-single, not yet totally divorced and flying to visit a man that I really liked and hadn't known for very long. I did not consider myself to be cheating on Darth. As far as I was concerned our vows to one another were over, but it was difficult to imagine myself with anyone else. I had absolutely no idea where my life was heading but I knew that I could soak up Rod like an ultra-dry sponge on water. He was fun, kind, and affectionate plus we shared several common interests. The fact that he was a successful trial lawyer with weekends off and stood almost six feet tall didn't bother me either.

Rod had assured me that he knew where the airport was and could drive directly to it. I was excited to see him and simultaneously afraid that this happiness would not be mine to hold indefinitely. For the moment, I told myself that I would take what I could treasure.

Rod's bachelor pad had five bedrooms. I chose the one down the hall nearest the full bath, away from Rod's master suite with sliding doors to the disintegrating deck. I patiently waited and studied the artwork while the stereo sang as Rod changed into jeans and tennis shoes. He told me that he wanted to take me for a boat ride, even though it was raining. I told him I would try just about anything once.

We stopped for deli sandwiches and drove to the marina. I had no idea where I was, but I could smell the salt air in the frothy mist. I supposed working on my tan was out of the question. Rod's boat was like his house, bulky and in need of a decorator's touch. I worried about how capable he would be at the helm, given the size of behemoth boat. Rod explained the difference between bow and stern and left me to observe procedures. The two diesel engines coughed and rasped, sputtered smoke, and started to life. We were going to sea, somewhere along the horizon. Rod discussed the boating instruction he'd previously taken, maybe he could read the hesitant thoughts in my expression. In my mind, I debated about how I was a good sport and a horrible swimmer.

We talked and ate our sandwiches and were dressed warm enough that Rod wanted to pilot the boat from the breezy damp upper deck. He had one hand on the steering wheel and pulled me beside him with the other. Being physically close to him made me feel safe and protected and scared the beegeezuz out of me all at the same time.

Far away on Darth's turf there was a hearing scheduled for Monday, so Rod had offered to drive me to Gretchen's house, after our weekend of fun, where I could commute to my appointed hearing. Rod stayed just briefly to visit with his brother and sister-in-law. Giving me a brief kiss, he swung into his BMW, and backed out of the driveway waving goodbye. Gretchen and her husband had all kinds of, "inquiring minds want to know" questions. I beamed, psychologically hugged myself and talked about the court proceedings I needed to mentally prepare for.

The following morning Nellie and I were just leaving her house on our excursion to the courthouse when the phone rang. It was her husband on his way to work telling Nellie that he'd passed Darth's brother in a company truck full of filing cabinets heading toward town. I wondered what kind of pandemonium loomed ahead.

The day's theme would be about carving up the assets Darth and I owned jointly. I mentally speculated about what Darth's blustery attorney would accuse me of today. After stating our case number, she rose and addressed the court telling his honor that she wanted to be released from Darth's retainer. I didn't even know that an attorney could do that. I knew they had a fiduciary obligation to look after their client's best interest. However, Ms. Frumpy claimed that she could not be held accountable for her client because he was so irresponsible that she could not communicate with him. In the same sentence she also expressed concern about his outbreaks of anger and his exceptionally delinquent bill. When she finished pleading her case she waited for the judge's response, and I realized that he would have to grant her pleas.

Once again, Darth was in contempt of court because he had not shown up and he was not out in the anteroom waiting. I took it as a good sign. The judge dismissed Darth's attorney from her obligations and my lawyer requested that he and I continue. The judge approved.

Darth's dad Dick was not waiting to be ushered in, but Darth's younger brother was. He was abiding by his subpoena from my lawyer because my bother-in-law owned the same amount of stock in the company as Darth and I did. Apparently, none of the subpoena servers had been able to locate and serve the court documents to Dick.

Dick, my stocky built father-in-law had been a boxer in the army, yet he had hidden from the subpoena server. Over the years there had been qualities about Dick that I had liked and many that I didn't. I think the quality I detested the most was his immaturity. Aside from Darth, Dick was the most immature adult that I had ever encountered. He recognized that I saw the immature browbeater in him. When he would sweep his dinner to the dining room floor, flex his biceps and pound his fist on the table, everybody shook in their shoes, but I always just sat there, his temper tantrums frightened me, but I refused to run from him. He might smash tableware or throw hot coffee on me, but I didn't think he would dare to hit me. Now, he didn't dare to be present for the court appointed stockholder's conference.

Among many items my attorney had legally requested was a current list of all company holdings. We'd also asked for profit and loss statements and company tax returns, etc. Before Darth changed the alarm system and locked me out of the business complex, I knew as much about the company financials, if not more than the other stockholders. I could easily recollect that many fights between Darth and I were about board meetings. When he had presented bogus information to his dad, brother and mother. I did not tell lies or intentionally mislead the other family members. Seated in front of them as mutual stockholders I would question the information Darth fed to them. Darth's family would sit silently and let Darth lead them onward with his erroneous equations.

As closely as my lawyer could calculate, considering assets, income and potential earnings for future years, my share was worth about two million dollars. I didn't expect to get two million dollars. I didn't want to bankrupt the business and I was not going to ask them to sell assets to buy me out. I did intend to receive something. Darth started the business with the money I was awarded from my neck injury almost six years before. I still suffered with my neck problems, and I'd originally worked for the company for free until it could afford to hire a secretarial bookkeeper. I would have settled for a monthly payment from the business over a period of several years. It was the only security that I had for myself and Joey. He needed braces and a college education and better shoes than I had been able to provide.

Seated around the court provided table was Darth's irritated brother and another man I had never seen before. He was an attorney who specialized in corporate conquests, and he was there on Dick's behalf. So, that was it. I was wrong in contemplating Dick's motives. I had misjudged him where his grandson, was concerned. He'd hired an attorney to take over the business that I still legally owned. Dick was guilty of many things, but I had never dreamt that he would foul the play yard where his grandson's future lay. I had never anticipated that he would intentionally cheat me out of what was mine.

Dick's corporate henchman asked me specific questions about the business finances. Initially he was stern and abrupt and then he eased back a bit with his verbal onslaught. Possibly, he recognized that I was not the bad bitch he had been told. He had questions regarding correspondence and acquisitions. He specifically quizzed me about the pension fund proceeds that were routinely withheld from each of the journeymen's pay checks.

The previous year Darth had convinced all our union employees to go non-union and then he had proceeded to wade through the wake of union exclusion. Darth preached that the employees could wave their union dues and better invest their pension proceeds themselves. I knew that pension funds had originally been withheld from their paychecks, but I had never seen any evidence that the funds had been invested or returned to individual employees. I had subsequently questioned Darth about the withholdings, but he had never given me a straight answer. We were never personally paid his pension monies and I didn't know where those funds were held or who controlled them. From the corporate attorney's questioning, I assumed that no one else knew either.

I told Mr. Corporate Attorney the truth about information I knew from first-hand experience. Obviously one of my problems in life was that I was honest. I always did what I said I would, and unconsciously assumed that everyone else did the same. I now had questions that I couldn't answer. No one else could answer them either. Darth was the only one who knew the truth. In my heart I suspected that Darth had also shortchanged and lied to his dad and brother, but there wasn't a thing I could do about it. I'd pleaded for their assistance with Darth, and they had treated me like an addle-headed blabbermouth. Darth's visions and hard work had originally grown the business and now his dirty dealings could run it into the ground. Since both, his father's and brother's families relied on the income from the same corporate entity, I seriously doubted that they would let a good thing go under. I did not want to cheat them, nor did I want to be cheated.

When my attorney requested the compiled documentation that he had ordered for the court date, Darth's brother tartly told him he could go look at any files he wanted. All the company file cabinets were in the back of the pickup truck he had driven in from the office complex. In other words, no documentation had been compiled or specific court orders complied with. If my lawyer wanted information, he'd have to dig it out of the filing cabinets and compile the information himself. My attorney turned his attention to me and asked if I wanted to search through all the files outside in the pouring rain. Before I could reply, Dick's hired gun slinger spoke up and informed me that any company information was no longer relevant anyway.

I was informed that I no longer legally owned any company stock. I was simultaneously shocked and ransacked in swift swoop. I explained that Darth and I owned forty three percent of all company stock and assets. In a crippling blow Dick's attorney laid paperwork in front of my useless attorney and explained that Darth had sold all our holdings to his father and authorized the proper documents with his own signature.

Darth's father had kept ten thousand dollars cash on hand. Dick knew that Darth would eventually knock on the door of his parent's house. With the cash on hand, Dick also kept the necessary paperwork that his corporate counsel had prepared per his request. It was only a matter of time before Darth would present himself whining for money. It was a simple exchange. Darth got his cash, and Dick got the company, for a basement bargain price, while I got nothing. They made the tidy transaction a family affair and legally got away with it.

I could not believe this. My lawyer had repeatedly assured me with the court restraining orders, no one could transfer company stock until it was permitted in the divorce decree, yet I was currently being corporately reamed. At this juncture my attorney abruptly stood facing the corporate lawyer stammering, "You can't do that!" Dick's legal representative responded, "It doesn't matter, because we did it anyway and the documents are legal." I slumped in my polished wooden chair in total disbelief. Now I had nothing to depend on, absolutely no type of monetary aid. Dick's attorney rose, excused himself and headed for the solid, raised panel door. I tried but couldn't sit up straight.

I was losing every flicker of financial hope, and I had a bad feeling that Joey was never going to get braces.

CHAPTER THRITY-NINE

Rod provided plane tickets for Joey and me to spend Thanksgiving at his house. Gretchen and the vacation family from the previous summer, arrived for turkey and stuffing. Joey tried not to have a good time. Agewise he was right between Gretchen's two boys. She had happy, well-adjusted kids and I was ever hopeful that just a smidgen of it would rub off on Joey, even if he did resist. I would always wonder if Joey felt that he had absolutely nothing in common with regular kids, raised in normal functioning families. I didn't know if it was his personality or a covert idea he harbored, but he only appeared to relate to other children with backgrounds similar to his own. I preferred to revel in the wonderful family hour. I knew that I was on the verge of falling in love with Rod and that it probably wasn't such a good idea.

Remembering his statements of unwillingness to make a permanent commitment to any female, made my insides rumble their complaints. I knew that a marriage commitment wasn't something that Rod was searching for, even though he seemed to be very dedicated to our relationship. This was constantly confusing for me because everything he did smacked of promise and assurance. He referred to commitment as the big "C" word and swore up and down he would never remarry. I tried to convince myself that he would recognize me for the person I was, and that I would never compromise our relationship like his ex-wife had. I thought he could get over what she did to him if he really wanted to. Here I was having difficulty trying to change a man again. The new guy didn't drink, but it was obvious he toted emotional baggage. I could appreciate not trusting your own ability to judge another person's integrity.

As Christmas gradually approached, I had a profound sense that Rod was pulling backward, out of our relationship. I suspected that he was having more in-depth feelings than he had initially intended. It was painstaking, but I had no other choice than to let him draw backward and away from me. I busied myself with selling roof packages and tried desperately not to think about him even though that was all I did.

An opportunity presented itself for me to ask my brother what he thought. I was sure he was listening to my explanation when he paused and said, "Give him his space, the last thing the guy needs is some blonde bugging him." Well, I could do space, especially since Rod was in another state. I visualized him being strapped to a projectile missile, aimed for unknown planets as he lifted off, bound for a different universe, never to be seen again. Almost three weeks later Rod phoned on Christmas Eve. I made sure I was out. Joey and I were walking the dog in the chilly winter night around the neighborhood. A stroll around the surrounding area gave me one-on-one, quality time as I attempted to goad Joey into conversation.

We came inside to a blinking red light on the answering machine and my heart skipped a beat as I ignored the pulsating red dot. I waited until the following day to return the call. Rod explained to me that he was trying to decide what he was going to do about us. He stated that he had previously promised himself through his divorced single years that he was never going to fall in love again. He wasn't sure what he thought, which was most likely another way of avoiding commitment, but he knew he wanted to keep seeing me. Well, that was a huge relief, but I didn't like the way he pulled backward and clammed up. It was painful, and I detested analyzing what the status of our relationship was.

Joey was in his usual defunct mood because he had not been able to reach his father on the pay phone and there were no presents under a festive tree to cheer him up.

I felt that I understood some of Joey's feelings. They couldn't have been that much different than mine. Legitimately I probably could have blamed Darth but that was a futile waste of emotional energy. Instead, I put on imaginary rented rubber lips and forced them to turn upward into a smile. I talked a ridiculously hard line and finally convinced my brother and his wife to bring their young kids out to the horse barn and hand feed carrots to my horse who had finally fully recovered from his bout with strangles.

That first Christmas evening without a father, Joey settled onto the sofa to watch MTV. I decided that I should re-read a book I'd purchased earlier that summer. I'd already devoured the material between its hardbound cover more than once. The book was titled, "Women Who Love Too Much", authored by Robin Norwood. I had never contemplated that I could love someone too much until I read this book. It was a suggestion at the Al-Anon group from one of the other alcoholic's wives. It was exceptionally interesting to me because I was remarkably guilty of loving too much. As explained in several chapters the material was geared mostly toward women, but that didn't mean that men were not exempt from the problem.

Women who love too much are good hearted, selfless women who proceed to love someone more than they love themselves. Loving selflessly can be an awesomely wonderful thing but does not apply when the selfish loved one does not appropriately reciprocate. When the loving woman is doing all the giving and none of the getting, the entire relationship is bound to be out of balance. I remembered many times when I had struggled to go the extra mile for my husband while he was feeding me lies, and I was so predictable that I continued to play right into his deceptive plans.

How many times had my instincts told me something was off, what Darth was saying or doing didn't make sense and neither did his excuses or explanations? I should have trusted myself instead of Darth. If I could read this book and learn just one simple lesson, I would understand the main mistake that I had made with Darth when we were just teenagers. Although I'd been taught to never give up, keep the faith, and work hard at being perfect, my worst error was believing that because of who I was I could change Darth for the better. According to my reading material, telling myself that I could change someone, especially a potential mate was the worse lie possible. This lie to me was also one of the most common mistakes that women tended to make, and repeat concerning the opposite sex. I had thought that I could change Darth, because of who I believed I was. In retrospect, I may have accomplished that goal to a degree for a little while, but ultimately, I would fail.

If I had been attracted to one of the "nice" boys in high school, I would have discovered a passageway to happiness in a relationship with a pleasant and slightly boring man. Instead of living with pain and rejection I would have found the opposite, comfort, and commitment. As defined in the book, boredom is the sensation that women who love too much so often experience when they find themselves with a "nice" man: no bells peal, no rockets explode, no stars fall from heaven. In the absence of excitement, anxiety, and challenge I would find myself feeling very awkward in the presence of a sincerely even-keel, good guy. My personal skills for relating on a normal level were honed for a challenge and I simply did not know how to enjoy the presence of a man who considered my best interests as important as his own.

The book was written about thousands of women who made the colossal mistake of misjudging their situations. We thought that because we were virtuous, kind, and loving, trying to do the right thing that we could mold the imperfect man into the perfect mate. A basically simple concept yet difficult to adhere to, I knew in my private mind's closet I was doing this with Rod. I clung to the idea that I could change him, or that he would want to change to be with me. I thought that he would surely recognize that I was not a thing like his ex-wife and if I could love him enough, he would give me what I wanted, love in return. I believed that I could change Rod into wanting commitment because sooner or later he would trust his realization of how much I loved him.

I reread the book highlighting pertinent statements with a pink felt tip marker. I completely understood the concept and I even recognized it in my internal thoughts of Rod. Yet, I couldn't stop telling myself that I was the one. I would be different to him than the others. Instead, I should have appraised him realistically, accepted him for who he was, and appreciated his good qualities. Instead, I harbored the thought that I was more talented than the loving women in the book. If I tried hard enough, I could change Rod's mind about marriage.

At the first of the month, when I was desperate for the necessary rent money, that was swiftly becoming past due, I received a phone call from my attorney informing me there was a buyer for my house and that the real estate agent had delivered an earnest money offer to his office. I had to decide on whether to accept the offer, counter back or wait for another purchaser. There was absolutely no question that I really needed the money. The fact that the house would be gone forever made me incredibly sad and I decided that it was just another piece of the puzzle that needed to be dealt with.

I opted to accept the offer, even though it was one hundred and fifty thousand dollars less than the house had appraised for two years before. The realtor had already acquired Darth's signature of acceptance on the sales contract. With this pending news I had a decision to make. Would I stay in Arizona and continue to work for my brother? I loved the weather but felt as if I didn't belong, leaving me with just a few choices. I could start my own cleaning and preserving roof business. My brother had told me, he wouldn't charge me the usual franchise fees that he required from his other sales associates when they ventured out on their own. If I did start my own business, where would I want to work that boasted an abundance of shake roofs.

Net proceeds from the house would barely give me enough funds for an inexpensive work truck, the custom-built pressure cleaning machine bolted to a trailer and the preserving equipment mounted in the bed of the truck. If I moved, I'd have scarcely enough money to get started with a new business and a new life. The house was supposed to close in February and that same month my lease would be up on the apartment with Joey's school year almost completed.

That night when Rod phoned me, I explained my plans to him. He had known all along that moving north would probably be my wisest choice, but now it was becoming a reality. He asserted, "I can't let you move near me because if you fail with your business, my family and I would feel responsible for you and your welfare." I hesitated, "You know, I really like our friendship and I don't want to do anything to screw it up, but I have to fend for myself first." I continued to tell him that I'd carefully thought it through and moving north was the wisest decision that I could make for Joey and myself and if that meant that he and I would discontinue our relationship, then that was that.

Rod was dead silent for the longest time. "Well," he said, "since that is the way you put it, when will you be here?"

CHAPTER FORTY

I pressed on with the necessary trip I had planned. It would give me a slight reprieve while Vonnie and Joey tended to one another. I needed to file the paperwork for my small roof cleaning corporation and search for a new place to live. I'd make the three-day drive north pulling my old horse trailer loaded with my gelding. My travel plans were in order, and I could stay in a hotel while I was out of town. Rod suggested that I stay with him and save the hotel expenses. When I hesitated, he promised there would be no strings attached and I trusted him enough to be comfortable with his offer. Wasting no time, I turned his accommodating dining room table into my private office and went about filling out forms and preparing contracts for printing, as I plagiarized copies of my brother's brochures.

For seventy-five dollars, I rented an experienced pilot and a single engine plane and tried not to look down during takeoff. We flew around for an hour at fifteen hundred feet. As the pilot mentioned which town we were above, I made mental notations of the neighborhood roofs. I was pleased to see thousands of cedar shake roofs all in immediate need of cleaning and preserving. I had come to the right place.

Around six o'clock, when Rod would arrive home from his office, my workday would revert into a mini vacation. We'd go out for dinner because he didn't think I should have to cook. We dressed up and went dancing downtown. On the edge of the dance floor Rod left me for a minute to find the restroom. He told me if someone asked me to dance to go ahead, but to remember he brought me.

We were having a very romantic time of playing house, as Rod referred to it. He asked me if we could sleep together. I'd spent enough time with him that I trusted the suggestion but not myself. I knew that if we maintained our relationship, we would end up doing more than just dancing together. The only teenager, husband, and demented man that I had ever slept with was all rolled into one, Darth. Since I was thirty-one years old it was safe to assume that at some point in my life there would be another man and Rod was certainly very tempting.

Putting on a simple silk nightgown that hung straight to my calves attached to spaghetti straps that did not stay on my shoulders, I brushed my teeth and pattered barefoot to Rod's bedroom. I didn't think he was surprised to see me. He smiled his boyish grin and held back the covers inviting me to climb in.

The next morning, we lay snuggled together between the fuzzy flannel sheets and talked about everything we could think of. I told Rod I must be the first married woman that he had ever slept with who wasn't his wife. He smiled at me, but for once, didn't have a clever reply. I felt marvelous but didn't have a clue of what I was getting into, nor did I want to spoil my good time by worrying about it.

That weekend before returning to my Arizona apartment, we went downhill skiing. I had never inspected a pair of skis or had them attached to the bottom of my boots. Rod was un-affected, as he had been skiing since he was a kid. I was a decent water skier, so I decided water couldn't be much different than snow. I was in good spirits and sportsmanship until I realized the ski lift did not stop for me when I got on. The lift grabbed my behind, plucked me up, swooping me high and away on the cable line. On the ride up, I realized that it wasn't going to stop to let me off either.

Rod told me not to worry about it, to just snowplow so I would not pick up too much speed going down the bunny slope. Our chair lift was fast approaching the touchdown mark. We scooted forward on the unstable swinging seat. My rented skis felt like heavy two by fours strapped to my stiff weighted boots. I was supposed to jump down on Rod's command. Much to my own amazement, I jumped. I stayed upright, and I was downhill skiing, well sort of. I veered right, and Rod disappeared somewhere off to my left. I hadn't gone very far but I was afraid of how far I could go. I did not know how to stop myself, so I ker-plopped directly onto my insulated rear end.

Still rotating on my downhill slide, I could not stay straight as my skis swiveled sideways. Other out of control skiers were frantically trying to maneuver around me. I did not think they could stop or turn either, even if their feet weren't in mid-air. When I finally stopped my snowbound travel, I was backward and my stiff, ill-fitting heavy boots with my tangled skis were up hill of my head. Other beginners were desperately trying to avoid being in my position with me. I spotted Rod down the hill as he was yelling at me to get up. Lying upside down I yelled back, that if I could get up, I would. He mimicked for me to watch him as he rolled over sideways and popped effortlessly straight back up like one of those old-fashioned spring-loaded puppets in a box. I laid upside down with snow compressed down the back of my pants imagining Rod as a mechanical child's toy. Lying upside down I couldn't even move my feet downhill from my head.

Two cute, buffed guys skied down to me and asked me if I needed some help. I most certainly did but I wasn't going to accept it from them. I explained to them that the old guy, repeatedly falling and getting back up at the bottom of the bunny slope was my date and this was his fabulous idea, so he could help me. Rod side-stepped on his skis all the way back up the bumpy hill to give me a hand up, he yanked me hard, straight uphill and erect onto my skis with one hand while his other handheld his ski poles. I didn't know where mine had gone.

Gazing up into his face I saw the first time he was exasperated with me. Looking down I realized that my two cheap, beat up rental skis were standing directly on top of his expensive brand-new skis. All I could say was, "I'm not supposed to be standing on your skis, am I?" Rod never took me skiing again. I suppose it was a good thing I never sunk his boat.

Playing house with Rod was like living in a fantasy for me. The conversations, the fun, the warmth and affection, I think I could have stayed for an eternity, but I had to go home to Joey, especially since I had called and talked to him the night before. Joey was excited because his dad had entered a treatment program. This would change everything. Now the divorce was being finalized and I knew that I would never return to a relationship with Darth; he was finally in treatment of his own accord. I'd had excellent reasons for excluding him from our lives, but soon I would have to deal with him on a parenting level.

I left my truck in Rod's garage as he took me to the International Airport because the next time, I drove upstate it would be in a U-Haul truck. In the interim I could use the inexpensive Mazda work truck I had purchased on credit. I was going to be faced with passing through the eye of the needle. Joey's father was in treatment, and I'd promised Joey he could go visit, if his father would just make the correct choices. I still didn't trust Darth, but I trusted that treatment would work for him for the sake of his son. I was going to give it several weeks and see if Darth would indeed honor his treatment program.

When I'd talked to Nellie, I knew Darth was still in treatment because the center was right next door to the assisted living facility where she was the activity program director for the elderly. The treatment center's cyclone fenced basketball court was adjacent to the parking lot where Nellie went to work every day. Instead of playing basketball like a good boy, Darth would stand inside the fence and stare across the parking lot at Nellie. She could see him through her office window. I'd moved thousands of miles away and left Nellie in the same town with Darth. Now she went to work and watched Darth watching her.

The day arrived for me to be true to my word, but I was not going to just let Joey go visit his dad. I was going to call on his father first. I wanted an answer to my question. Would Darth be reliable as a parent? I had an appointment to meet with Darth and his counselor. The closer I drove north to my appointment the less I wanted to be there, but I'd made a promise to a ten-year-old boy who could trust me, and I was going to honor my word.

Wearing the sweater that Rod had given me for Christmas, I pulled into the treatment center's parking lot. The long sleeved, softly knit feminine sweater had become the favorite in my wardrobe. It seemed silly, but I thought of my Christmas present as my invisible force field shield.

I parked and walked up the simple sidewalk lined with spring grass leading to the treatment facility's entry. The doors swooshed open, and I boldly stepped through a portent where I'd never gone before. I noticed how the linoleum floor glowed with a sheen of fresh wax and I couldn't believe how many patients were milling about accomplishing nothing. I had crossed an undetectable passage to another world full of addicts.

Briefly scanning the large public mess hall, I noticed how most but not all the patients were male. The few females that were present looked as haggard and wrung out as the men. Many of the men wore their long, ratty hair in ponytails. All the patients, who were close enough for me to notice, hosted bloodshot rheumy eyes and a repelling weariness.

I knew that most families of addicts must give up in the end. Despite their heartaches and devised good intentions, most family members had to reconcile themselves to the truth, that many addicts were ultimately a hopeless case. Perhaps the addicts just hadn't had enough to drink, yet? They seemed to insist on pursuing their self-destructive behavior until something apart from any other effort changes radically within themselves. Their desire for the chemical high is replaced by a yearning for something even greater, their higher power.

While I was lost in my private thoughts, Darth approached me. I had the distinct feeling he thought he still owned me. I guardedly thought of him as a pestilence that could not be sprayed with Raid. I didn't sense that he understood how much I had changed and that I was never going back to him, nor did I invite him to invade my personal space. I remembered my sweater armor and walked toward Darth's counselor, turning my back to escape Darth the menace. I had expected a man. Strange, Darth's lawyer had been female also. Who knew what kind of sob story he fed the women around him? I presumed that his female counselor was possibly an ex-addict herself. I expected that whatever Darth had to say was not the whole truth and nothing but trash.

I thought there was still a strange way about how he physically moved and held himself. He didn't look very healthy to me. His skin was pasty and more of his thick dark hair was receding from the top of his head. I wished I were anywhere else. I anticipated the counselor taking us to her office, but instead she pulled up a well-used plastic chair and sat down right in the middle of the public commotion in the oversized cafeteria room. Darth grabbed an identical chair and sat down beside her, facing me. I found an empty chair and drug it away from them to a comfortable distance and sat down strategically facing both. I placed my purse in my lap to facilitate my invisible shield, crossed my legs at my knees and waited.

Darth started first, no apology, no explanations, no reasons, just that he was glad he had been hooked on cocaine because its addiction process was quicker than alcohol. I assumed that drugs made Darth feel better, and more powerful than anything else he could ever imagine. I was under the impression that Darth saw his drug and drinking habits as an intellectual desire rather than a physical need. He pronounced, "Why, if I would a stuck to drinking, I'd still be drinking instead of be'un in treatment," so he was thankful for his drug addiction and acted as if I should be thankful too.

I thought that was so like him. He turned his slight admission into something that he perceived to be good that was excusing his past actions. He still was not acknowledging responsibility for his delusional, deranged self. Lost in my thoughts I kept quiet for the moment and let Darth continue. He talked about how many of his problems stemmed from his father. I knew there was a percentage of truth to that statement, but it didn't matter to me. Darth was an adult and should be accountable for his own actions. There was no point in blaming good old dad at this juncture. According to Darth all of Dick's problems were really his wife's fault because he wasn't sexually satisfied.

Ah, sex, the root of Darth's tribulations. I thought to myself that Darth was still full of bull puck. He had to be the most self-deluded human being that I didn't want to know. Then I pondered something that I doubted I would ever really know. If alcoholism is a progressive disease that is not caused by a virus or germ, then what kind of illness was it? Was addiction a choice? A choice that was made every time the potential addict swallowed a swig, snorted a line, or plunged the needle.

I was drawn back into the conversation when the counselor asked me what I thought. "Oh, I think Darth is going to be a very sick puppy for a very long time." As I knew he would have to stay totally clean of drugs and booze for three years before the effects could dissipate from his system, and I doubted he would ever really be normal. I couldn't recall that being his old self again would even be a good thing. I also stated that if I were his mom, "I wouldn't sleep with Dick either, you know, really my only concern is whether or not Darth can be a responsible father." I pretended that Darth was not present, and I explained about the court dates and custody battle and what I had promised to Joey. I told the counselor, "I just don't think Joey, for his own sake, should visit his father until Darth has stayed clean for at least a year.

Darth began to blubber, as if he were in actual pain. He bawled about how he couldn't make it if he wasn't allowed time with his son. I realized that his statement was no doubt intended to make me feel responsible for his demise if I withheld his child from him. I told him the last time he had a chance to visit with his son, he'd left trusting little Joey sitting and waiting endlessly on the neighbor's porch; knowing that Joey would be moving far away the following day. Darth claimed he had been completely out of control on cocaine and that he wouldn't do that again. He said he went to treatment, so he could be with his son. Darth promised that he would make it up to Joey. He said he knew he could never make things up to me and that Joey was all he had left. I considered that for once Darth was right.

Even though I didn't believe that he was good for Joey, he was his father. I knew if Darth got his act together his parents would eventually forgive him. I thought I should forgive my enemies, but never forget their names. Darth was so pathetic that I felt sickly sorry for him. The golden boy with the American dream only had one person left who really wanted to be with him and that was my son. What a huge responsibility to burden a ten-year-old boy with.

Personally, I found Darth to be despicable and for the duration I decided those feelings were healthy. After years of being married to Darth I'd lost my sense of self-worth while the effects of his abuse had diminished my confidence. If having loathsome feelings toward Darth helped me to remember who I really was, I'd continue to safeguard myself in that fashion.

The counselor mentioned that it was obvious from my attitudes and comments that I had been through some counseling of my own. I admitted that I had, and I was working awfully hard to avoid any further enabler pitfalls, yet here I was feeling somewhat sorry for Darth. Both Darth and his counselor agreed he would stay in the outpatient program for one year. They thought he could do it. I hoped they were right. I explained that I would be moving to a new job and location the following month. If Darth stuck to treatment, I would bring Joey to visit him. Darth was mewling like a wet kitten while his therapist kindly nodded and patted him on the back. I knew he wanted to pollute my thoughts with his guilt. Emotional sabotage had always been one of his strongholds.

Darth's counselor ventured, "Let's talk about his other problem, his sexual compulsiveness." I mentally gagged and wanted to projectile vomit into their faces. I remembered the things the bastard had tortured me with as he'd triumphed over me, and I couldn't believe his counselor could call it something as petty as compulsiveness. Even the word "obsession" was too mild in my opinion. Maybe the counselor was as much of a sicko as Darth, and here I was trying to have a sane conversation with them. Later, I would learn that over 50% of patients in treatment for addictions were also in treatment for sexually abusive acts.

I ended the discussion; said I'd be checking on Darth's status again and left. I wanted a lot of distance between me and the treatment center. I walked as fast as I could without appearing hurried and fumbled for the keys in my purse. When I inserted the key in the truck door, Darth was right behind me, invading my personal space again, on purpose no doubt. Sneering and biting my tongue, I turned around and told him to go back inside where he belonged. Darth grinned at me like a poised python eyeing a cornered mouse. He casually leaned up against the hood of my vehicle with his hands stuck in his pant pockets, as he admired my truck. Dubiously, he stated that he wished he had something nice to drive. I thought he'd steal my truck if he could.

My heart clenched, knocking hard against my chest as I opened the truck door to stand behind it. I thought a metal barrier between Darth and me was an outstanding idea. I told him he used to have a nice truck, lots of them. He'd thrown them all away along with his family for his alcohol and illegal drug habit. I told him I'd be in contact about Joey, and I drove off. I thought about running over him, but I knew there were too many rehabilitating druggies witnesses in the adjacent basketball court watching our episode.

CHAPTER FORTY-ONE

After the moving van was loaded to capacity, we hitched Vonnie's compact pickup truck to the tow-dolly and disengaged the transmission. In the back of her truck bed, we loaded all of Joey's bedroom furniture and personal belongings along with the portable television. I wasn't sure if Darth would have one. I hopped behind the oversized steering wheel, and ground the gears searching for second. Joey who was sitting between Vonnie and me, straddling the gearshift with the terrier on his lap, complained about my driving abilities. As I pressed the clutch in, gunned the engine at the traffic light and ground the gears again, we were out of town and on the freeway. I'd figured out how to shift the giant ogre of a vehicle. I was confident that after three solid days of steering, braking, and shifting, I would be an expert.

During the drive, I had plenty of time to contemplate how this was probably the first time Darth had ever stuck to a promise and faithfully remained in his outpatient program. I knew that Darth had gone back to work at the business. He was no longer the lofty president with the big extravagant desk making all the corporate decisions, but he was clean and sober, and he had a job. There was no longer a viable reason for me to keep his son away from him. I felt a slight spark of chance that Darth might succeed at keeping his promises and his life on track.

After hundreds of monotonous miles, we arrived at the work shop's parking lot, I asked Joey if he wanted to keep our terrier with him during his visit. I felt she would be a good friend to have, and he might enjoy her companionship during the day while he was at the shop with his dad. He agreed as I gave him a big hug. I felt that Joey was focused on his dad and not worried about his mom leaving him. I had already given him a slip of paper with my parents' phone number and some quarters, so he could call my mom if he needed. Our plan was for me to get settled, start my new business, make some money, and then have Joey return at some point that summer.

Darth made a chauvinistic statement about me driving the behemoth rental truck as I tried to concentrate on feigning indifference. It would have been personally rewarding to remove his liver and other significant boy body parts, but I faked being immune to him while doing a princess wave with a robust smile. I said a prayer that Joey would be alright with his father. Then I convinced myself that Darth really did love his son enough to keep his act together. But uncertainty clung to my chest like powerful plump fingers.

In the next five hundred miles I kept the pedal down as I passed Rod's exit and had amazingly fantastic thoughts of him. He didn't need to worry about being responsible for my welfare. I could prove it. I wasn't going to live anywhere near him. I was moving in about thirty exits further up the freeway. I'd found a house in a small new development on the edge of a prosperous and popular town surrounded by neighborhoods full of shake roofs. It was the smallest house in the neighborhood, which made it an excellent investment.

Being new it smelled of fresh paint and clean carpet. It needed a landscaped backyard, but I could work on that eventually. This was going to be my refuge, my haven. What Rod really didn't understand was that I needed a nest. I genuinely wanted to feel like I finally belonged somewhere. I was staking my claim, to live free of dependence on someone else, especially a man.

Previously my attorney who allowed Dick to steal my share of the company, had explained to me that the only way I could receive the net proceeds from the sale of my old family home was to finalize the divorce. This was a bit difficult because Darth no longer had an attorney representing him. My lawyer made a motion to the court to finalize the divorce without Darth who had never returned any of the paperwork that had been forwarded to him. Basically, my choice was this; if I wanted the proceeds from the sale of the house escrow, I could take them if I finalized the divorce. To finalize the divorce, I would have to agree that I held no future claim to my portion of the company stock and assets.

My attorney knew that I did not have any money and my current debt to his office we well over ten thousand dollars. My divorce decree awarded me the shirt on my back, and my horse. I had to sign a legal agreement that I would never lay claim to the company stock and equities that Dick had scammed from me. The big bonus was that I could have a one time, free of charge name change. I took the deal and attempted not to feel stripped and cheated.

Now that Darth had what he wanted, I phoned Nellie and gave her my new telephone number. She would never give it to anyone that she shouldn't, and we didn't think that Darth would bother her now that Joey was with him. Nellie had been my best of friends for years and we had seen each other through a lot, including growing up, but she seemed annoyed with me. She did not feel that I should have let Joey stay with Darth for part of the summer. Nellie had asked, "How can you just give Joey up?"

I explained, "I'm not just giving him up, I still have full legal custody and Joey will be coming back to live with me for the school year with occasional visits to Darth." Nellie still did not like it and she made it clear.

I did not like it either, but there was no way on Earth I could change who Joey's father was. That was a colossal mistake I had made years ago and would have to live with the rest of my life. My son wasn't just an infant like hers. He was going on eleven, he had feelings and attachments that I couldn't change and didn't believe that I should. If my son were less than two years of age like hers, I could tell him someday that his father had died and leave Darth dead as dust in Joey's memories.

The way Nellie felt really bothered me, but I told myself that I could not expect her to understand. No one could really comprehend my situation. I still did not get it myself most of the time. I just kept putting another foot forward. If I weren't moving forward, then I was backsliding, and backsliding was something I absolutely could not afford to do financially or emotionally. I was afraid of so many unknown things. I couldn't let fear get in the way or I would flounder in it.

Maybe the planets were aligning, and I wouldn't have to move again for a long time. I couldn't decide which boxes to tackle first. My shoulder blades were agonizing over every movement, my truck that I hauled my horse trailer with was still parked in Rod's garage where I'd left it when I transported my horse during the previous trip. I dropped onto my unmade sofa as a temporary bed and slept like a rock until the sun peeked through the bare windows.

Deciding to skip the shower since I did not know where the bath towels were packed, I started with the cardboard box positioned directly in front of me. I'd been unpacking for a few hours when the doorbell rang. My hair was a mess, my clothes were slept in, and I didn't feel like inviting company inside and being cordial. I opened the front door thinking I would tell them to go away, and there stood Rod beaming at me with the magnetism that drew me to him. I was sure his aftershave smelled better than I did, and his professionally pressed suit looked a hundred times neater than my wrinkled tee-shirt.

He was gazing at me with his fresh-faced grin, "Hi, I found you; I wasn't sure I could remember exactly where your new place was. I was in the area, so I thought I'd stop and ask you to dinner and I thought I'd share my bed with you since it has sheets on it and yours probably doesn't. You can drive your truck home, so you have wheels." I peered down at him from my perch in the doorframe and told him I would accept, unless I got a better offer. I'd see him when he came to pick me up after work. I closed the front door thinking he seemed awfully pleased to have me in the same state and in his life.

I called Joey every couple of days, and we visited long distance. He would start out sounding cheery and then downslide into a griping and grievance syndrome. It sounded like his dad and his grandfather weren't getting along at the workshop. No doubt, Darth wanted to take over again and his father was not going to take the financial risk. It was difficult to know if Joey was genuinely happy or not, he was so vague in our discussions about himself. He said that he would be happiest if I would come back home to his dad.

Damn Darth, I knew he was promoting that idea. I paused for excuses and reality pushed back at me as dreadfulness washed over me. I flinched at the thought of living with Darth again. Just the idea made me feel as if I were permanently out of order. I did not wish to be stymied in an endless loop of further dysfunctional conduct and abuse while forced to live with a man that I'd learned to detest. I now understood that as an incredibly young woman I had deemed myself capable of changing Darth for the best, through the sheer force of my devotion. I'd even thought that it was my obligation to do so.

Silently, I shrouded my thoughts as I stood next to the kitchen counter talking to an expectant little boy who could not understand why I could not live with his father, so we could all be together again. For years I had evolved, functioning in constant turmoil. I'd adapted to concentrating on the mayhem instead of my own panic and pain. The additional burdens of struggling with inconsistencies strangled my growth as a human being and a parent but offered me a reprieve from my marital problems all at the same time. I'd developed a Savior complex for rising above difficulties while simultaneously attempting to rescue those around me. Now I was concerned that Joey was learning to live the same way. Darth was manipulating his son as a tool to get what he wanted from me. Joey thought that his dad loved him, but to Darth, Joey was just a toolboy and a willing player giving up his own needs to get what he thought his father needed. There was no way I could possibly explain that to an eleven-year-old.

I had previously explained to Joey that his father was not honest or fair with me and I could not continue to co-exist with a person who treated me in that manner. I would never tell Joey about the true ugliness of living with his father. I didn't think that was the right thing to tell a child. Every time that I talked to Joey on the phone, he pleaded with me to speak with his dad. I didn't want to visit with Darth, but Joey seemed to be impervious to my feelings so occasionally I would relent and hold the line while Darth came to the phone on my nickel.

Darth started telling me that he knew he could never find another me, and if I would just give him another chance, he would prove to me that I had wrongly judged him. In all honesty and fairness, I decided that I needed to level with Darth in a fashion that he would understand. In tortured triumph I told him point blank, "I've started a new life and even if you were the last man on earth, I'd never reconcile with you." He had the audacity to ask me why. "Because I could never trust you again, please, you really need to focus on your own life and not hold onto hope that I'll be in it." He didn't respond. He just hung up. I guess Darth could have an evening to think things through, and possibly the power of deductive reasoning would prevail.

The next day I picked up my business cards and contracts from the printers. My fresh new household was organized, and my employee was being trained so I went every afternoon and cleaned my horse's stall and rode in the arena. I told myself that life was good.

During daylight hours I'd scouted the local neighborhoods and decided where I would start knocking on doors. I was well practiced at the door knocking routine and people seemed delighted to have someone volunteer to climb up on their roof to inspect for damages. It was still extraordinarily difficult to walk down the sidewalks of family homes and see families happy together. I did it anyway. I ignored the heartfelt pangs of separation, regret and forlorn. Instead, I kept in mind that I had to be emotionally clever enough to remember hard learned truths and reality. I strove to be a professional with a service to sell. I was going to make a decent living and find my own way. I didn't need a husband to be happy. I put the bounce back into my step. In less than forty-five minutes of door knocking, I had acquired permission to do nine roof inspections for the following day.

The subsequent evening, I sold two jobs, which we could start the following week when my new employee finished his job training and arrived with the equipment. I'd been careful not to fill my garage full of unnecessary junk so that I had ample room to park the Mazda and the equipment trailer under cover.

There was abundant parking room out front around the cul-de-sac island with the deciduous trees, but I did not want any of the neighbors to complain about me running a business out of my home in a residential neighborhood. I also had two deposit checks in my hand. Not only did I have payroll to make, but I had a house payment and all the utilities, plus I had to purchase chemicals for the roof preserving and they were shockingly expensive.

I usually quit knocking on homeowner's doors after about eight thirty in the evening, as I did not want to annoy anyone. When I drove home, I decided it wasn't too late to phone Joey. The telephone did not even ring, but there was an answer. The pre-recorded operator's voice said the line was disconnected. I couldn't believe it. I had not planned or prepared for this. I felt as if my insides had been rearranged.

The pre-recorded message gave no forwarding number and because I could not trust Joey not to give his dad my new home number, the only way Joey could contact me was to phone my parents. That is what would happen. Joey would reach me through my parents. He was a smart creative kid. I knew he would find a way to phone my parents.

As the days rolled into weeks with no word or message from Joey, I knew that I would have to face the difficult reality. There would probably be no word. I'd checked, and Darth was no longer working for his father at our old place of business. Worrying about Joey became a mainstay in my mind. I began to repeatedly wonder if he was in school or if he had enough to eat. I gave serious consideration to hiring a private detective. I knew that I couldn't afford one, but if I could hire a detective on credit, perhaps he would find my missing child. Grappling with my feelings I felt a growing pressure of crushing magnitude. After contemplating the hired private investigator, I finally decided that it wouldn't work. If an investigator found Joey what good would it do?

I could bring him home again, kicking and screaming. I'd rescued him from his father's plans before and he'd never forgiven me. If I put all logic aside and did what I thought was best for my son, then what? The real sticky-wicket was he'd tell his father where we lived again. I tried to get my mind wrapped around the idea that if Joey stayed with his father long enough, the best thing might happen. Joey would decide of his own volition that he would rather be with his ordinary mom than his dysfunctional father. The only way I could do this was to let time run its course. I just didn't feel right about any of my options.

I decided to recognize that the answer could eventually be what I didn't want to even imagine, that Joey would simply want to remain with his father. Joey couldn't have possibly known that kids who grow up or are raised in alcoholic homes are the same children who are most likely to develop alcoholism. I'm positive he believed that it would never happen to him, because he knew better. I doubted that Darth was holding Joey in a hostage type of situation and unleashing terrorist tactics to scare him into submission, at least no physical tactics, just the mental ones. On the contrary I suspected that Joey had become the parent and felt that he was obligated to look after his father. Perhaps Darth spoiled and bribed Joey to buy his affections. Possibly Joey was being mentally corrupted as Darth taught him how to manipulate and con people in illegal matters. I certainly had never thought about Joey being kidnapped after his father had undertaken treatment.

Was Joey the companion that he thought his father wanted? Joey's father was probably his hero, and in a demented way Darth was using him as an excuse. My guess was that Darth was using a custody issue as an opportunity to re-victimize me. It seemed logical that court fights, custody battles, and kidnapping could extend my abuse beyond the divorce, and miles of separation.

I mailed letters and packages of items I thought Joey might like. I had a post office address from the shop secretary, and I assumed that if it wasn't current, perhaps by chance, my letters would be forwarded, and Joey would receive them. After several months of no response I decided Joey wasn't coming back for a long time, maybe never, so for economical reasons I ran a "roommate wanted" ad and leased out the third bedroom that I had saved for him.

CHAPTER FORTY-TWO

My business venture was working out. I was keeping Vonnie and my one-man crew going five days a week and then some. I'd tried hiring additional sales staff, so I could grow my company, but I couldn't find sales reps that were sufficiently motivated who could truly sell. If they did close a contract, it was usually an underbid on the job, so I finally opted to be the single-handed sales team. It kept the bills paid and generated enough profit that paying board on my horse was affordable. Housing two roommates, one in each hallway bedroom, paid for better than half of my house payment. The roommate experience could be very inconvenient and sometimes intolerable, but not as unpleasant as living with Darth had been. I certainly would have preferred my home to myself without other parties coming and going, encroaching on my privacy, and leaving dirty dishes in the sink, but I needed the additional income.

Rod and I saw each other once during midweek and then we spent Friday evenings through Sunday together. Neither one of us could get enough of each another. We experienced constant detonations of mutual desire igniting on a regular basis. We both baked in the sun during our weekend outings on the boat. There were two cushioned benches on the upper tier, and I'd claimed one as my private sunning lounge. It was not private, because it opened to the vastness of the hovering sky. Anyone peering down from a bigger boat had a bird's eye view. We had the entire Bay Area to ourselves until a yacht or freighter passed, at which time Rod would reach for his opened newspaper and give it a toss to cover my bare chest.

Gretchen sent me a magazine article that she had clipped about women marrying older men. Rod was mature on many levels. His legal practice was secure and successfully advanced which gave him the liberty to spend time with his kids and me. I told Gretchen that no matter how old I was, Rod would always have more wrinkles than I did. I considered that a bonus. Before all of Rod's hair could turn grey, we flew to Hawaii for five days. PDA was a new term that Rod was teaching me, and I'd been a willing student of "public display of affection". We practiced everywhere we went.

Although Rod understood many of the residual feelings that I struggled with from my divorce, I don't think that he could fully comprehend what an intimidating cocky jerk Darth had been. There were many things that I didn't explain to Rod about Darth because I saw no point in dredging it up, though I had the impression that Rod thought Joey was safe from harm's way with his father. Rod felt that I should give them a little time and they would eventually turn up as if they'd just returned from a male bonding sabbatical. I knew better, but Rod thought that I should give Darth a break and some credit in the fatherhood department.

Instead of constantly worrying about Joey, I tried to focus on Rod's annual family vacation. I was contemplating how Rod and I had been an exclusive couple for a year. I had never been in a relationship as fantastic as this one and I was excited about the vacation with the rest of the family. Gretchen would be hauling her own horse this time and I would take my horse along with Rod's daughter's steed. Her 4-H leaders claimed that he could not be loaded into a trailer. I assured Rod that I could load her horse.

Then four weeks prior to the vacation departure, Rod had phoned me on a Friday night. I was expecting him in the next hour to attend our regular country western dancing lesson. He told me he wouldn't be picking me up. He needed time to think. I said I understood. I didn't understand a thing other than Rod was backing off. I wondered if my mettle was being tested.

Two weeks passed, and I had not heard a peep from Rod. I imagined him concealed in his man-cave. Exactly what was he doing in there, I didn't know. I was tired of the psychologically exhaustive contemplation, so I went to work. In addition to selling jobs and doing inspections, I started doing a lot of the roof repairs, I always did this in the heat of the day, and it is always the hottest on top of a roof. I was trying to purge suffering from my system through sweating and zealously swinging a hammer. I climbed my ladder with huge bundles of cedar shakes on one shoulder and my carpenter's belt fastened around my waist. With every hammer strike, I tried to drive my fears away as I rebuked myself for wanting the sensations that came with being in love.

By the third week, my new horse trailer had arrived at the dealership. I was ready for our vacation, but I hadn't heard a single word from Rod. I didn't know if his daughter was planning on me hauling her horse or if I was even still invited. All of us were supposed to leave that Friday morning so on Tuesday night of the same week I decided to arrive unannounced at Rod's house. With flip-flops in my stomach, I was determined to talk to him face to face.

He was somewhat surprised but seemed delighted to see me. He hadn't expected a visitor knocking on his door at nine o'clock in the evening. Just watching him I realized I'd missed him even more than I thought I had. Before I imploded, I cut right to the chase and told him, "I don't know what to plan for this weeks' vacation." "Well, I'd intended to call you tomorrow, so we could talk."

Rod said his fourteen-year-old daughter Sadie, had been excited about getting to take her horse and he was hoping that I would still go on vacation with him, and his kids and we could all caravan down together. Rod rationalized that he had done a lot of thinking about the two of us, but he still didn't know what he thought. I should have recognized this as a handy stall tactic regarding commitment on his part. However, I was willing to readily accept his admittance of his desire for us to remain a couple and go on holiday together with his family. I told him I was glad he wanted to remain an item because I did too, and I'd be on my way. It was a long drive home and I'd see him in a couple of days. I started to move toward the kitchen door as Rod wheeled around to my side of the table and asked me not to go. He tenderly took hold of one arm and then the other; he kissed me as if he had missed me a lot. I really loved this man. The passion was always so intense, just simmering below the surface where I could slurp up every drop.

In exchange for feelings of intense passion, I had deliberately forgotten all about one of the latest passages that I read in my book about Women Who Love Too Much. The text explained two different types of love; a partnership based on love where two caring people are deeply committed, where the depth of the love is measured by the mutual trust and respect they feel toward each other, where each individual exhibits a willingness to look honestly at oneself in order to promote the growth of the relationship and the deepening of intimacy, an association with real love, where shared feelings consist of serenity, security, devotion, understanding, companionship, mutual support, and comfort.

The other type of love described was all consuming, desperate yearning for the beloved, who is perceived as different, mysterious, and elusive. The depth of love is measured by the intensity of obsession with the loved one, where often there are great obstacles to be overcome, representing an element of suffering in true love by enduring pain and hardship for the sake of the relationship leaving you with feelings of excitement, rapture, drama, anxiety, tension, mystery, and yearning. To continue my relationship with

Rod I was willing to feel frustrated and anxious thinking that it would ultimately contribute to a stable and reliable relationship. I thought our passion for one another would eventually lead me to what I really wanted, a stabilized commitment full of security and safety.

I should have gone back to my book and re-read this paragraph. "When we are involved with a man who is not so much of a challenge, the sexual dimension may also lack fire and passion. Because we are not in an almost constant state of excitement over him, and because sex isn't used to prove something, we may find an easier, more relaxed relationship to be somewhat tame. Compared to the tempestuous styles of relating that we've known, this tamer kind of experience only seems to verify for us that tension, struggle, heartache, and drama truly do equal real love."

Cemented in emotional mayhem, I arrived on a brilliant pre-fall summer day. I'd conveniently left my man-junkie book at home and packed my suitcase. At Rod's we loaded our ten speeds onto the bike rack on the back of his car and I followed him to his ex-wife's house, pulling my horse trailer. I would have appreciated a lot of Rod's qualities that I suspected the "ex" viewed as weaknesses. I supposed that I had changed a lot of my attitudes about what made up a real man. Boasting, bragging, and bullying were no longer characteristics that I viewed as admirable. My "man pendulum" had swung a long way in the opposite direction of where it had been.

While Rod was showing me the barn, Sadie was catching her quarter horse gelding. I could see that what he made up for with a bigger belly he lacked in horse etiquette. I'd loaded other horses that people claimed wouldn't load. Usually they were just spoiled, and they had gotten away with not having to get in the trailer. When I loaded my horse, I tossed the lead rope over his neck and stepped back while he calmly addled up and into the stall space. My trailer walls and partition were extra safe with lots of rubber padding and tempting grain lay in a mound on the manger shelf.

I recognized human nature well enough to know that I should patiently let Sadie and all her family members attempt to load her horse, if they opted to. When they were finished making my job even more difficult, I would load him. Sadie coaxed him with carrots, her brother pulled on the lead-rope as hard as he could with the ex-wife pushing from behind. Then Rod yanked on the halter and whacked him a good one with the end of the rope. I tolerantly waited, while the gelding got away with every horse trick in the book. He wasn't afraid. He was just bigger than everybody else and he knew how to use his weight. I had always been certain that my brain was bigger than a horse's brain, even though the horse outweighed me by over a thousand pounds.

When Sadie's horse had convinced everyone that it was impossible to load him, they all gave up. I said, "OK" and pulled the syringe with a needle out of my jeans pocket. I'd picked it up at the vet's the previous day. It was a few cc's of Acepromazine, a nifty horse tranquilizer to take the edge off any physical fight. While I administered the inner muscle injection, I explained what it was and how it would work and that it would take a few minutes to kick into his system.

Her gelding was having a siesta in the sun tied to the side of the trailer. His head hung a little low and his eyes were barely closed. He wasn't drooling, so I knew I hadn't overdosed him. Perfect, he'd wake up enough when I told him to get into the trailer. I brought my twenty-inch stud chain and properly ran it through the halter rings, adjusting it under his chin so I could yank and release as a reminder of who was boss.

He walked nonchalantly beside me up to the back of the trailer. I didn't look back at him or hesitate. I expected him to walk right in beside me.

He stuck his head and neck into the stall opening beside my horse and stopped with all four feet planted squarely on the ground and grunted. I gave a firm yank on the chain, and he took a few steps backward. That backward step earned him a harder yank and then release on the shank. He took one step forward and up, right into the trailer where he merrily munched on his crimped oats.

CHAPTER FORTY-THREE

It was a harmonious holiday road trip. Sadie did not seem to have much to say, but I had found that was typical of her. I wondered what she had thought of her father's other girlfriends over the past five years. She had been nine years old when her parents divorced, the same age Joey had been. Then I contemplated what Joey thought of his father's girlfriends or the way his dad conducted himself in general. My wish for Joey was for him to grow up with sufficient self-worth and respect for significant females that he would eventually encounter throughout his life. I worried about how he was all the time.

At a fueling point Sadie announced, she wanted to ride with her seventeen-year-old brother, so Rod switched vehicles to travel with me. Watching them through the back windshield, I noticed they appeared young and blameless. The sunroof was wide open letting streaks of sunlight dapple Sadie's blonde hair. I could hear the radio blaring music only teenagers could commune with. I wished Joey were one of them.

That evening at Gretchen's, we all gathered around the backyard swimming pool and listened to the kids' squabble. We were lounging in the recently purchased patio furniture from my previous backyard and marriage. There hadn't been enough room in the U-haul truck when I'd moved, so I'd asked Gretchen to pick up the patio furniture and table and take it to her house. I felt as if I'd been catapulted into a fantasy charade sitting in furniture from my past married life, in another family's backyard with a boyfriend holding my hand.

After downing a quick bowl of Cheerios, Sadie and I were up in the early morning headed to the boarding barn to load our geldings. Just as I'd predicted, her horse got right back into the trailer that morning with no hesitation. We were all in high spirits for the last leg of our trip. I scrolled forward in my mind already relishing the week to come. Arriving at our destination, in northern California Gretchen and I went straight to work bedding our equine's stalls, rationing feed and filling water buckets. I noticed that Sadie was content to let her aunt and me do all the work for her horse.

After dinner on the deck, the men did the dishes and Uncle Craig appointed sleeping quarters to all the adults and children. Rod informed me that there was no way he could sleep with me with his parents present in the house. I found his morals and conscience amusing. The following night we argued. It started out as regular discussion and turned into a commitment crisis with me wanting us to be together all the time. We'd spent a lot of quality time together over the last year and I was ready for an assurance of where our relationship was headed. The source of my frustration and fear was that Rod had previously said he would never make the commitment to remarry again. I reminded myself that he had told me this initially and I had hoped that in time, this would change about him.

Not having the wisdom or strength I needed, I had not been capable of admitting to myself that in some ways I only knew how to be with a man, if he needed me. I was refusing to accept who Rod really was, just like I had denied who Darth was for many years. In the back of my mind, I was convinced that both would be much happier, if they would just allow me to show them how. Possibly, I was searching for an insurance policy against pain and my perception of full coverage was having a man bound to me through need, so I could teach him how to overcome himself, if he would just cooperate.

Since his ex-wife had deeply hurt him, Rod promised himself that he would never be in that vulnerable position again. One of the side effects that I tried to explain to Rod was that his ex-wife didn't respect him. He seemed astounded and insisted that she had indeed respected him. I persisted that she did not respect him, or she never would have cheated on him repeatedly, without remorse. I tried to implant in Rod that cheating did not exist in the fabric of my moral fiber.

Things were a bit taught and unresolved between us for the next few days, but we had a lot of fun bicycling together into the fast-fading light and solitude of the darkening desert. I dismissed some of my misgivings, thinking that perhaps the taught-ness was just my imagination or insecurities, or whatever else was wrong with me. We stopped on top of a small knoll and Rod told me I was the most incredible woman he had ever known.

Through my prism our relationship was full of promise. I knew a commitment would liberate my future happiness. I was worrying about the future wishing that I could simply let the moment in the present be enough. Because I still wasn't strong enough within myself, I wanted guaranteed relationship security. I wasn't ready to admit there were no such guarantees in life, no matter who I was in love with.

Early the next morning Rod had helped me hitch the horse trailer and load up my tack. As usual, Sadie had made herself scarce when it came to doing barn chores. She was sweet in her appearance, a blue-eyed blonde that resembled her mother, and she was also very spoiled. We were loaded up, ready to depart before Gretchen hitched her rig. All of us said our goodbyes as our group would drive the homebound trip straight through. Sadie wanted to travel with me again so both Rod and his son drove down the dirt road kicking up dust in front of us.

Once we had driven beyond the timeshare neighborhood, we picked up the narrow-paved road that wound down and around the mountain side leading us to the freeway. We had to slow to a crawl for a road construction crew. The road crew had just finished digging a ditch across both lanes of pavement. Always cautious of my horse's well being, I slowed down to a snail's pace to cross over into the one lane with a dip and bump in the ditch line. When the road construction was behind us, and we'd reached the bottom of the next ascending hill I began to accelerate. Rod and his son had already disappeared over the top of the rise.

Midway up the long slope, I had picked up speed when the truck shuddered. It felt as if the back end had been grabbed by the bumper, yanked hard and then immediately released as the vehicle lurched forward. Before my brain could assimilate the problem, I heard a loud clank and thunking noise. Glancing up into my rearview mirror, to my horror and astonishment I couldn't see my horse trailer. Turning to look over my right shoulder I could see it descending backward of its own accord down the hill. The trailer was no longer hitched to the truck, and neither were the hefty safety chains. As the trailer continued its descent, it picked up speed as it was gradually veering left toward the oncoming lane of traffic and the craggy shoulder. The graveled edge of the road disappeared off into a steep stony ravine with a six-hundred-foot drop straight off the mountain side.

Neither horse would survive such a crash. My horse was all I had left in the world. I loved him as if he were a human. He was better than most humans and he trusted me every time he loaded into the trailer. I didn't waste time stopping the truck. I slammed the automatic transmission directly into park and jammed on the emergency break while the truck was still moving uphill. I was out of the vehicle running down the pavement chasing the horse trailer as if I could catch it like Wonder

Woman. Adrenaline coursed through my body like rocket fuel. I felt my feet intermittently slapping the pavement, and my legs felt like churning pistons. My heart pumped faster.

The trailer was still rolling backward and swerving toward the death-threatening cliff. It started to careen sharper and fortunately it was beginning to slow. The automatic electric brakes had locked on, the tandem tires were laying thick rubber tread marks, but they were still rolling. I could hear the blackened tires screeching and I was close enough to smell the stink of burning rubber. I raced over the skid marks in my pursuit. Just as I reached the trailer it lolled to a complete halt right next to several of the men in the road construction crew. As I stopped with my sides heaving beside the trailer, half of it was positioned on the graveled shoulder, beside the life-threatening edge.

Thanking God, I kept moving since I did not know how long the brakes would hold. A sturdily built crewman with a bull neck and beer belly asked me what he should do. I knew there might not be time to tell him. Puffing air, I told him to get the hell out of my way. I bent down and lifted a hefty egg shaped medium sized boulder. I knew under normal circumstances I would never have been able to heave it. I planted it firmly under the back tire on the road's shoulder.

If Sadie lost her horse, I thought she would get over it. I was not going to lose mine. The tongue and hitch end of the trailer was sticking straight up in the air because the trailer was tilted downhill on the slope. I needed it to stay that way until I got the horses out. Backing my horse out, I handed him directly to the crewmen in the plaid shirt and suspenders who'd offered help. I ran to the other side of the trailer and unloaded Sadie's horse. By that time Sadie was at the resting spot and she could hold onto her own horse. She was panting and looked pale.

Going back to my horse I took charge of his lead line and the road crew clapped and cheered. I thought I was going to pass out from the possibility of what could have happened. I'd purchased a new trailer to keep my horse safe and it had come unhitched. I didn't know how that could have happened. I scanned the hillside and saw my truck had stayed where I'd thrown it into park. It was still running, and both the doors were wide open. It looked like a bulky square bird, flapping its wings for flight.

Just cresting the hill was Rod's car. It was coming toward us down the slope. Both the passengers could see what had just happened. I walked my horse down the pavement to see if he was possibly limping while the road crew helped Rod connect the trailer hitch and tied the newly designed coupling clamp which had malfunctioned, down with baling twine. We reloaded the horses. I was amazed when even Sadie's horse got back in the trailer like a trooper. Rod looked at me and said some of the color had returned to my face, but he thought maybe he should drive.

CHAPTER FORTY-FOUR

Both of our vehicles pulled into a bumpy parking lot next to a local small-town mini mart where we stopped to quench our thirst. Rechecking the coupling on the hitch we looked up in time to see Gretchen merrily waving as she pulled by in her rig. We continued traveling for several hours and I slept as we went. Silently I was trying to decipher if I was more distraught over the near fatal accident or the fact that Rod and I were going home to two separate households.

I needed to face my own reservations about what would happen to our relationship if I remained convinced, we should unite in a permanent commitment. I wanted to work on eliminating my own insecurities, rather than trying to manipulate Rod, but I was positive that if I stopped trying to help him commit, he would simply disappear into another realm. I'd repeatedly convinced myself that with commitment Rod would not withdraw emotionally to protect himself. I wish that I could have appreciated Rod enough to allow the struggle to be his, not mine. I did not fully comprehend that it was best to let Rod be what he wanted, and if I could not live with that, I should move on.

We arrived and unloaded teenage offspring, suitcases, bicycles and one penny-colored, fat horse. I would continue with my favorite four-legged friend. Rod went to his house on the lake near the airport. As hard as I tried, I couldn't completely understand his refusal to get past his unwillingness to share in mutual trust. Loving each other was not the issue because I believed that we did. If I pushed the commitment topic, he ran in evasion leaving me with a feeling of imposing need.

I'd promised him that I would never hurt him. He said that he believed that I wouldn't hurt him intentionally. I assumed that meant that there were hundreds of ways I could hurt him unintentionally and we both knew that no one could possibly guarantee otherwise. I wanted us to do the best we could and make an intelligent leap of faith and commit.

The following weekend was my birthday. We drove to a lodge in the mountains to have dinner and feed colored M&M's to the chipmunks. We meandered about the hiking trails, holding hands, and admiring the commandingly vivid view. It had been a magnificent lazy day when we returned to Rod's place on the soundless, smooth lake. He ceremoniously presented me with a birthday card which made a ridiculous dumb joke which he had simply signed, "Love you, Rod". Then he handed me a secondary card which was preprinted with a warm and sweet sentiment on which he had signed, "Love you more, Rod". I knew that he did. I knew this man really did genuinely love me, he'd said so a hundred times, even after he'd explained that he had promised himself he would never use those words with a woman again.

The next day was Monday morning, a workday for both of us necessitating my drive thirty exits up the freeway to my house. I was so happy and dejected all at the same time. Whenever I left Rod at his house I felt as if I had been unplugged from life. I deliberated about how I had thought that I knew all the black and white answers when I was younger. Now I privately claimed to know nothing at all.

The following weekend directly coming forth with his thoughts he told me that he knew that I wanted a commitment from him. He didn't seem to think that I understood that he was very committed to me. I reticently admitted that in many ways he was very committed to our relationship and that was one of the many things that endeared him to me. Then he totally stunned me, I had not expected this question. "Would you live with me?" Perhaps living together was a steppingstone that he needed, to wiggle his toes in the water before he plunged into the deep dive. I did not think I should back pedal. I believed in compromises, but not this one. I didn't want to just live with him. I thought he needed to understand how serious I was when I told him, "I don't know if I can just live with you?" Trying to quell my panic attack, I thought about how my mother would disapprove, which seemed absurd to me because she would have disapproved of our sexually intimate relationship anyway. Attempting to repel distress, even though Rod was attempting a partial commitment, I bumbled over my words, trying to be honest, but creating a catastrophe and told Rod I did not think that living together was what I wanted.

To my surprise, he seemed stymied. I'd never seen him react in this way. Before I could express anything further, Rod told me he wanted me to think about it and if living together didn't work for me that would be all right. We could keep our relationship intact like it was. Picking up his car keys he started to walk toward the front door. I grimaced because I didn't want him to go. I needed to discuss this decision some more.

He turned in the hallway as I followed him to the door and told me, "You can think about it all week, but you need to let me know your decision by the weekend," and he left. The last and final statement landed me somewhere between shock, disbelief and being really perturbed at him. Who did he think he was? He couldn't just give me orders and candidly walk out the door. In my arsenal of defensive decisions, I bolstered my feelings by remembering that Rod was the person who handily disappeared into his man-cave without notice whenever he felt like it.

My wavering emotions drove me nuts all week. I worked as hard as I could, but long hours offered no reprieve. The grueling work week came to pass, and Rod's imposed time limit was up. I knew that he expected to hear from me, and I intentionally did not call. I wasn't going to let him force me into a time allotment I had not agreed to. By design I let the weekend pass and I missed him so terribly I could hardly stand myself. I'd already predetermined that I wasn't going to phone him. Just two more days to touchdown Tuesday, and then I would talk to him.

Posturing my potential conversation, I waited until our usual nine o'clock phone session hour and I dialed his number. The only answer was from his voice on the machine. It sat in his bedroom on top of his antique walnut dresser. I thought he was there laying in bed reading while he ignored me. Despondency slithered down my spine and seeped into my feelings. The impact was devastating. If he were gone, he'd be home in the next hour or so from the gym and he'd return my call, but he never did, not even later in the week when I left another message. I began to feel that I'd made an enormous mistake. I also felt that he was out of line. Perhaps he was just getting even by forcing me to wait. There'd been slight situations in the past where I had suspected that he liked to get even. I'd decided to be patient through the next weekend, that maybe he'd gone out of town with his kids.

Another week passed by as I slogged through time and there was never a call. Why give up too soon? We really needed to talk. I'd try again. This time I drove down late at night, and he was there. He motioned me through the backdoor, with a quick glance about the room I noticed that the framed photo of me that sat in the windowsill was missing. So that was it. He had mentally disposed of us.

He insisted that I should go. When I reached the garage steps, he was behind me as he flipped on the overhead light. If he wanted me to go, I didn't understand why he was following me? I turned to face him in front of my truck and started to speak. He shushed me as he deliberately closed off all potential for communication and understanding. There were huge alienating tears in both of his eyes that spilled over the rims and rolled down his cheeks. Perhaps this was not my problem? I felt that I should have been allowed to verbalize my feelings and the topic should have been open for discussion. I didn't know what the crying was supposed to tell me.

I hoped that the tears represented the depth of loving feelings that he held for me, but I was probably wrong. I had learned that life is not as perfect as I wanted it to be. I thought that commitment required energy and hard work. Possibly it was just easier to blame the other person for our own shortcomings. I tried to speak into the forced silence, and he told me to leave. When I hesitated, he turned and left the garage without saying a single word. I was stunned, so this is how we would end up. All the love I felt was unraveling before me. I pondered if I should have allowed Rod to be who he was, not expecting him to change to commit to me, and then simply respected his feelings enough to have walked away of my own accord.

CHAPTER FORTY-FIVE

Aside from Rod, and his family, the only other person I knew within state boundaries was Vonnie, the gym-buffed roommate, and that was not working out so well. I'd hoped that she would be capable of continuing to sell roof jobs, but her closing abilities weren't consistent. She had still never paid me the rent monies she owed from our Arizona tenancy, so I had chosen to just let it slide. Most of the time she did pay her rent for the bedroom at the end of the hall in my small rambler.

She was entitled to her own privacy, but I had been privy to different parts of conversations she held with our other roommate. Vonnie was guilty of backstabbing, and she had begun to blatantly break the house rules that all of us had agreed to honor. Her attitude was deteriorating to the point that she no longer just quibbled behind my back. She'd begun to confront me in physical ways where she could subtly push her weight around and she had more weight to push around than I did. I'd contemplated for several weeks about how I could ask her to move out and I didn't think asking would work.

Upon returning from the horse barn late one evening, I intentionally parked in the street knowing Vonnie would pull into my parking slot in front of the garage when she came home from partying. Early the next morning while Vonnie was sleeping off whatever she'd taken the night before, I abruptly woke her explaining that she needed to get up and move her vehicle. I told her I'd donated the old sofa I'd moved into the garage to Goodwill and their donations pick-up truck would be arriving shortly. She rolled over mumbling, and I suggested that I could move her truck out of the way if she would give me her keys. She grumbled and pointed to the top of her dresser. Bingo, now I was in possession of her house key that fit the deadbolt in my front door. I quickly removed it from Vonnie's key ring and with sneaky bravery, buried it in the potted plant near the patio deck.

I pounded as loudly as possible on Vonnie's bedroom door. She was now very cranky but not as ornery as she was going to be. I told her to get up and move out. I knew she had friends she could stay with, or she could return home to live with her parents, the next state over. I told her that I would no longer ignore her insubordinate defiance about house rules and her attitude in general. Then I mentioned that I knew she had been using drugs and I shouldn't have to tell her that I had zero tolerance for users. She admitted that my assumption was correct while she marched down the hall in protest slamming doors. She loaded her mattress into her truck and left.

Two weeks prior to booting Vonnie, I had replaced the guy I'd trained to pressure clean roofs because he said his back was bothering him and he wanted to collect workmen's compensation. Completing the required state paperwork, I learned that he had a history of cocaine use. Was there no end to weak-minded people bent on mucking up everything or was I just another addict's magnet?

Thinking that I needed to hear a voice I could rely on, preferably male, I phoned my brother. I only phoned him sporadically. I understood that he was busy with his own family. I'd always wanted to have a more in-depth relationship with him. Like anyone, he had his faults but at least he did not drink or do drugs. Late that evening he answered when his phone rang. We spoke briefly about my roofing business, and I inquired about my sister-in-law, nieces, and nephew. I wanted my brother to give his permission to let his wife come and visit me for a few days.

Pensively, I claimed that I wished we could spend some time together. He rolled right into his reasons of business and busyness, and I explained to him that he was really all the family that I had access to. Mom and Dad were in a campground in Nevada with no phone for the winter. I had absolutely no idea where Joey was or when I would ever hear from him. I was my brother's only sibling.

He replied with a concept I'd never thought about, "All the females in the world are Biblically my sisters." I felt the verbal smack. That simple sentence had reduced me to being less important to him than all the other women in the world. Yielding my brother, a multitude of sisters that he did not have time for, my only defense was spun from my mouth about how I was his only sister from the same mother. He didn't seem to be affected by that fact.

I continued to spend my free time on the weekends with my trusty steed. While riding, I frequently pondered my solitude and sadness over the loss of my home life and family. In my heart I knew that the feelings of loss I constantly experienced were still preferable to living as a captive with an emotional terrorist. Brooding over thoughts of being held prisoner in a marriage where I felt that I could not leave or protect my family, I knew I couldn't stay and protect myself. I had been traumatized in a variety of ways, yet I had promised myself that I was going to create a new healthy life and I refused to turn back to the familiar securities that I thought the terrorist could offer. Hollowed out and empty, I felt as if I were intentionally living disengaged emotionally.

Knocking on locally owned housing and climbing onto shake roofs was not my preferred career choice. I'd taken the liberty to phone one of my brother's friends. I knew this guy was expanding and growing his business territory and I thought he might be interested in purchasing my cleaning equipment. It turns out he was also interested in purchasing my self-made company in its entirety including all contracts for cleaning with repairs and the remaining balance of contracts still waiting for the preservation chemicals. This would buy me time to complete the state-required real estate licensing program and get to work.

Clocking my hours for the state examination was excruciatingly tedious. I caught myself nodding off a few times at each class, which was better than thinking about Rod. I thoroughly missed him. I could still see, smell, and feel him. I couldn't begin to imagine how I was ever going to get completely over him. As much as I loved him, I gave serious contemplation to the idea that for the long haul, my life would have been less painful without ever knowing him. Ever since I could remember all I had wanted from life, besides a horse, was to be loved and to have someone to love back.

As a previously abused married woman, I had surrendered most hopes. With resignation to my abusive marriage, I was unconsciously dosing my own pain during the years that I stayed. Darth had frequently intimidated me into one type of submission or another. One of his favorite tools for control had been isolation. When he manipulated me away from contact with friends, family and even the outside world, I had become even more dependent upon my relationship with him. My forbidden outside social resources deprived me of inner strength to resist his controlling maneuvers that were intended to alienate me. I couldn't imagine feeling more alone.

CHAPTER FORTY-SIX

While preparing for the Real Estate licensing test, I had been clocking additional hours that would eventually be required over the next two-year period to keep my license current. I was eager for all the real estate language and education I could consume.

Working arduously seven days a week with my formulated strategies, I succeeded in fatiguing myself. There was no allowable time to power down and submit to rest. I was in overdrive pushing myself toward success and a paycheck.

Then I succeeded in taking my first listing my third week in business. That weekend I proudly held my first open house for which I had also taken classes. With my first listing in the first hour of my first open house I sold my first home to my first buyer. I didn't benefit from the knowledge and wisdom of working with a seasoned listing agent because I was inexperienced and also the listing agent.

Once I had effectively muddled my way through the twenty-page contract and traveled back and forth between negotiations, I closed the deal. This was a word I had been pointedly instructed to never use because it made me sound like a used car salesman. I swayed with relief when all signatures were properly applied to each dotted line. I had just earned two commissions which was a most prudent accomplishment because my house payment was due the first of the month, although I learned not to call them house payments. Realtors properly refer to them as the monthly investment installments.

Shot in the arm with success, I was not to be subdued. The following month I made agent of the month for top producers and the month after that I won the listing contest the broker promoted in the office of thirty plus agents. This was good for my pocketbook but tended to distance me from other new licensees. It did not matter because I was working so hard, I didn't have time to worry about it. The fear of having no money drove my motivation and the pleasure of success inspired me onward. Busy hands and a busy mind afforded less time for me to lament over Rod. I hung on my horse's neck a lot and found his muzzle to be even more kissable than it was.

Missing and worrying about Joey was another burden. I berated myself for not realizing that he had been in cahoots with his father as a small child. Did I know where Joey was? Did I know what he was doing? Did I know anything at all? Sometimes, my disbelief was still just beginning to set in. I couldn't possibly fathom what lay dormant for the future. I worried that his daily experiences with Darth were not advancing Joey's paramount interests.

For me to allow total despair over him, was an abandonment of my hope, so I tried to believe in the power of destiny as I wrote him letters and sent him packages but didn't ever receive a response. I did send a note to Rod. Months had passed, and I was feeling melancholy and ambivalent. I made up my mind that I owed Rod some clarification.

I was reading about men who are good for you and men who are bad for you and how to recognize the difference. In my simplistic handwritten note, I told Rod the truth, that most of the time I really did not know what to think, say or do. I told him I was sorry that I'd lost the relationship with him and that I had probably been reading too many self-help books. I sincerely wished him well and expressed my hopes that his life was the way he wanted it to be.

I rationally sought a response for the first few weeks, I regularly checked my post office box for an envelope with Rod's handwriting. After being repeatedly disappointed, I forgot about it most of the time. At least I wasn't checking the box frequently. I didn't have that kind of time to waste.

Approximately four weeks after my message of confession and regret, I received exactly what I had given up on, Rod's response. He had written a casual, brief update of what he'd been busy doing. He mentioned remodeling his office and the hard to dock, old wooden boat. In his last sentence he wanted to know if I would like to go out for a boat ride. (Yeah, I could be there with bells on).

I phoned and got the black voice box setting on top of his dresser. Later that evening I received a return phone call. Weird and wonderful feelings ebbed with my pulse when I heard his voice. I had always thought of it as secure and sexy and now I worried about what I was getting myself into. The singular feeling that I knew beyond doubt was how much I had missed that voice and the man that went with it. Conversation was somewhat awkward, yet so familiar. He kept the communication brief and to the point and set a date for our reunion on the recently remodeled, seaworthy vessel.

The logical compartment of my besotted brain wanted to focus on all the hazards I could encounter, re-encountering Rod. My female feelings wanted to run rampant without reason. Being female, I chose to ignore the logical thoughts. Still, I knew that history generally repeats itself and when cornered, confused, or feeling guilty, Rod would probably retreat. I would have been completely daft and dense not to know his patterns. Yet, I was unbelievably willing to try again. He might change, it could happen.

For a month, we dated. Some dates and conversations were regal and reserved. In other instances, our relationship felt as if we had been comfortable together without interruption through all time. I noticed that Rod would frequently refer to us, as we, and make some sort of small future proposal. One evening I realized that he had pre-set the radio station in his car to all the country stations I had sung along with the previous year. He seemed to reach out to me on intermittent levels and hold himself at a distance all at the same time. I couldn't begin to comprehend all of it, so I just went with the flow.

After my office Christmas party, we had driven to my house and sat on my sofa drinking carbonated apple juice from plastic stemware in front of a red foiled poinsettia, which served handsomely as my Christmas tree. The setting was serene and pleasurable until Rod made a comment I had not been expecting. He straight forwardly informed me that I was ripe for the picking. "What?" I said, simultaneously choking and swallowing carbonated fumes through my nose. He chuckled, "You know, you're like a matured berry, ripe and ready to be plucked from the vine. Some lucky guy should nab you and commit."

Was Rod talking about himself or some other guy? I was now just as confused as ever and tried to accept his comment as a compliment while my brain froze, and my heart palpated. I didn't know what to say. I felt as stupid as a stump. I had not planned for this conversation. As I was emotionally gasping, Rod presented me with a beautiful gold bracelet. I exhaled that it was beautiful and feminine yet appeared strong and durable in its workmanship. Rod said, "Yeah, kinda like you, beautiful and strong."

I did not hear from him again that week or the following week until the late end of a difficult day when the phone rang. I had been agonizing over whether he would phone. He was calling to let me know that he needed time to think. He was taking his daughter on a cruise to a warm beach with sparkling sand dunes and guided tours. I dreaded that the excursion across salty waters, and lolling waves wasn't going to change a thing. But, Rod was going to decide our destiny on his vacationing cruise. He informed me, "I'm either going to fish or cut bait." Being an intelligent girl, I told him, "I understand the meaning of, "cut bait", but I'm not exactly sure what "fish" means."

A new verbal experience for Rod, he stuttered and stammered his tongue around in his mouth until he could actually say the big "M" word, "You know, Mmmarriage. I'm going to decide if I should marry you." He went off to his man-cave cruise to make a monumental decision about me, without me. Trying to decipherer and digest where he was coming from, I opened my motor mouth. My overactive oral cavity might frequently discharge defiant thoughts, but it generally spoke the truth. "So, you've got a decision to make about us, but what do I get to say about it?" With that exclamation, Rod countered that he would call me when he returned from the decision-making voyage, and he hung up.

For a mini-millimeter, nano-second, I was elated, but I knew I had re-read it in self-help paperbacks, I'd constantly repeated it to myself and someday I would learn to live by it. Leopards do not change their spots. I, of all people should recognize that concept, as it was one of the unbearable lessons Darth had taught me.

If Rod had to cross the ocean to determine a decision, when he had already had over two years to do so, what exactly was there for him to regurgitate in his manly multi-leveled thought process? What dangled within my reach was his promise to phone when he returned.

He never did pick up and dial.

CHAPTER FORTY-SEVEN

In my attempt to get over myself I tried to focus on the future. Independence Day was looming, and independence was most worthy of celebration. Holidays tended to be lonely and depressing, but I planned to haul my horse to go riding with Gretchen at the barn where she boarded. Then I could trailer up to my trainer's homestead and take some lessons. I would spend several segments of time visiting with Nellie. I was excited to get a break from my heavy work schedule and left instructions for my roommates to feed my fur ball cat.

The coupler hitch on my new horse trailer had been inspected and repeatedly tested by the manufacture's authorized dealership. It was guaranteed to be in perfect working order. All I had to do was load up and hit the road to my old familiar stomping grounds.

It had been too long since I had the opportunity to ride with my trainer, Debbie. When our lesson was over, we both headed for the house as I'd been invited to stay for supper, which is what they called dinner in Texas where Debbie was born. Her husband Jerry was already comfortably occupying his reclining lazy boy chair in front of the television. Over the years he and I had rehearsed a relationship of friendly bantering.

Jerry mentioned Darth, who had apparently visited their ranch a few times over the past two years. What was Darth doing up here? He had never attended lessons with me and to my knowledge he'd never held much of a regard for my friends. As far as human beings went Debbie, and her husband didn't have much in common with Darth. Jerry had no way of knowing that I still practiced concerted efforts to keep my past behind me, nor would he have any reason to know just how hard I was working to rebuild what life I did possess. I listened as he proceeded to tell me that Darth had previously come up to their place looking for me and asking questions. Apparently, Darth thought that Debbie would know where I could be contacted.

Like Rod, I doubted that Jerry could truly identify with Darth since he would never be able to relate to the physical abuse, much less the emotional cruelty and exploitation that Darth routinely practiced. Jerry was genuinely sincere when he told me he knew Darth still loved me. I wasn't drinking coffee so there was nothing to choke on other than my real knowledge of who Darth was. I reminded myself that Jerry simply had no comprehension of what he was telling me.

Jerry was not easily dissuaded, halfway into his discussion I could tell that Jerry totally bought into Darth's gobbledygook. Jerry seemed to feel that it wouldn't hurt me to give Darth just one more try. There was no point in continuing to persuade Jerry to my way of thinking. I finished by telling him that I would never be able to trust Darth again because he had repeatedly betrayed my trust and love in every possible way. Darth needed to move on to a more understanding woman.

Unhitching my horse trailer, I left the tires blocked and the hitch elevated in the circular drive, smacked a juicy kiss on the good old gelding's nose while promising another on the following day and departed for Nellie's house.

Her husband was not home from work, which gave us a chance to catch up on girl talk. It turned out that there wasn't much talking for us with a busy toddler around. He was so cute, and he'd grown since I'd seen him the previous year. He had tufts of fine blonde hair with lazy looping curls and huge round twinkling blue eyes with pudgy baby cheeks. I thought he should be a Gerber baby.

Her toddling package of bubbles was in a better mood than his mother. I wasn't certain exactly what was eating at her. Maybe she would share it with me when she had an opportunity. I longed for the days of our past friendship when we always knew each other's thoughts. Now, she was busily trying to do dishes, dinner, and diapers all at the same time.

I slept on the sofa in the living room that night with a flashing blip on my mental radar screen. Something was bugging Nellie, I didn't know what it was, but I was worried that it was me. I was enjoying being with a normal family, even though I felt displaced. The next morning, I left my second riding lesson and turned my horse out in one of the cow pastures. I hung around the barn with Debbie for awhile watching her ride one of the two-year old's she'd just started under saddle. Then I headed back to Nellie's taking a different route. The paved street curved around to pass the end of my old driveway. I slowed down to a crawl as I stared.

All the buildings, shop with turret and enormous horse barn stood on their foundations, every structure the same color as I had left them. The yard looked manicured and well maintained. The heavy wood fence that circled the outdoor arena was demolished. The fertile sandy loam soil used for quality footing was now growing six-foot-high corn stalks, row upon row. Throttling forward I felt undeniable loss and a shallow wave of calmness wash over me because I would never have to go home to the perpetual suffering that had existed inside those walls.

Mrs. Poe was not home yet, but as I had been told in past years, the door was never locked, and I was always welcome with no invitation needed. I had only planned to visit for a few hours and then return to

Nellie's to spend the night on the sofa, but I was reconsidering. Mrs. Poe's conversation was interesting and insightful about how she never wanted to remarry. She claimed she was no longer in possession of her libido and had no further use for a man of any sort. I couldn't blame her and wished that I could feel inspired in the same sense, but I didn't. I still yearned for a male companion. I wanted a good hearted, honest, kind man, not because I was lonely and not because a male with an income could make my house payment. I yearned for a companion to share in my life, a special someone to love. There wasn't anything wrong with that if it were the right kind of man. Someone so secure within himself that he possessed no urges to dominate me.

I left for Debbie's barn the next morning, I parked beside my trailer and headed for the barn to check on my gelding and ask Debbie if she had time for one last riding lesson. She was too tired from her son's wedding the night before. It had been extremely late when she and Jerry had gotten home, and I knew there was no sleeping-in allowed with a barnyard full of animals to feed. There were only two dogs wagging their tails against my leg in the barn aisle. I asked Debbie where the third dog was, and she said she had to lock him in a stall due to his wounds.

What wounds? All three mutts were healthy the other day. She led me to the stall full of fresh shavings and one afflicted dog. The wound was deep and ugly, an angry gash started just behind the left shoulder and continued across the high side of the ribcage beyond the left hip. It was a fresh laceration where the surrounding hide had been shaved of all brown doggie hair. I could easily count the stitches made of thick black surgical thread.

Together, Debbie and I observed man's best friend before entering the stall, she showed me the secondary wound that started midpoint of the animal's abdomen and ran down his underside. The second set of stitches was just as revolting as the first. I was surprised the dog hadn't died of its injuries and I wondered how this could have happened.

The vet had told her it was a knife-inflicted wound. Who would stab her dog, twice? Shaking her head Debbie talked about how she and Jerry had lived in their place for over a dozen years, and no one had bothered any of their animals. Since there were three barkers, strangers never dared to get out of their vehicles unless one homeowner would attend to the dogs. Some unwelcome trespasser had been at their house the previous night and the most aggressive and protective of the three dogs was the same one with the stab wounds.

I hitched my trailer and double checked the coupler, said my goodbyes, and loaded my horse. We had a long drive and tomorrow the work schedule would begin to unfold in a flurry. I put my truck in first gear to descend the steep grade of Debbie's gravel driveway and puttered down their country road until I came to the stop sign where I would turn directly onto a four-lane highway. Waiting at the stop sign took a few minutes due to all of the Fourth of July traffic.

The highway traffic was so heavy that I could not safely maneuver over the intermittent white lines to the far right, so I decided to accelerate as fast as possible in the left center lane. As I was speeding past a row of old-fashioned fruit stands with enormous watermelons, I heard a clunk, thonk, clank noise. My memory seized, searching the faint recognitions, I knew that distinctive noise from my last trailer accident.

My brain waives were already in denial, could not be, never could happen twice, impossible. Looking up into the rearview mirror I could see identical smoky green eyes filled with dread. My new horse trailer was no longer hitched to the back end of my truck. Searching beyond the blank spot directly behind my vehicle where my trailer held my most trusting equine there was nothing except black pavement passing from underneath my truck. Frantically searching in the rear-view mirror, I found it. Appearing to be the front end of a silver fuselage with no wings the trailer was doing loop-dee-dos in the freeway. It had crossed the center dividing line and was still spinning in front of oncoming traffic.

I could hear startled motorist's horns blaring as if their honking would remove my horse from their pathway. I saw an opening in southbound traffic and cut hard to the left over the center line into on coming vehicles and pulled directly in front of my trailer as it began to slow into a resting position. Automobiles in all four lanes were braking and swerving, a few were skidding sideways into the wrong lanes. I had enough forethought to jam down on my emergency blinker button on the steering column, I was afraid flashing lights weren't going to keep us safe.

Horns were still screeching as they blew past me. I could feel the suction and drag of the compressed air as motorists whizzed by. Please God, don't let anybody hit my trailer, not until I get my horse out. Last summer when my trailer had come unhitched and descended on its own journey down the hill along the craggy ravine, it had stayed balanced on its tandem wheels with the back of trailer dragging on the pavement and the hitch pointing skyward. That position made unloading the horses a scary proposition but not impossible, even though my trailer now rested on flat ground, it was in the center of a freeway with traffic buffeting both sides and the trailer was not positioned on its back end.

The hitch was down, on the pavement. I could smell the frying metal as it had slid unhindered, coupler against concrete at fifty miles per hour; showering spectacular firework sparks as it went. With the hitch downward on the blacktop the backend of the trailer faced upward about thirty-two inches from ground level. This meant my horse was basically standing on his head. His neck could be broken, his legs could be broken and if they weren't, I had no idea how I was going to get him to back straight uphill out of the back of the trailer where his feet and legs would drop off in one gigantic step before finding purchase on the ground.

I didn't know how I could possibly unload him or even if I could get him to pay attention to my commands. Surely, he had no clue of what just happened to him other than it was terrifying. I could see the side of his head through the feed door window. His left eye was the size of a saucer, and I could hear his labored breathing.

Climbing up the far side of the wheel well, I unlatched the back-trailer door. Swinging it completely open I pulled myself up the back of the trailer and into the empty right-hand stall compartment. It was next to impossible to move quickly due to the downhill slant of the trailer making it extremely difficult to balance and stand upright. My horse's shoulder and massive chest were compressed against the feed manger and hind feet were straddling his front legs. His entire body was trembling. He was desperately trying to maintain his balance. From the opposite side of the dividing partition, I grabbed hold of the cheek piece of his nylon halter and tried to maintain my own balance. I could feel burning hot tears rolling down both sides of my face. I told him to back up. He struggled but could not go backward because the rising grade was too steep.

I felt the trailer rock sideways when an eighteen-wheeler zoomed past with his horn blaring. I wished the stupid jerk would drive straight to perdition. We had to get out before another idiot killed us both. We had spent thousands of hours together over the years as a honed working team and I needed him to respond to me now.

His metal shoes shuffled and found traction on the rubber floor mats. The first hind foot out the back door reached for contact and found nothing but airspace. I pushed backward harder on the halter as both hind legs dropped out of the back of the trailer, hide scraped along the metal edge and he high centered with his twelve-hundred-pound body stuck on the elevated butt end of the trailer. Now was not the time to stop, all feet clamored for solid ground.

Crossing oncoming traffic, we made our way to the parking lot in front of the old-fashioned fruit stand where looky-loos were gathering. Checking hairy legs and scraped belly I knew that the life-threatening situation was over. Spectators had pulled off the road and into the parking area offering their assistance. I handed my lead rope to a stranger, told him not to move my horse, borrowed a quarter and walked to the conveniently located payphone. I was only a few minutes from Debbie and Jerry's. They would know how to get my trailer out of the middle of the busy highway.

Both of my friends arrived in their flatbed dually which they would use to remove my trailer from the center of commotion. The bystanders slowed traffic to a lull while I turned my truck around and crossed both southbound lanes into an available parking spot. Traffic continued to slow somewhat while Jerry and a half dozen broad shouldered farmer good guys in baseball caps heaved on my trailer until it could be successfully hitched to Jerry's truck.

Debbie and I impatiently waited with the crowd of expectant onlookers as I rubbed down my horse's legs searching for bumps that would swell. Both of my hands quivered. Doctoring my horse seemed to help steady my nerves. I still could not believe I had lost that trailer a second time.

Approaching us from where he had left his dually hitched to my trailer, Jerry wore a look that gave me the impression he was not certain what he should say. "Your trailer didn't come unhitched". Sure, the safety chains had broken away from the underside of my truck frame and yes, my trailer had been in an accident that was potentially life threatening, but there wasn't one single problem with the manufacturer's coupling mechanism on my trailer hitch. Jerry knew this beyond a shadow of doubt because as he explained it, "That heavy duty hitch and ball are still connected to the coupler mechanism on the trailer tongue Rylee, even after getting scorched while skidding down the highway blacktop, the coupler didn't fail."

I stood there clinging to my horse, certain that my mouth was open, unable to verbalize any words. My frozen moment in time must have been obvious to Jerry because in his next breath he spoke, "I'm positive that your truck hitch was sabotaged." My mouth worked around my tongue and the hinges on my jaw moved up, down and sideways, but no sound escaped my throat other than a low, pitiful moan.

Switching my focus to Debbie I read in her expression what I could not articulate from my own lips until her mouth parted and formed the one word that was simultaneously escaping from mine, "Darth". Someone might say that the concurrent recognition was divine from the Holy Spirit; others might insist that it was the all-knowing female intuition and logically it could have been my ever-functioning subconscious mind never at rest. Whatever just happened was one of those seemingly knowing moments that I intuitively realized were true, the instant I thought them.

Both Debbie and I knew whom the unwelcome intruder had been the previous evening when her family pooch had been viciously slashed. Jerry continued with an inspection of my truck as he summoned me to look for myself. It was obvious that the thick polished steel pin that had always kept the hitch from sliding out of the towing frame was missing. When the appropriate pin is inserted through the pin holes in the hitch box and through the drop hitch with the mounted towing ball there is absolutely no way it can become disengaged on its own. There is a second retainer clasp that can only be removed on purpose, by a hand with strong fingers.

Instinctively I knew that I must decide not to give Darth any more power than he already had. It was pointless to hate him or fear him. Nonetheless, I wanted to kick Darth's ass to kingdom come.

CHAPTER FORTY-EIGHT

I concentrated on an ancient passage I read, "If you stand on the bank of the river long enough, you will see the bodies of your enemies' float by." Although I did not wish to view Darth's bloated body bobbing downstream, the idea of it, did offer appeal.

Darth had committed the unthinkable in my book. Premeditated and with vengeance, he had stabbed an affectionate, loving animal that was domesticated and solely dependent upon humans. Darth had repeatedly crossed the line and injured my horse, the last possession that was truly of value to me. It wasn't enough for Darth to have ruined our marriage, manipulated my friends, stollen my share of our profitable business, caused the loss of our home, driven me from the state I'd grown up in, threaten to kill me, physically and emotionally abuse me and then disappeared with our son, the only child I would ever have.

I questioned if Joey would ever recognize the unfailing love his father claimed to have for him was nothing more than an orchestrated verbal façade that Darth had been rehearsing for years. Darth's transgressions had finally disintegrated our entire family. I'd been a loyal, dutiful wife even though there were many times I was tempted to thoroughly trounce him, I was raised to believe I should save him first. I had spent over a decade functioning in confusion and depression in my abusive marriage and I now thought that my attitude towards handling disappointment would determine whether frustration was a mere inconvenience or if I were going to be consumed by it.

Breathing an audible sigh, I felt like mashed potatoes that had been boiled too long. My relentless past and my home state could belong to Darth. I wouldn't expect him to share, and I wouldn't come back. Hands and limbs still trembling I had returned my gelding to Debbie's barn. No doubt she and her husband would be on the lookout. I didn't think Darth could get past the loaded twelve-gauge shotgun. Besides, he was a bully, and all bullies are really nothing more than crummy cowards. I drove down the highway heading toward Nellie's house. She would understand how I felt, and I needed to purge myself of my emotions and talk to her.

When I entered Nellie's house, I felt tainted, even though what had happened that morning on the highway wasn't my fault. No matter what the cause, the effect was the same. My friends were not safe from Darth's diabolical activities if I were around. I pulled my horse trailer with the same vehicle that we had purchased over five years ago, when we were still married. My truck had the metal Ram emblem turned backward on the hood. I kept it this way on purpose because it was something that Joey had started, so I left it backward as a token reminder of him. Darth could easily recognize my truck.

Nellie's previous mood had seemed sour. Now her mood was unpalatable. I wondered if it was just me sensing an undertow because I felt guilty about my connection to Darth. Then Nellie told me she had seen him outside her house the night before. She did not mention it to me because she thought she was being predisposed to sightings of him since I was in town. Now she was certain that she had seen Darth sneaking about her neighborhood spying on her home.

I knew I should go. I was contaminated. Being the main attraction of Darth's attentions had turned me into a creature that was now fouled, and infected and nobody else wanted to catch it. They could end up like Debbie's eviscerated dog. I did not blame anyone for being uncomfortable in my presence. I didn't think that Nellie was mad at me, but it sure felt that way. I told myself that it wasn't anger that fueled her acidic mood, it was fear. She worried about who Darth would sabotage next. I did not blame her, but I still needed her friendship.

I did not feel that I belonged anywhere. I sensed I was an intrusive trespasser trying to be normal. I spent that night tossing and turning at Mrs. Poe's house and left the following morning. My first stop was a hardware store where I purchased a new metal pin for my hitch. This new version of a pin had a predrilled hole in it where I could permanently attach a heavy-duty padlock. No one could ever pull my hitch pin again as it was now a permanent attachment.

All was well at Debbie's farm where I retrieved my trailer and horse. His front legs were swollen, and he was lame on a stiff shoulder. I hauled him home as carefully as possible and he healed up as good as new, but never did relax again when hauled in a trailer, forever after that was a problem.

As I drove, I dramatized facial expressions as I talked to myself. I repeatedly told myself that a woman should not need a man. No man in my life was better than a bad man. Gleaning the most potent lesson of all, I had learned at my own expense that I was the most important emotional investment that I could make for myself. When it came right down to it, I could count solely on myself. I could trust myself. Of all the people in the world I must surely be more important to myself than I was to anyone else. No matter how many times I repeated my self-coaching, these self-evident truths were still difficult and foreign for me to accept.

I promised to live my life by my own personal standards. No matter what, I would honor all my commitments, or I would honorably terminate them. Never dreaming that I could honorably divorce a spouse, I knew

I had. It was the one thing I didn't have to feel guilty about. Prior to my divorce I had sincerely tried absolutely everything imaginable within my power to make our marriage work. For several years I'd thought we'd shared the same goals, but we really hadn't. My superb beliefs in sharing, trusting, loving and commitment had been nothing more than an illusion that Darth had intentionally created to ultimately control me.

I felt I had failed Joey. All those miserable years I stayed with his father because I thought I was doing the right thing for him; in retrospect I was convinced that staying with his father through his adolescent years had been the worst thing I could have ever done. Any home life with the influence of a manipulative monster like Darth was a far worse example and training for a small boy than never knowing his father at all. Looking back, I now knew that I should have left Darth when I was five weeks pregnant, and he hit me the first time. Better yet, I should have been educated about the warning signs of addiction and abuse and never married him in the first place.

Doing a perusal of my memories, I could organize them neatly into designated file folders and store them away into my personal file cabinet of remembrances and stack them on a forgotten shelf in a far corner of my mind. Joey continued to remain a tremendous loss that I didn't know how to deal with. He was deeply seated within his father's mire; a place Darth had created for Joey years before I had understood.

I held steadfast to my belief that someday Joey would attain adulthood and be capable of making his own decisions. Perhaps then he would want to know his mother. He wasn't just Darth's flesh and blood. I clung to the hope that there was enough of me flowing through his veins that he would grow up making honest choices. My heartache was in knowing that he wasn't getting the childhood he deserved.

I worried that he was being cultivated to be a repeat of his father. Textbooks claimed that alcoholism was a disease you could blame on how your liver processed enzymes and you either inherited that type of liver or you didn't. Scientifically I was sure there was something biologically correct about that theory. Mentally, I'd decided that alcohol inflicted irresponsible people who were the guilty parties of drinking to the point where they could not stop. I believed a profoundly responsible, selfless person would never allow themselves to step that far over the line. A responsible person would be too concerned about their everyday tasks and loved ones to throw their lives away for the inside of a bottle. As for drugs, they were just another mind-altering chemical, as lethal and dangerous as alcohol.

All the pain and suffering would have been preventable if I had not made the number one mistake that most women make; convincing myself that I was so good-hearted that I could change my man's faults. I could not, and it was not my place or responsibility to do so. Making assessments that led me to believe that I could change someone was selfish on my part as I wanted them to change for the betterment of my own life and theirs.

Typical of most people, my perception of a significant other must have been partially warped when in love. I had viewed my man in a shaded light that made him look better than he really was. I vowed there would be no more Savior complexes for me. I did not want to be a woman redeeming men through my gift of selfless love. My responsibility was to myself. It would be a struggle, but I was going to break the cycle of needing someone else because I did not stoically believe in the one person I would always have, me.

An abusive, sick personality had manipulated me into thinking foremost about him and then he had continued to feed on my naïve nature for as long as I had allowed him to do so, while I never realized that the person who needs the relationship the least has the most control.

There never was a response from Nellie, not even to my second and third letters. Since I was an advocate of actions speaking louder than words, I decided that I had no choice other than to accept and hear her actions loud and clear. It was ironic really, all those years where Darth had done his deeds to ruin our friendship and we had vowed never to let him. Now it seemed that he had won again.

I sincerely wished that I could wear glittering red pumps, click the heels together three times and return home to normal, whatever that was. I pondered thoughts of really losing oneself in Kansas, only to be found again. I was determined to blaze my own yellow brick road, destined to an emerald city no matter how scared I was. I knew that in my moments of weakness I would find my strong suits, because where I was going with my life, was much more important than where I had been.

Time would touch us all, Darth wasn't dead, yet.

I would ultimately discover and fill a most important void.

Joey would be yet another story.

* * The Story Lives on In The Next Book * *

ABOUT THE AUTHOR

Rylee Ryder unequivocally understands abused women because she was for decades, until she learned that denial of her circumstances could only harbor bitterness, distrust, and dread. Making it easier for the alcoholic druggie to continue to control her, while she constantly found herself repeating the same recuperative tactics to cure the offender.

When she learned that people who abuse can also be attentive and affectionate as well as cruel and conniving, she understood that deep, dark, dirty denial wanted to convince her that she could not possibly change her life, so she conveniently adapted to live in physical, emotional, and sexual terror.

Along her journey Rylee forgot how to believe in herself, her intuition, and her own self-trust. As her abuse worsens, without realizing, she simply acclimates to it. In Rylee's case she felt morally obligated to try everything she could muster to withstand the insanity, still trying and thinking she was saving her family.

Ultimately, she does save herself and worked hard for years to persevere. She now loves a healthy life with good friends, neighbors, and church support group. She still likes men, still rides her horse, and lets the dog sleep on the sofa, knowing that the journey can be more fulfilling than the destination.

FEEL A CONNECTION WITH THIS BOOK?
CONSIDER SHARING THE MESSAGE.

Mention my book on social media platforms. You do not realize how many people you know that are silently struggling in dysfunctional relationships.

Could this book be helpful to someone you know? Consider purchasing them a copy or less expensive e-book.

Please recommend this book to a friend, relative, classmate, neighbor, co-worker; anyone in your sphere of influence.

CONTACT ME DIRECTLY
At my website:

www.KisstheBully.com

Should you have questions, comments, or concerns, I will give my best efforts to respond!

Most sincerely, Rylee Ryder

Printed in the United States
by Baker & Taylor Publisher Services